# The Fourth Discontinuity

# The Fourth Discontinuity

The Co-Evolution of

Humans and Machines

**Bruce Mazlish**

**Yale University Press** New Haven and London

Designed by Sonia L. Scanlon.

Set in Trump with Helvetica condensed display type by Keystone Typesetting, Inc., Orwigsburg, Pennsylvania.

Printed in the United States of America by Vail-Ballou Press, Binghamton, New York.

Library of Congress Cataloging-in-Publication Data

Mazlish, Bruce, 1923–

The fourth discontinuity : the co-evolution of humans and machines / Bruce Mazlish.

p. cm.

Includes bibliographical references and index.

ISBN 0-300-05411-4

1. Human information processing. 2. Artificial intelligence. 3. Man-machine systems. I. Title.

BF444.M38    1993

155.7—dc20 92-38075

CIP

A catalogue record for this book is available from the British Library.

The paper in this book meets the guidelines for permanence and durability of the Committee on Production Guidelines for Book Longevity of the Council on Library Resources.

10    9    8    7    6    5    4    3    2    1

To **Jacob Bronowski**

# Contents

# Acknowledgments

While writing this book, I incurred innumerable obligations. It would be impossible to acknowledge them all. However, to satisfy my conscience, a few must be recognized. I would like to state my appreciation to my colleagues James Paradis and Harriet Ritvo for reading earlier versions of this book. To Mary Smith, research librarian at Widener Library, Harvard University, and Paul Vermouth at the MIT Humanities Library, I owe a special debt of gratitude. To Eric Kupferberg, who is fast finishing his own doctoral thesis in the MIT program in science and technology, a special debt is owed for his most informed, careful, and collegial reading of the entire manuscript. Gerald O'Neill never read any part of the manuscript, but hiking on trails on Mount Desert Island, he and I talked out crucial parts of the argument. Although he is now dead, his lively spirit endures. Special thanks go to Charles Grench, senior editor, and to Richard Miller, manuscript editor, who made this publishing experience a most pleasant and productive one. Last is Neva Goodwin. It is impossible for me to separate this book from her, for we have talked about it almost line for line and argued about its theses over breakfast, lunch, and dinner. I should add that the computer obeyed her touch when mine faltered in getting the incantations right. She and the computer alone know how much I owe her.

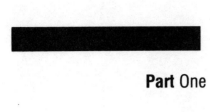

# Part One

## **Chapter** One

In the eighteenth lecture of his *Introductory Lectures to Psychoanalysis,* originally delivered at the University of Vienna between 1915 and 1917, Sigmund Freud suggested his own place among the great thinkers of the past who had outraged man's naive self-love. First was Copernicus, who, according to Freud, taught that our earth "was not the centre of the universe but only a tiny fragment of a cosmic system of scarcely imaginable vastness." Second was Darwin, who "destroyed man's supposedly privileged place in creation and proved his descent from the animal kingdom." Third was Freud himself. On his own account, Freud admitted, or claimed, that psychoanalysis "seeks to prove to the ego that it is not even master in its own house, but must content itself with scanty information of what is going on unconsciously in the mind."[1]

After completing these lectures, in 1917 Freud repeated in his short essay "A Difficulty in the Path of Psychoanalysis" his sketch concerning the three great shocks to man's ego, discussing in greater detail these cosmological, biological, and psychological blows to human pride.[2] I shall be arguing that the human ego is undergoing a fourth shock, similar to those administered by Copernicus, Darwin, and Freud.[3] We are now coming to realize that humans are not as privileged in regard to machines as has been unthinkingly assumed.

The most interesting extension of Freud's self-view has come from the American psychologist Jerome Bruner. He stands Freud on his head, so to speak, substituting the notion of continuity for what Freud considered to be a break. The way Bruner phrases it, establishing a belief in nature as a continuum can be seen either as creating continuities or eliminating discontinuities (where discontinuity means emphasizing breaks or gaps in the phenomena of nature—for example, stressing the sharp differences between physical bodies in the heavens or on Earth or between one form of animal matter and another).

According to Bruner, the first continuity was established by the Greek physicist-philosophers of the sixth century B.C. rather than by Copernicus. Thus, thinkers such as Anaximander conceived of the phenomena of the physical world as "continuous and monistic, as governed by the common laws of matter." The creating of the second continuity, that between humans and the animal kingdom, was, of course, Darwin's contribution and a necessary condition for Freud's work. With Freud, according to Bruner, the following continuities were established: the continuity of organic lawfulness, so that "accident in human affairs was no more to be brooked as 'explanation' than accident in nature"; the continuity of the primitive, infantile, and archaic as coexisting with the civilized and evolved; and the continuity between mental illness and mental health.[4]

In this version of the three historic smashings of the ego, humans are placed on a continuous spectrum in relation to the universe, to the rest of the animal kingdom, and to themselves. They are no longer discontinuous with the world around them. In an important sense, once humans are able to accept this situation, they are in harmony with the rest of existence. Indeed, the longings for a sense of "connection" seen in the early-nineteenth-century romantics and all "alienated" beings are, unexpectedly, partially fulfilled.

Yet, to use part of Bruner's phraseology—though not his idea—a fourth and major discontinuity or dichotomy still exists in our time: the discontinuity between humans and machines. Once again, we are confronted with the human need to be special, to feel superior—but in this case in regard to the machine. Such a need satisfies important psychological and social purposes yet is a crutch that is best discarded, in order to move closer to reality and away from disabling fantasy.

To put it bluntly, we are now coming to realize that humans and the machines they create are continuous and that the same conceptual schemes that help explain the workings of the brain also explain the workings of a "thinking machine." Human pride and its attendant refusal or hesitation to acknowledge this continuity form a substratum upon which much of the distrust of technology and an industrialized society has been reared. Ultimately this distrust (for which there are good reasons as long as we think of the machine as alienated from us, instead of a being created by us and thus potentially under our control) rests on the refusal by humans to understand and accept their nature—as beings continuous with the tools and machines they construct. Once the discontinuity is overcome, we will be in a better position to decide more *consciously* how we wish to deal with our machines and our mechanical civilization.

As with Man's* animal nature, evolutionary theory provides the needed perspective on his "mechanical" nature (leaving open for the moment the exact nature of that theory as well as its applicability to cultural change).[5] The evidence now seems strong that humans evolved from the other animals through a continuous interaction of tool, physical, and mental-emotional changes. The old view—that humans arrived on the evolutionary scene fully formed and then proceeded to discover tools and the new ways of life that they made possible—no longer appears acceptable. As one anthropologist has put it, "From the rapidly accumulating evidence it is now possible to speculate with some confidence on the manner in which the way of life made possible by tools changed the pressures of natural selection and so changed the structure of man." The details of the argument are fascinating because they link tools with such physical traits as pelvic structure, bipedalism, brain structure, and so on, as well as with the organization of humans in cooperative societies and the substitution of morality for hormonal control of sexual and other "social" activities. The author concludes that "it was the success of the simplest tools that started the whole trend of human evolution and led to the civilizations of today."[6]

Charles Darwin had glimpsed the role of tools in human evolution, but one of his contemporaries, Karl Marx, a social rather than a biological scientist, first placed the subject in a new light.[7] Accepting Benjamin Franklin's definition of Man as a "tool-making animal," Marx suggested in *Das Kapital* that "the relics of the instruments of labor are of no less importance in the study of vanished socioeconomic forms, than fossil bones are in the study of the organization of extinct species."[8]

In the spring of 1873 Marx sent Darwin a copy of the second German edition of *Das Kapital*, with an inscription and a letter; until recently it was also believed that Marx had tried to dedicate the English translation of his work to Darwin and had been turned down.[9] But it is clear that the cautious English scientist wished to keep his German admirer at arm's length, whereas Marx wanted to stress the connection to evolutionary theory of his own work.

---

*Occasionally I shall use the term *Man* capitalized, for linguistic convenience and out of historical tradition; in such cases, I mean by it a generic term, which includes both sexes equally of the human species.

We can see part of Marx's reason for this desire in the following revealing passage:

> Darwin has aroused our interest in the history of *natural technology*, that is to say in the origin of the organs of plants and animals as productive instruments utilised for the life purposes of those creatures. Does not the history of the origin of the productive organs of men in society, the organs which form the material basis of every kind of organisation, deserve equal attention? Since, as Vico [in the *New Science* (1725)] says, the essence of the distinction between human history and natural history is that the former is the work of man and the latter is not, would not the history of *human technology* be easier to write than the history of natural technology? (italics mine)[10]

Marx's brilliant imagination had led him to perceive a part of the continuity between humans and their tools. Indeed, he might almost be given a place in the pantheon of Copernicus, Darwin, and Freud as a destroyer of Man's discontinuities with the world about him. Anticipating present-day anthropologists, Marx had sensed the unbreakable connection between Man's evolution as a social and cultural, if not physical, being and his development of tools. He did not anticipate, however, the second part of our subject, that humans and their tools, especially in the form of modern, complicated machines, are part of a theoretical continuum.

My first thesis, then, is that humans are on the threshold of decisively breaking past the discontinuity between themselves and machines. This thesis consists of two parts. On the one hand, humans are ending the discontinuity because they now can perceive their own evolution as inextricably interwoven with their use and development of tools, of which the modern machine is only the furthest extrapolation. We cannot think realistically any longer of the human species without a machine. On the other hand, the discontinuity is being bridged because humans now perceive that the same scientific concepts help explain the workings of themselves and their machines, and that matter evolves—from the basic building blocks of hydrogen turning into helium in the distant stars, then fusing into carbon nuclei and on up to iron, and then exploding into space, which has resulted in our solar system—developing on earth its intricate patterns into the structure of organic life, and now into the architecture of our thinking machines.

It is absurd, of course, to contend that there are no differences between humans and machines, as absurd as claiming that there are no differences between humans and the other animals. The differences, needless to say, are ones of degree.[11] What is claimed here is that the sharp discontinuity between humans and machines is no longer tenable, in spite of the shock to our egos.[12]

As I have suggested, this change in our metaphysical awareness, this transcendence of the fourth discontinuity, is essential to our harmoniously coming to terms with an industrialized world. The alternatives are either a frightened rejection of the Frankensteins we have created or a blind belief in their "superhuman virtues" and a touching faith that they can solve all our human problems. Alas, in the perspective I am suggesting, machines are mechanical—all too mechanical, to paraphrase Nietzsche. But, in saying this, I am also saying that they are all too human as well. The question, then, is are we to repeat the real Frankenstein story (see chapter 3) and by turning from the "monsters" we have created also turn away from our own humanity or, alternatively, are we to accept the blow to our egos and enter into a world beyond the fourth discontinuity? In taking the latter path, I am arguing that then we would be free to reconfigure the relationship between humans and machines in various ways—for there is, of course, no single right way.

The fourth discontinuity and the hope of ending it form my first thesis. My second thesis involves evolving human nature. I shall be arguing that human nature is not fixed, not a kind of Platonic ideal, but is rather an evolving identity, secured in the process of adaptation to "nature."

Such evolution in humans increasingly has unfolded in terms of culture—our "second nature"; indeed, human physical change has largely ceased except, as I shall try to show, in the form of prosthetic adaptation, that is, mechanical means.[13] Machines, of course, are a major part of human culture; as part of that culture, though created by humans, they seem to take on a life of their own. To understand human nature more fully, we must understand this complex new way in which Man's evolution has been proceeding.

In seeking a theory by which to understand evolution, Darwin started from domestic breeding (see chapter 5). As he conceptualized the matter, in selecting, and thereby modifying, animals, whose variations Darwin took as a given, humans are the "cause" of such "evolution." Who, or what, Darwin asked himself, plays this role in nature? His answer, as we know, was "natural selection" or "survival of the fittest," a process that operates without conscious intent. What humans consciously are to domestic breeding, survival of the fittest unintentionally is to natural breeding.

The "evolution" of machines as it turns out is closer to domestic than natural selection. Humans create machines; in this sense, they choose and select what is to come into being and to survive. In short, when we consider machines from an evolutionary perspective we must reverse Darwin's steps and retreat from natural selection in its ordinary sense to some version of domestic selection as our model. The analogy used here is, of course, an imperfect one, but at least hints at the way we must proceed.

As we try to understand evolving human nature, our guidelines tell us that human nature not only evolves but does so in intimate connection with humanity's creation of machines. Whether machines are now poised to undergo an "evolution," or to use a more neutral term, development, of their own, partly independent of humans, their creators, becomes a pressing issue. (There is a question whether the term *evolution* can be properly used in regard to machines; I shall give sustained attention to this issue in chapter 11, when the full historical context of the question will be available to us.) Though this issue was first raised only ironically in the late nineteenth century by Samuel Butler, it is an issue that I shall try to take seriously as part of my examination of evolving human nature.[14]

In discussing the purpose of the great eighteenth-century *Encyclopedia*, d'Alembert stated that it was intended not only to supply a certain body of knowledge but "pour changer la façon commune de penser"— to change the way people think.

My hope is that readers of this book will henceforth be persistently conscious of the machine question and will thoroughly and constantly perceive the meaning in their own lives of the interconnected nature of humans and machines. More pointedly, my aim is that readers will then feel deeply that they are that particular evolutionary creature whose origins are to be found in both the animal and the machine kingdoms, with the animal and mechanical qualities together incorporated in the definition of human nature.

One inspiration for the *Encyclopedia* was Sir Francis Bacon. I should like to hark back to something he said in his *Advancement of Learning* concerning arts and mechanics:

> The history of arts should the rather make a species of natural history, because of the prevalent opinion, as if art were a different

thing from nature, and things natural different from things artificial: whence many writers of natural history think they perform notably, if they give us the history of animals, plants, or minerals, without a word of the mechanic arts. A further mischief is to have art esteemed no more than an assistant to nature, so as to help her forwards, correct or set her free, and not to bend, change, and radically affect her; whence an untimely despair has crept upon mankind; who should rather be assured that artificial things differ not from natural in form or essence, but only in the efficient: for man has no power over nature in anything but motion, whereby he either puts bodies together, or separates them. And, therefore, so far as natural bodies may be separated or conjoined, man may do anything.[15]

Here, at the beginning of what we have come to call the Scientific Revolution, in confident Elizabethan tones, combining utility with Promethean aspiration, we hear the premonition that any dichotomy between the natural and the mechanical is a false one, which, at the hands of Man the maker, can and will be eliminated. In statements such as these by Bacon, extravagant and tendentious (especially in the eyes of radical critics today) as they may be, I have found part of my evidence, as well as a confirmation of my general thesis.

Humans have been struggling, in various ways, with this matter for many, many hundreds of years. Their efforts prefigure my thesis here; and like the authors of the *Encyclopedia* I will be supplying a certain body of knowledge as the basis for my hoped-for change in the mode of thinking. Thus, I try to supply a rich context for my major theses rather than simply pursuing a lean, straightforward, unencumbered argument. I want to share with the reader the fullness of the debate—to spend time on small points, for example, concerning Babbage or Pavlov—even though at first glance such a procedure does not seem always immediately to address the larger question about humans and machines.

The task is to immerse ourselves initially in the far-flung materials themselves. Out of such an immersion I have formulated the theses advanced in this book (perhaps, more modestly, they should be called themes). These theses did not generally lie nicely separated or even labeled in the original texts. Though I have had to treat them discretely for purposes of exposition, I have also tried to preserve something of the messy connectedness found in the originals.

A critical part of my inquiry is to probe whether the Baconian claim that "Man may do anything" is true or is mainly the expression of Western hubris or fantasy. I have had to grapple with fantasy being as important as reality; indeed this, too, is a false dichotomy, for fantasy *is* part of human reality. Angels as such may not exist; but that humans aspire to be angelic does "exist." Humans may or may not be machines; but that humans have been creating an increasingly mechanical civilization, especially since the Industrial Revolution, and perhaps even aspiring to be machines, is part of reality. It is into this category of a merging of fantasy and reality that the statement "Man may do anything" must be placed.

The nature of issues such as the relationship between fantasy and reality, then, helps dictate the kinds of evidence to be used. I shall appeal to myth and legend, as well as to history; to science fiction as well as to scientific statement; to social and economic developments as well as to the anxieties and hopes that they may arouse; and so forth. Through these appeals I wish to establish the contexts in which discussions of these issues have taken place in the past and that must weigh upon any such discussion in the present.

I should add that though my approach focuses on the varieties of discourse found in history, my presentation itself is devoid of the terms that dominate so much of current postmodernist and poststructuralist writings. Similarly, I will not engage in the debate about the social construction of science. These other approaches are of interest and importance, but they do not serve me in this task. My effort in this work is more to construct than to deconstruct.[16]

Yet I must acknowledge my own fascination with Michel Foucault. Although I disagree with much of his work and his approach, one must respect his erudition and his dedication to trying to understand at the deepest level the epistemology of the human sciences. As a disciple of Gaston Bachelard and Georges Canguilhem, he furthers their work in an original, if frequently polemical, fashion, and his work is especially pertinent to some of the topics in this book.[17]

I differ from Foucault on his frequent dismissal of the conflict of different ideas and forces—polarities—which, in fact, constitute the whole he is studying. His ignoring of unintended consequences means that he also offers a rather monophonic history.

Though I share with him an interest in epistemology, I come at it less from a philosophical than from a historical perspective. We know ourselves in large part by knowing what we are not—or so humans have thought over the centuries. It seems useful to study what humans historically have believed about themselves as they sought to establish their own sense of identity in contrast to those other "beings": bestial and mechanical. Thus, though my study is primarily historical, it is also philosophical.

This means rooting my inquiry in the thoughts of other people—historical figures, whether individual or group—rather than in "pure" thought. Again, this means also paying attention to humanity's actual relations to animals and to machines as these have developed and changed over time. In the end, then, the two inquiries, into human nature and into the historical study of human nature, are intertwined. To know what we know, we must also examine closely the ways in which we have tried to know.

As will readily be seen, the elements of my inquiry are not particularly new. There are many excellent studies of humans' relations to the other animals and many similar studies concerning our feelings and thoughts about machines. What is new, I hope, is my attempt to synthesize and perhaps reconcile the studies on animals and the studies on machines, and to indicate the similarities and differences between them.

If all of these studies on animals and on machines did not already exist, my task would be hopeless. As it is, I shall have to be enormously selective. My first selection grows not out of choice but out of my parochial limitations. In talking of humans, I shall, in fact, be talking of Western civilization. Though I shall try to glance at other cultures and societies, this outreach will necessarily be limited. Allusions to examples from other cultures may have to serve as warning comparisons, or vital background, rather than as integral parts of the story I am trying to tell.

In taking this tack, I recognize that I may be skirting a serious problem: the human-machine interface may be very different in non-Western parts of the world, yet I am generalizing about human nature and the "evolutionary" nature of the machine.

My response is in two parts. First, for example, though the ways humans use clothing are different in various cultures, they all more or less have clothes; the same is true with tools and machines. Though attitudes to the machine vary, they do so around certain relatively common tropes.

Second, the West is a machine-driven society; and because the West has imposed its dominance on most of the world, largely because of its machines, more or less all of humanity, willy-nilly, has been caught up in the fourth discontinuity: the computer-robot as a possible "evolutionary" form can no longer be viewed simply as a Western creation.[18] It is now, for better or for worse, a "human" possibility. So emboldened, I have moved forward into my materials.

My starting point is the absorption in the seventeenth century with what was called the "animal-machine." Here the debate swirls about the Cartesians and the anti-Cartesians and their attitudes to both animals and machines. Descartes, however, who distinguished humans from the other animals by their possession of a soul, nevertheless argues that the other animals are mere machines. When the soul is removed from the Man-machine, as it is in the eighteenth century by La Mettrie, Man, too, becomes only a machine.

In chapter 3, I focus on machines, going back to the early Greeks and Chinese and then forward in a wide-ranging discussion of automata, the forerunners of modern robots. I shall analyze Shelley's *Franken-stein*, as well as such works as L. Frank Baum's *Ozma of Oz* and Isaac Asimov's *I, Robot*, not to mention Capek's famous *R.U.R.*, the source of the term *robot*.

Chapter 4 is on the Industrial Revolution, where humans pass, or begin to pass, the boundary between the animal and the mechanical. Henceforth, human evolution seems to point in a new direction. Humans themselves become more mechanical; as Carlyle says, "Man becomes mechanical in head and heart as well as in hand." Existence is now mechanized in a way unknown before. From these circumstances comes the possibility of a new direction in "evolution" itself: toward machines, with humans as their godlike creators but perhaps no longer their controllers.

Then I shall engage in a more extended discussion of biological evolution in order to establish a firmer context for the leap I want to make in discussing evolving human nature. In Part II, chapter 5, I will look first at Linnaeus and his attempt to name all the inhabitants of the world, and thus to command them; and then at Charles Darwin (with a side glance at T. H. Huxley), who breathed life into Linnaeus's static classification and thereby set the entire animal kingdom into motion, with the human now one among many other evolutionary animals.

Chapter 6 follows two of Darwin's disciples, Freud and Pavlov, as they pursue the implications of how his work relates to the nature of humans. Both, of course, are concerned with the animal roots of that nature and how it functions. For Freud the key word is *culture*, though for Pavlov it is *conditioning*; for the former, the animal in humans must become subordinated to the ego, though for the latter the animal, properly conditioned, becomes, as I shall argue, a machine. (In fact, Freud, to a limited extent, also moves in this last direction.)

After chapter 6, we are poised again at the junction where the two parts of humanity's evolving nature, as animal and machine, meet. To come to grips more directly with this development, I look in chapter 7 at three figures: Babbage, Huxley, and Butler. Charles Babbage is the father of the modern computer, crafting it in the very heart of the early Industrial Revolution; in its primitive beginnings we can see with special clarity the shape it will later take. T. H. Huxley, Darwin's "bulldog," wrestles with the animal-machine problem in evolutionary terms that continue but go beyond the Cartesian definitions. Samuel Butler, more novelist than scientist, is an anti-Darwinian Darwinist who takes Darwin's evolutionary scheme to its furthest conclusion, with machines potentially dominating human beings.

In Part III, chapter 8, I shall try to estimate and evaluate what is involved in the so-called biogenetic revolution of our time. Here, we encounter the culmination of human efforts, up to our era, to "mechanize" the other animals. It is the Pavlovian effort in an entirely new guise.

Chapter 9 takes the opposite approach. It focuses on the computer and brain sciences, and especially on the question of artificial intelligence, which deals with the "animalization" of the machine, for example, the computer-robot. The machine, some now claim, has become human, or at least gifted with human attributes. The further Carlylean development, of course, is that humans have now become "mechanical" in a new way.

In my last two chapters, 10 and 11, I will seek to evaluate all that has gone before. By estimating what of the animal and what of the machine exists in humans, and what uniqueness resides only in humans, if any, we may be able to secure a reasonable assessment about the present condition of our evolving nature. Finally, we can also consider seriously the question whether, broadly defined, *evolution* is taking a new direction with the increasing presence of machines.

## **Chapter** Two

For thousands of years humans have wrestled with the question of their "human" nature. On one side they have had to define themselves in relation to the animal kingdom, mainly creating but sometimes breaching the second discontinuity. Yearning either to take on some of the superior attributes of other animals or to rise above their own animal nature by becoming angelic, humans have mostly sought to define themselves as a special sort of creation.

Humans have also created machines, and their new creations, in turn, have raised the question of whether animals are merely a variant of the machine and whether the machine, as a kind of Frankenstein monster, can turn against its creator and either "take over" or make humans over into its own image.

These concerns about Man's animal and mechanical nature came forcefully together in the West in the seventeenth century and did so in terms of a debate over what was called the *animal-machine*. Were animals mere machines, and were humans the same, that is, Man-machines?

In order to set the stage for that debate, I shall first look briefly at its anticipation by artists and illustrators. There are many ways to science; we tend, because of Francis Bacon and René Descartes, to think that there are only one or two (or a mixture thereof): the empirical inductive, or the rationalist deductive, with both emphasizing a form of logical reasoning. That much of science was rooted in magic and in art has thus often been forgotten.[1]

We get a somewhat different perspective when we look at the role played by Leonardo da Vinci, who so splendidly combined scientific and artistic interests. Leonardo's extraordinary sharpness and quickness of sight made his eye almost the equivalent of a microscope or camera. He could literally "stop" motion. Thus he was able to analyze the flight of birds and sought to devise flying machines based on the principle of a flapping wing.

Analyzing animals and machines in terms of function, he saw the similarities beneath the surface. He recognized in the structure and working of the bones and sinews of both animals and humans the same mechanical principles that were applicable to machines. All three—humans, animals, and machines—were explicable, he argued, in mathematical terms, as they found their expression in mechanism. "Mechanics," Leonardo wrote, "is the paradise of the mathematical sciences because by means of it one comes to the fruits of mathematics." He went on, "Thus a bird is an instrument working according to mathematical law, which . . . is within the capacity of man to reproduce."[2]

So inspired, Leonardo simulated mechanically a number of animal functions and forms. Thus he invented a military tank that, he wrote, "takes the place of the elephants."[3] From the form of the spiral, as in a shell, he devised a helicopter operating on the principle of an aerial screw. In his notebooks he designed other kinds of machines to mint coins, polish needles, bend beams, lift weights, gear various devices, and measure humidity, distances, inclinations, and the force of the wind. The illustrations of these inventions, and subsequently of "animal-machines," most concern us here. Leonardo, a skilled draftsman, used drawings that utilized exploded, rotated, and transparent views—that is, were three-dimensional—to work out his mechanical contrivances. In so doing, he was part of a larger contemporary development of new methods of dealing with scientific illustration.[4]

In this development, three-dimensional linear perspective based on geometric principles opened up a whole new world to human sight.[5] Even before Leonardo, a Sienese, Mariano di Jacopo, called Taccola (1381–c. 1453), applied perspective rules to designs for machines. He was not a very good artist, but what he wanted, as Samuel Y. Edgerton, Jr., tells us, was "to invent machines not by making expensive three-dimensional models but by working out their problems in drawings." Even working models would not allow him to "look inside," say, into a suction pump. However, by imagining the pump as if it were not only three-dimensional but transparent, and so rendering it, Taccola gained and communicated a new understanding of how things function and work.

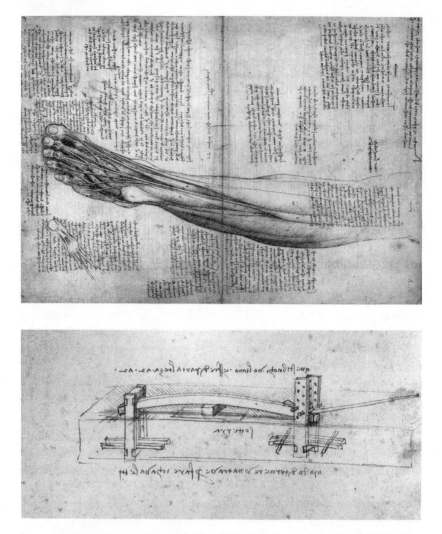

Leonardo da Vinci, *The superficial anatomy of the foot and lower leg, c. 1510* (Courtesy Windsor Castle, Royal Library © 1992 Her Majesty Queen Elizabeth II), and *Design for a device for bending beams, c. 1488* (Courtesy Pierpont Morgan Library, New York. 1986.50, Gift of a Trustee). The beam-bending device, with its combinations of supports and levers, is analogous to the forms and functions in Leonardo's anatomical drawings of the bones, tendons, and muscles of the human body. The descriptions accompanying the designs are in Leonardo's famous mirror writing.

So, too, the unknown illustrator of Agricola's classic treatise on mines, according to Edgerton, "cut open the ground to expose the bowels of the earth, illustrating the otherwise impossible-to-see interior of a mine-shaft."

The same techniques were applied to the human figure by Hans Wechtlin (c. 1480–1530) in a set of wood-block illustrations made in 1517–1518 for two surgery textbooks. Here we have some of the "earliest printed pictures of an anatomical dissection which seems literally to have been drawn from 'life.'" Wechtlin modified the transparent view to a kind of cutaway view, showing a cadaver's head separated and "in various stages of having the brains and nerves removed."

Vesalius's treatise on the working of the human body was a superb combination of science and art. Vesalius and his illustrator, a minor Flemish artist, literally drew the parallels between the functioning of the human body and simple machines. As Edgerton describes it, "At the bottom left, his artist illustrated some examples of carpenters' joinery, which Vesalius likened to the sutures of the skull; on the right, he showed some iron door hinges which he likened to other bone joints in the body."

Ambroise Paré (1510–1590), the great French physician, carried this approach one step further. Anticipating modern prosthetic devices, he "seemed even to be thinking that the human hand could be replaced by a machine working on the same principles of gears and levers" as those found in various treatises on machines; the hand, cut open to show the mechanical contrivances equivalent to muscles and nerves, in his *Dix livres de chirurgie* (Paris, 1564), is breathtaking in its implications.

The moral is clear. Renaissance scientific illustrations make us "see" that humans and machines function in the same way and that they may be made to share interchangeable parts. The continuum is envisioned even before it can be thought.

The next step, however, was, indeed, to think about it. The one who was prepared to do so most systemically was René Descartes. Edgerton agrees with my conviction that scientific illustrations and theorizing are part of the same methodical approach—and I find it exciting confirmation that he does—when he writes, "It would be interesting to speculate that pictures like these, from the numerous followers of Vesalius and the many 'Theater of Machines' treatises like Ramelli's, were seen by René Descartes, the great French philosopher and one of the fathers of the modern scientific method." Then Edgerton continues, "In 1640 . . . almost as if he were thinking about these two pictures [Vesalius's and Ramelli's], Descartes wrote:

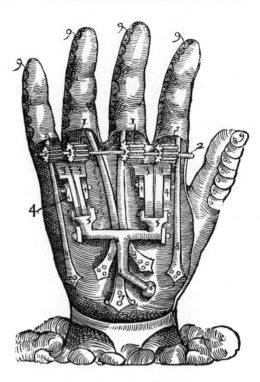

Ambroise Paré, *Design for a prosthetic hand*, from *Dix livres de chirurgie*, Paris, 1564 (Courtesy Francis A. Countway Library of Medicine, Boston).

> We see that . . . artificial fountains . . . and other machines of this kind, although they are built by men do not for this reason lack the power to move by themselves . . . even the machine (of man) which I suppose can very well be compared to the pipes of those fountains, the muscles and their tendons to the other various contrivances and springs that serve to set them in motion; and their animal spirits to the water that moves them, and . . . the heart to the fount and concavities of the brain the tanks. In addition, respiration . . . can be compared to the movement of . . . a mill which the flow of water can render continuous.

Suddenly, the illustrations have taken on a philosophical guise; and philosophy has become illustrated.

According to George Boas, the seventeenth-century debate over animals as machines, in which Descartes figured so largely, can best be seen as starting from the theriophily, or love and admiration of animals, in Montaigne.[6] Montaigne's work, in turn, is rooted in a long tradition, going back to Plutarch and running through the Middle Ages and Saint Thomas Aquinas, that gives the beasts superiority over humans.

In Montaigne, the argument is put forth as a series of provocative paradoxes. The beasts, he asserts, are more natural than Man; hence they are superior. Man's vaunted reason is merely another facet of his true inferiority; for reason can be misleading, resulting in, for example, the Fall from Paradise. Mainly in the *Apology for Raimond Sebonde*, but also in his *Autobiography*, Montaigne deals explicitly with animals as our fellow creatures, to be respected: "We owe justice to men and kindliness to other animals: there is an intercourse and mutual obligation between them and us."[7]

Montaigne's aim was to humble human pride. In page after page, he cites examples of animal intelligence (sometimes questionable) and claims for them emotions as well. Then, as if anticipating Darwin and Huxley, he declares that "there is a greater difference between man and man than between man and animal."[8] Passages such as these lead Boas to treat the French essayist's writings as part of primitivism, that is, the extolling of Man's precivilized state. The primitivist message is that humans should aspire to be more like the animals.

Montaigne's version of this message provoked two different responses. On one side, the *beaux-esprits*, or libertines, took up his suggestion and advocated following nature, that is, giving in to the animal part of Man. This line of thought, "lowering" humans to the level of the beasts, eventually culminated in the Marquis de Sade. On another side, more significant for our purposes, a number of prominent thinkers attacked Montaigne, claiming that animals were simply machines and had no feelings, and hence were quite inferior to Man.

The revolutionary thinker on this side of the question was Descartes. Of course, he had predecessors—I have already cited artists and scientific illustrators—especially in the scholastic philosophers whom he had studied in his early years. Thus, Saint Thomas Aquinas, discussing dogs chasing a deer rather than going home, argues that "the animals act like machines made to run in a certain way by the sagacity of their maker, who is God. Thus God is, so to speak, their reason." In another passage, Aquinas, denying free will to beasts, likens their natural functioning to that of a clock.[9] Was Descartes influenced by these passages? We know only that he had read Aquinas's *Summa Theologica* at the Jesuit College of La Flèche.

We do know, however, that Descartes was fully aware of the Aristotelian position on which Aquinas also drew. Aristotle had conceived of three distinct souls: a vegetative, or plant soul; a sensitive, or animal soul; and a rational soul, the last being unique to Man.[10] Before Descartes the debate over the "Beast Machine" had mainly been in terms of the "animal soul." If beasts merely had an animal or "sensitive soul," giving them a degree of knowledge that was restricted to sense perceptions and memory, there were no real problems. If, however, beasts had a rational soul, that is, the ability to reason, differing from humans' only by degree, then all kinds of difficulties followed: would animals then, like humans, have a claim to immortality? But not having participated in Original Sin, how could they be involved in the great Christian drama leading to immortality? How could they be made to suffer, through no fault of their own?

Descartes faced these problems head-on. As Leonora Cohen Rosenfield suggests, Descartes placed the question in a new light: "In the first place, he rephrased the old question about animal soul to make of it an inquiry into animal intelligence, since to the author of the *cogito ergo sum* the word 'soul' spelled reason. Secondly, the scientific connotations he lent to the controversy were new."[11] As Rosenfield points out, "the growth of modern science opened up fresh approaches to the age-old enigma" of the animal soul. Descartes, of course, played a major role in "the growth of modern science," and we must now continue our examination of his contribution to the question of the animal-machine.

Descartes's revolutionary shift was to place in the forefront of the discussion the question of an animal's ability to reason, rather than its possession of a soul. He argued that the very perfection of the animal, which was instanced by the Montaignists—its superior industry, skill, and speed—pointed to its mechanical nature, its lack of reason. Pursuing this point, Descartes, according to a number of historians of science (though challenged by at least one, Georges Canguilhem), anticipated Pavlov, actually coining the term *reflex* long before the Russian scientist used it (see chapter 6) by perceiving in the animal a mere mechanical reflex action system.

Human superiority is therefore saved in a most paradoxical fashion: according to Descartes, Man is a machine that, unlike the animals, has reason (or soul), and can therefore err; nevertheless, the French scientist spent his life working out rules of reasoning, as in the *Discourse on Method,* to give Man rational certainty. It is as if, denying Man the perfection of the animal-machine on one level, he wished to endow him with this "inhuman condition" on another, higher level.

In fact, by so doing Descartes allows Man to achieve the animal-machine's certainty and perfection by means, not of mere reflex, but of rational free will. Descartes's first reference to the subject strikes this very note. "From the very perfection of animal actions we suspect that they do not have free will," he wrote sometime between 1619 and 1621 in his private notebook (*Cogitationes Privatae*). In short, Man, not being innately perfect (or else falling out of perfection when he errs in the Garden of Eden), has free will and must strive for perfection through his reason.

Descartes's basic assumption is that Man's will is completely under the discipline of his reason—for the great mathematician there is no Freudian struggle in the mind. As he pontificated, "Since our will neither seeks nor avoids anything except as it is judged good or bad by our reason, good judgment is sufficient to guarantee good behavior."[12] Shortly after this statement comes the famous Cartesian reduction of Man to a thinking being, at least as a thought experiment—"I concluded that I was a substance whose whole essence or nature was only to think."

The method by which Man thinks is to doubt. *Cogito ergo sum* is really *Dubito ergo sum*. It is important to note that doubt is the tool by which reason uncovers (rather than discovers) truth. It does so by freeing us from prerational conceptions and from misleading sense perceptions: "It delivers us from all sorts of prejudices and makes available to us an easy method of accustoming our minds to become independent of the senses."[13] In doing so, reason then does away with doubt; this is the task of reason.

And again we are left with a paradox: reason, operating by means of doubt, does away with doubt, and thus leads us toward perfection. Listen to Descartes as he tells us that "I reflected upon the fact that I doubted, and that, *in consequence* [my italics], my spirit was not wholly perfect, for I saw clearly that it was a greater perfection to know than to doubt."

Perfect knowing was to be found in God. Descartes's proof of the existence of God is a piece of not very convincing scholasticism. What is important for our purposes, however, is that in reaching to a "greater perfection," Cartesian Man aspires to a God-like state. Reason becomes the religion whereby Descartes can free himself from the material world and the dross of animal nature and become pure, rational spirit.

Having earlier told us that Man differs from the animal-machine because he can err, Descartes now proposes that Man transcend his own nature. By reason—and in accordance with Descartes's famous method of reasoning—Man "acquires the habit of not erring . . . since this comprises the greatest and principal perfection of man."[14] Is it too much of yet another paradox to say that Man apes the perfection of the animal-machine by becoming more mechanical than the animal but does so, for Descartes, out of free choice and the exercise of God-like reason? Moreover, even God has to exist and to "think" in accord with Descartes's "Method" for thinking.

On the night of November 10, 1619, in a now famous episode, Descartes had the extraordinary sequence of dreams that revealed to him the true nature of the universe. He realized literally in a blinding flash (for lightning figured in one of the dreams) that the universe was rational and was comprehensible by reason's most powerful tool, mathematics. We must note one last Cartesian paradox: Descartes had come to his "reasoned" insight by means of an "irrational" dream.[15]

Descartes immediately saw, like Leonardo before him but with a far more technical understanding of mathematics, that mathematics was linked to the mechanistic nature of the world and could penetrate its innermost nature. Everything in the universe except reason—for mathematics was a tool of reason—could be explained in the new mathematical-mechanical terms. As Descartes remarks, "The rules of mechanics . . . are the rules of nature."[16]

Intrigued with the mathematical-mechanical possibilities, Descartes very early on imagined a Man-machine to be activated by magnets and is reported to have planned machines to simulate a flying pigeon and a pheasant hunted by a spaniel.[17] In addition, even before he came to practice dissection (probably in the 1630s), he would have become acquainted with the work of the scientific illustrators whom we have discussed.

With such a background he could affirm most confidently in the *Discourse* that Man, though mechanical in every other way, was a superior creation of God's because Man alone of the animals—and machines—possessed reason. As he wrote, the fact that animals do better than humans only proves "that they are not rational, and that nature makes them behave as they do according to the disposition of their organs; just as a clock, composed only of wheels and springs, can count the hours and measure the time more accurately than we can with all our intelligence."[18] (One of Descartes's critics seized on his comparison of animals to clocks and asked rhetorically, "But do we caress our watches?")[19]

The key issue is the nature of reason, and of reason's God. Let us follow further than we have Descartes's cogitations and meditations on this subject, looking ahead to their relation to present-day work on "thinking machines." In his *Discourse on Method*, for example, he had set up God and the soul on one side, being without spatial location or extension, and the material-mechanical world in all its aspects on the other side. Only insofar as Man's mind or soul participates in reason—which means God's reason (happily, reason is common to all humans)—can Man know this division or dualism of mind and matter.

Once having established his God, and Man's participation through reason in God, Descartes could advance daringly to the very precipice of a world without God. Thus he conjures up a world in imaginary space and demonstrates that it must run according to known natural laws.

Even further, he imagines a world in which humans are simply machines: that "God formed the body of a man just like our own, both in the external configuration of its members and in the internal configuration of its organs, without using in its composition any matter but that which I had described [that is, physical matter]. I also assumed that God did not put into his body any rational soul."[20] Descartes defines *rational soul* as that part of us distinct from the body.

Analyzing this purely mechanical Man, Descartes boasts of how he has shown "what changes must take place in the brain to cause wakefulness, sleep and dreams; how light, sounds, odors, taste, heat, and all the other qualities of external objects can implant various ideas through the medium of the senses . . . I explained what must be understood by that animal sense which receives these ideas, by memory which retains them, and by imagination which can change them in various ways and build new ones from them."[21]

In what way, then, does such a figure differ from a real Man? In a manner that looks back to ancient automata (which I shall treat in chapter 3) and forward to the Turing Test (concerning the possibility of a machine being similar to a human in its responses, and thus being indistinguishable—see chapter 9), Descartes confronts his own created "Man" forthrightly:

Here I paused to show that if there were any machines which had the organs and appearance of a monkey or of some other unreasoning animal, we would have no way of telling that it was not of the same nature as these animals. But if there were a machine which had such a resemblance to our bodies, and imitated our actions as far as possible, there would always be two absolutely certain methods of recognizing that it was still not truly a man. The first is that it could never use words or other signs for the purpose of communicating its thoughts to others, as we do. It indeed is conceivable that a machine could be so made that it would utter words, and even words appropriate to physical acts which cause some change in its organs; as, for example, if it was touched in some spot that it would ask what you wanted to say to it; if in another, that it would cry that it was hurt, and so on for similar things. But it could never modify its phrases to reply to the sense of whatever was said in its presence, as even the most stupid men can do. The second method of recognition is that although such machines could do many things as well, or perhaps even better than, men, they would infallibly fail in certain others, by which we would discover that they did not act by understanding, but only by the disposition of their organs. For while reason is a universal instrument which can be used in all sorts of situations, the organs have to be arranged in a particular way for each particular action. From this it follows that it is morally impossible that there should be enough different devices in a machine to make it behave in all the occurrences of life as our reason makes us behave.[22]

Simply put, Descartes's two criteria for discriminating between humans and machine are that the latter has (1) no feedback mechanism ("it could never modify its phrases") and (2) no generalizing reason ("reason is a universal instrument which can be used in all sorts of situations").

But it is exactly in these points that, today, we are no longer able so surely to sustain the dichotomy. The work first of Norbert Wiener and then of his followers, in cybernetics, indicates what can be done on the problem of feedback. Investigations into the way the brain itself forms concepts are basic to the attempt to build computers that can do the same, and the two efforts are going forward simultaneously. As we shall see in detail in chapter 9, the gap between Man's thinking and that of his thinking machines has been greatly narrowed by recent research.

Descartes, of course, could not have foreseen such developments. Nor would he have been happy to acknowledge them. For to eliminate the dichotomy or discontinuity between humans and machines would be to banish God from the universe. Instead, the rational soul, Descartes insisted, "could not possibly be derived from the powers of matter . . . but must have been specially created."[23] Such special creation, in turn, requires—and hence proves—the existence of God. The shock to Man's ego of learning the Darwinian lesson that he was not "specially created" is, in this light, only an outlying tremor of the greater earthquake that threatened Man's view of God as well as of himself. The obstacles to coming to terms not only with the Darwinian shock, where humans become one with the other animals, but also with what I am calling the fourth discontinuity—that between humans and machines—are, clearly, deeply imbedded in human pride.

Paradoxically, the result of Descartes's work was to undermine the bases of the very pride he extolled. Descartes had struck a sturdy blow at the vitalists' view that organic life does not fall under the same mechanical principles that govern inorganic life. In opposition, he argued that physiology was a part of the general physical sciences, governed by the same mathematical-mechanical laws that ruled the latter. Thus, though it is true that Descartes placed theological and metaphysical restraints throughout his treatment of the animal-machine question, these were trappings that could be pushed aside easily by those who wished to make the question one simply of physiological psychology.[24] A defender of the uniqueness of humans versus both animals and machines might well have said of Descartes: God save us from our friends, we can take care of our enemies ourselves.

In his own time, Descartes had enemies on two sides. Traditionalists rejected his view that animals were machines without souls and moved the animals closer to humans. More radical thinkers accepted his mechanistic view of the animal and extended it all the way to humans. I shall give only enough bits and pieces of the debate to suggest its nature.

For Descartes and his supporters, one serendipitous aspect of his view was that it allowed vivisection to proceed without guilt. Though he later qualified his view, Descartes more typically claimed that animals, without understanding, could not "feel" pain as we do, that is, be conscious of it. Characteristically, a story is told of one of Descartes's supporters, Malebranche, who, sweet and gentle man though he was, kicked a pregnant dog. When his friend Fontenelle protested, Malebranche replied coldly, "Don't you know that it doesn't have any feeling?"[25] Pavlov, as we shall see, could have spoken no more pointedly and automatically.

Descartes's opponents attacked him on this and other grounds. Mme. de Sévigné, in 1672, wrote, "Regarding machines that love, machines that have an affinity for someone, machines that are jealous, machines that fear! Come on, come on, you're making fun; Descartes never intended to make us believe so." And Fontenelle exclaimed, "You say that beasts are machines just like watches? But put Monsieur mechanical dog and Mlle. mechanical dog together, the result will be a third little machine; while two watches may be together all their lives without ever making a third watch."[26]

Animals felt pain, were jealous, and procreated: so Descartes's opponents argued. Descartes was therefore wrong on these matters. Did this then mean that animals also had reason? Yes, said the great fabler La Fontaine. The animals in his immortal fables are characterized by both cunning and intelligence; thus, typically, La Fontaine writes that the owl is a wise bird. "This bird reasoned, it must be admitted."[27]

Philosophers such as Gassendi, however, gave a more systematic form to these arguments. In his fifth *Objectiones* to Descartes's *Meditationes*, while agreeing that animals do not reason as well as humans, Gassendi declared that this was merely a matter of degree, not of kind. "In this respect, there's hardly any difference between them [animals] and us except according to degree."[28] Thus, he contended, human speech was simply a more highly developed form of the same mental operation involved in a dog's barking. We are clearly on the way to another continuum.

It was Julien Offray de La Mettrie who most vividly drew out the other side of the implications of Descartes's work and declared Man to be a machine, no different from the animal-machines except in degree; nothing remained to Man in the way of a unique reason, or soul. Adding the empiricism and sensationalism of Lockean philosophy to Cartesian rationalism, La Mettrie boldly advanced his "shocking" thesis, even arguing that if apes could be taught language they would not differ from primitive humans.

La Mettrie was a physician. Originally intended for the ecclesiastic life, he began to study natural philosophy, and then medicine (especially anatomy), receiving his medical degree in 1725. His subsequent life is unspectacular (except for his last moment, when he died from eating too much pâté).

His published work is not particularly extensive or, with the exception of one book, memorable. Thus, he first translated a treatise by the great Dutch thinker and his medical teacher, Boerhaave, who had also influenced Descartes; to this treatise, *Aphrodisiacus*, La Mettrie added a dissertation of his own, on venereal diseases. Somewhat later, during a violent attack of fever, experienced during a period of military service (and we have already noted Descartes's famous dream, during a similar period of military service), he had an illumination and became convinced that thought was a product of the body-machine. Inspired, he wrote *Histoire naturelle de l'âme* (The natural history of the soul, 1745), which was condemned to flames in Paris, and then, *L'Homme-machine* (1747). Even though this last book was published anonymously, La Mettrie was forced to flee for protection to the more "enlightened" court of Frederick the Great.

Here he died early in 1751, age forty-three. Elected earlier to the Prussian Royal Academy of Science, he was honored when he died by the composition of a brief Eloge by the king himself. His enemies, however, rejoiced at his demise and depicted him as a debauched sensualist (a fact, they argued, proven by the manner of his death).

In his last work, La Mettrie left a defiant and persistent assertion of humans as machines. He was not always consistent in his position—at one point, he seemed to condemn Descartes's "absurd system that animals are pure machines"—but when he embraced it, he did so in highly provocative terms.[29]

There was a touch of the libertine in La Mettrie. His interest in venereal diseases coincided with a prurient note in his *L'Homme-machine*. The most easily available English translation omits the frequent references to men's involuntary erections and to women's genital parts that La Mettrie sprinkles about his book.[30] Such references, though calculated to titillate and attract readers, also point to the central role sexuality is always given, explicitly or implicitly, in the human-machine discussion (we have already noted Fontenelle's allusion to dogs and watches procreating).

La Mettrie's central assertion, on which the rest is hung, is that Man is a machine; an "enlightened machine" (*"une machine bien éclairée"*), he calls him. In the Newtonian terms of the times, he also declares, "The body is but a watch." Appealing to scientific experience and observation as guides, he writes that the required empirical data "are to be found throughout the records of the physicians who were philosophers, and not in the works of the philosophers who were not physicians. The former have traveled through and illuminated the labyrinth of man; they alone have laid bare to us those springs [of life] hidden under the external integument which conceals so many wonders from our eyes."[31] Instead of a priori philosophy, he advises, we must turn to a posteriori anatomy.

We sense La Mettrie's personal experience in the military campaign when he goes on, "In disease the soul is sometimes hidden, showing no sign of life; sometimes it is so inflamed by fury that it seems to be doubled; sometimes, imbecility vanishes and the convalescence of an idiot produces a wise man. Sometimes, again, the greatest genius becomes imbecile and loses the sense of self. Adieu then to all that fine knowledge, acquired at so high a price, and with so much trouble! Here is a paralytic who asks if his leg is in bed with him; there is a soldier who thinks that he still has the arm which has been cut off." Continuing in this vein, La Mettrie argues that "the human body is a machine which winds its own springs. It is the living image of perpetual movement. Nourishment keeps up the movements which fever excites. Without food, the soul pines away, goes mad, and dies exhausted."[32]

If, as we shall see, La Mettrie anticipates much of Pavlov, and, before him, Huxley, he does so in a markedly different way, coming from machines to animals, rather than the reverse. Thus, where Pavlov concluded that because we cannot see into the minds and feelings of animals we must assume they have no consciousness, only reflex actions, La Mettrie draws an opposite conclusion. In a passage that must be quoted at length, he states:

> Have we ever had a single experience which convinces us that man alone has been enlightened by a ray denied all other animals? If there is no such experience, we can no more know what goes on in animals' minds or even in the minds of other men, than we can help feeling what affects the inner part of our own being. We know that we think, and feel remorse—an intimate feeling forces us to recognize this only too well; but this feeling in us is insufficient to enable us to judge the remorse of others. That is why we have to take others at their word, or judge them by the sensible and external signs we have noticed in ourselves when we experienced the same accusations of conscience and the same torments.
>
> In order to decide whether animals which do not talk have received the natural law, we must, therefore, have recourse to those signs to which I have just referred, if any such exist. The facts seem to prove it. A dog that bit the master who was teasing it, seemed to repent a minute afterwards; it looked sad, ashamed, afraid to show itself, and seemed to confess its guilt by a crouching and downcast air. History offers us a famous example of a lion which would not devour a man abandoned to its fury, because it recognized him as its benefactor.[33]

La Mettrie is not a systematic or unambivalent writer, but similar to the clocklike nature of Man he extolled, he struck with recurring consistency the fundamental note of humans' and animals' machinelike nature.[34] Indeed, one can make the case that La Mettrie was not really interested in the human-machine as a scientific question but mainly used the general idea, which he hardly explicated fully, as a weapon to oppose Descartes's egocentrism and thus to humble humans. Whatever La Mettrie's true intentions and interests, what persists is his becoming the symbol of the Cartesian (or rather anti-Cartesian) reduction of humans to pure machines.

It is important also to realize that La Mettrie was perambulating, or even sleepwalking, on the edge of an evolutionary vision—one very much in the air in eighteenth-century France; in fact, it was given initial form at the end of the century by Lamarck but was unable at the time to root itself either in the evidence to be collected so assiduously by Darwin a century later or in the breakthrough hypothesis of natural selection. Thus, characteristically, La Mettrie reminds his readers that "the transition from animals to man is not violent, as true philosophers will admit. What was man before the invention of words and the knowledge of language? An animal of his own species with much less instinct than the others. In those days, he did not consider himself king over the other animals, nor was he distinguished from the ape, and from the rest, except as the ape itself differs from the other animals, i.e., by a more intelligent face."

Almost at the end of his book, La Mettrie glimpses the relatedness of plants, animals, humans, and machines that I am postulating when he announces that "such is the uniformity of nature, which we are beginning to realize; and the analogy of the animal with the vegetable kingdom, of man with plant. Perhaps there even are animal plants, which in vegetating, either fight as polyps do, or perform other functions characteristic of animals."[35]

The explicit connection of Man and machines is made in a prophetic passage. "It [thus] appears that there is but one [type of organization] in the universe, and that man is the most perfect [example]. He is to the ape, and to the most intelligent animals, as the planetary pendulum of Huyghens is to a watch of Julien Leroy. More instruments, more wheels and more springs were necessary to mark the movements of the planets than to mark or strike the hours; and Vaucanson, who needed more skill for making his flute player than for making his duck, would have needed still more to make a talking man, a mechanism no longer to be regarded as impossible, especially in the hands of another Prometheus."[36]

Bold, ribald, polemical, satirical ("Fish have large heads, but these are void of sense, like the heads of many men,"[37] he commented about his opponents), and writing in an unattractive style, La Mettrie nevertheless pounded home effectively his message that Man was nothing more than a machine. He did so in what is for us old-fashioned terms. He was not thinking of computers and artificial intelligence—even Pascal, his earlier compatriot who invented a calculating device, seemed not to engage his attention—but of the simple animal machines depicted in the scientific illustrations of a da Vinci, a Taccola, and others of their craft. Man is mainly a clock—a system of levers, escapements, and so forth—and not a computer.[38] La Mettrie presented his mechanistic views in such primitive terms, and in such terms his position was embraced or repulsed by contemporaries and the following few generations as the notion of "L'Homme-machine" spread into the general culture.[39] There it remained to haunt many thoughtful humans as they have sought to hold on to their vaunted separateness from and superiority to (other) animals and machines.

## **Chapter** Three

Long before the seventeenth-century debate over the animal-machine, concern with the subject had been given practical form in the shape of automata. From antiquity to the present, these simulacrums of "flesh and blood," so to speak, put directly before humans the question of their difference, if any, from machines. Automata presented to all mankind what philosophy had otherwise reserved for the academies.

Because automata placed humans face-to-face with physical shapes rather than mere metaphysical speculations, they could call forth intense feelings of psychological identification. Such identifications might be positive or negative, promising or threatening.

Automata were the work of human hands; and, for many, Man's taking of creation into his own hands seemed, and seems, to bring with it the seeds of his and his creatures' death and destruction, thereby mirroring Man's own Adamic rebellion against his Creator and consequent condemnation to the fate of "dust to dust." For others, such creative power meant humans themselves were a god, omnipotent, perfect, and potentially free from death.

Fantasies or aspirations, such derivations from identification with automata have haunted the human imagination for at least the last few thousand years. In seeking to understand Man's relation to his machines, automata are of critical importance, for they seem to present Man's image to himself physically and not just in his mind. Such mechanical "creatures" seem to fuse theory and practice.

From antiquity, I am arguing that humans, the ingenious makers, have posed to themselves the question of their identity by making "doubles": mechanical figures and puppets that seem to be animated. If a machine, in the shape of an automaton, were to look and function exactly as a human, how would we know if it were one, or not? (The Turing Test, treated in chapter 9, is a recent version of this concern.) The animal-machine controversy thus takes on an android look.

It is difficult to know how many of the automata of antiquity were constructed only in legends or by actual scientific artifice. Icarus's wings melt in the light of historical inquiry, as they were reputed to do in the myth; but was the flying automaton attributed to a Chinese scientist of ca. 380 B.C. actually in the air for three days, as related? (The same story is told of Archytas of Tarentum.)[1] The mix of fact and fiction is a subject of crucial importance for the history of science and technology; for our purposes, the aspirations of semimythical inventors can be as revealing as the actual embodiments in levers and gears.

Chinese and Greek traditions are especially rich on the subject of automata. Indian and, somewhat later, Arabic sources are also copious. Western-centered and limited as this book is, I am compelled to note the preeminence of Chinese science and technology in this area. Joseph Needham has made this fact evident in his monumental work, *Science and Civilization in China*.

The wealth of mechanical toys cited in ancient China is awesome. In addition to the flying machine mentioned earlier, mechanized doves and angels, fish, and dragons abounded; automated cup bearers and wine pourers were prominent; and hydraulically moved boats, carrying figures of singing girls, animals, and men in motion are said to have amused the emperors. Of particular interest are the chariots that moved themselves—*auto*-mobiles—attributed by legend to the scientist Mo Ti in the fourth century B.C. Were they actually wheelbarrows, or "pedicarts"? A mechanical man of jade is reported, as well as all kinds of wooden dolls, gold Buddhist statues, and puppet orchestras.

What is Man? asked such automata by their actions. "Man is the mechanician" is the most obvious answer. Are humans also machines? Needham cites a long passage, which I repeat here, that vividly gives us the flavor of automata development in China and raises the questions of humans' dual nature. The passage, from the *Lieh Tzu*, whose probable date is the third century B.C., tells of how

> King Mu of Chou made a tour of inspection in the west . . . and on his return journey, before reaching China, a certain artificer, Yen Shih by name, was presented to him. The king received him and

asked him what he could do. He replied that he would do anything which the king commanded, but that he had a piece of work already finished which he would like to show him. "Bring it with you tomorrow," said the king, "and we will look at it together." So next day Yen Shih appeared again and was admitted into the presence. "Who is that man accompanying you?" asked the king. "That, Sir," replied Yen Shih, "is my own handiwork. He can sing and he can act." The king stared at the figure in astonishment. It walked with rapid strides, moving its head up and down, so that anyone would have taken it for a live human being. The artificer touched its chin, and it began singing, perfectly in tune. He touched its hand, and it began posturing, keeping perfect time. It went through any number of movements that fancy might happen to dictate. The king, looking on with his favourite concubine and other beauties, could hardly persuade himself that it was not real. As the performance was drawing to an end, the robot winked its eye and made advances to the ladies in attendance, whereupon the king became incensed and would have had Yen Shih executed on the spot had not the latter, in mortal fear, instantly taken the robot to pieces to let him see what it really was. And, indeed, it turned out to be only a construction of leather, wood, glue and lacquer, variously coloured white, black, red and blue. Examining it closely, the king found all the internal organs complete—liver, gall, heart, lungs, spleen, kidneys, stomach and intestines; and over these again, muscles, bones and limbs with their joints, skin, teeth and hair, all of them artificial. Not a part but was fashioned with the utmost nicety and skill; and when it was put together again, the figure presented the same appearance as when first brought in. The king tried the effect of taking away the heart, and found that the mouth could no longer speak; he took away the liver and the eyes could no longer see; he took away the kidney and the legs lost their power of locomotion. The king was delighted. Drawing a deep breath, he exclaimed, "Can it be that human skill is on a par with that of the great Author of Nature?"[2]

"Anyone would have taken it for a live human being"—here we have one of the key phrases. The robot making advances to the ladies and incurring the king's wrath presents the sexual threat so prevalent, as we shall see, in fears about automata. In the sentence "Can it be that human skill is on a par with that of the great Author of Nature?" is sounded what in the West we know of as the Promethean theme.

The Greeks, too, were absorbed with automata of one kind or another. The Delphic oracles spoke through a wind-operated "voice," and the god Hephaestus is said to have forged a sort of robot of bronze, named Talos, to guard Crete. Indeed, statues and effigies were themselves godlike, that is, filled with the voices of the gods. We catch this sense of the statue as divine in the writing of Callistratus, in the fourth century A.D., about an ivory and gold statue of the god Asclepius: "Shall we admit that the divine spirit descends into human bodies, there to be even defiled by passions, and nevertheless not believe it in a case where there is no attendant engendering of evil? . . . for see how an image, after Art has portrayed in it a god, even passes over into the god himself! Matter though it is, it gives forth divine intelligence."[3]

A true history of automata would give all the details and would cover the ground systematically.[4] I wish merely to highlight the topic and to pick it up again in more modern times. Note Needham's concluding comment that when the Chinese and European traditions of mechanical toys "came together in the middle of the +13th century, the European tradition did not show up to much advantage. The triumphs of the European 'Gadget Age' were yet to come."[5]

In the thirteenth century in Europe, for example, we find reports of exemplary mechanical doves and angels made by Villard de Honnecourt. In the fifteenth century, the mathematician and astronomer Johannes Müller constructed an eagle and a fly that astounded his contemporaries; the twentieth-century historian of science Pierre Duhem has proposed a tentative explanation: "The fly, for instance, would beat its wings by means of springs concealed within it, and make the tour of a dinner-table suspended from a hair invisible to the guests, finally approaching the hand of Regiomantanus [Müller] because of a magnet secretly held by him."[6]

In this account, Müller seems as much magician as mechanician. The connection is not accidental, as Frances Yates and others have argued, positing a "Hermetic Tradition" in Renaissance science. Her argument, for example, is that "the Renaissance magus was the immediate ancestor of the seventeenth-century scientist." In turn, the Renaissance magus "had his roots in the Hermetic core of Renaissance Neo-Platonism."[7]

It was especially Marsilio Ficino, along with Pico della Mirandola, who revived and carried forward the Hermetic tradition into the Renaissance. Ficino translated the collection of treatises that supposedly were written by Hermes Trismegistus, who he believed to have been a real Egyptian priest and who gave an account, like Moses, of Man and the cosmos. In the Hermetic story of creation, however, Man is given permission by the Father not only to dominate over the animals but also to share in the demiurgic powers, that is, to create and animate artificial beings, as we would call them, or, in my terms, machines. Thus, in the Hermetic *Asclepius*, as Yates informs us, "The Egyptian priests . . . are presented as knowing how to capture the efflures of the stars and through this magical knowledge to animate the statues of their gods."[8]

Alchemy was the Hermetic science par excellence. Mere matter could be transformed, for example, into gold, but life also could be distilled from the alchemist's retorts. The other means of creating life out of inanimate matter was through cabalistic conjurations. Small wonder that an air of mystery and magic hung over the Renaissance magus, who rapidly also gained the taint of charlatanism. John Dee, the Elizabethan scientist, is a prime example of the confusion of magic, "chemistry," and mechanics. Called the "great conjuror" for his magic summoning of angels, he was also suspect for his mechanical powers. In vain he protested: "And for . . . marueilous Actes and Feates, Naturally, Mathematically, and Mechanically wrought and contrived, ought any honest Student and Modest Christian Philosopher, be counted and called a Coniuror?"[9]

In the Hermetic tradition of the Renaissance, the ancient fascination with automata took on new life. Magic and mechanics were mixed, and an air of fear and wonder hovers over the statues and angels conjured out of the earth and air. Are they alive and real, or not? Are humans, indeed, mechanicians, who can then breathe life into what they have created, thereby imitating their own Creator? Or are they, in turn, merely machines themselves, working on mechanical principles? In the Hermetic tradition of the Renaissance, these questions are close to the surface, though enveloped in mythical and magical shapes.

A century or two later, having passed through the cleansing and brightening waters of Baconian and Cartesian thought, the automata giving rise to these questions take on, seemingly, a more secular, more reasoned form. In the eighteenth century, one of the most skilled technicians was the Frenchman Jacques de Vaucanson. He produced a duck, which we are told "drank, ate, digested, cackled, and swam—the whole interior apparatus of digestion exposed, so that it could be viewed; [a] flute player who played twelve different tunes, moving his fingers, lips and tongue, depending on the music; [a] girl who played the tambourine, [a] mandolin player that moved his head and pretended to breathe."

Even more spectacular were the automata of Pierre Jaquet-Droz, a

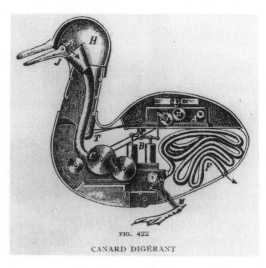

Jacques Vaucanson, *Canard digérant*, from *Le monde des automates* (1928).

FIG. 422

CANARD DIGÉRANT

Swiss, who "in 1774 . . . created a lifesized and lifelike figure of a boy seated at a desk, capable of writing up to forty letters." (He still functions at the History Museum in Neuchâtel.) Droz created another figure, called the "Artist," in the shape of a boy that could draw up to four different sketches, improving on the average work of his human counterpart.[10]

These mechanical figures were bathed, at the time of the Enlightenment, in the pure light of reason, and the discussions about them took place in unambiguous "scientific" terms. We have already listened to some of the discourse, ranging from Descartes to La Mettrie. Underlying these discussions, however, as I shall try to show later, ran the fears attached to the automata, for they posed an "irrational" threat to humans, calling into question their identity, sexual jealousies (the basis of creation?), and powers of domination.

Automata provoked not just fears but the promise of creative, Promethean force as well. The tension between these two aspects of the automaton is most interesting, at play in various examples of the genre. I shall try to explore the human ambivalence regarding automata in a selected group of literary examples: the nightingale of Hans Christian Andersen's *Fairy Tales*, the creature in *Frankenstein*, by Mary Shelley, the Tiktok of the Oz stories, the *R.U.R.* of Karel Capek, and assorted robots of Isaac Asimov.

I could have chosen from innumerable other examples, for tales of the automaton are legion. Those I have chosen, however, are classic examples (Asimov's is becoming one) and illustrate different aspects of the human encounter with the mechanical "other."

Thus, Andersen's tale hinges on clockwork mechanisms; Shelley's Frankenstein, perhaps the dominant Western metaphor for the fourth discontinuity, straddling both biological and mechanical fears, is self-evident in its importance and thus deserves extended treatment; Baum's Oz stories obsessively reflecting the childlike curiosity about "life" are hardly as innocent as they appear; Capek's *R.U.R.* gives birth to the term *robot*, and voices the fear of its taking over, a fear echoed today in countless films about menacing androids; and Asimov's varied cast of robots allows us to explore many of the intellectual dimensions of a predicted coming of a robotic age.

Let us begin with Hans Christian Andersen's "The Nightingale," a famous tale from the nineteenth century. It reflects both the scientific concern with automata and the Romantic revulsion against the mechanical Newtonian worldview. Newton had imagined the universe as a clockwork. The clock, with its intricate, precise, and more or less unfailing machinery, as we shall see further in chapter 4, symbolized the new age of scientific method and industrial discipline. It also prompted additional speculation about the relation between the internal "works" of human beings and clocks.

In Andersen's tale, we are presented with a "real nightingale" and one that requires a "watchmaker."[11] The tale itself is a simple one. The real nightingale charms a Chinese emperor and his peasants alike. Its song brings tears into their eyes. Then an artificial nightingale appears, even handsomer than the real one because it is ornamented with precious stones. It appears to sing with equal skill and more repeatedly and is as well received as the original. Banished, the real bird flies away. After a year, however, the artificial nightingale begins to break down and cannot be fully repaired. A few years later, the emperor lays dying, and only the nightingale's song can save him. But the artificial bird has now completely wound down. Suddenly, the live nightingale appears, sings to the emperor, and he comes back to life.

In Andersen's telling, the tale has a poignancy and meaning that cannot be conveyed in this précis. Looked at closely, the short story also takes on unexpected ambiguities. The compelling note is the constant comparison between human-made and "natural" things: at the beginning, the croaking of frogs is mistaken for church bells by the courtiers, the nightingale's song for glass bells. The artificial bird and the real nightingale cannot sing well together, "for the real Nightingale sang in its own way, and the artificial bird sang waltzes."[12] At first, the palm seems to go to the mechanical contrivance for "three-and-thirty times over did it sing the same piece, and yet was not tired." Praising it, the artificer explains how "with a real nightingale one can never calculate what is coming, but in this artificial bird everything is settled."

In fact, the artificial bird is neither untiring nor settled. It breaks down and cannot be repaired. In contrast, the nightingale goes on living, as if for eternity. (While I do not know how long a nightingale can live, I suspect not too many years; of course, new ones can be produced, but so can machines.) Thus the qualities normally assigned to animate (living) objects and inanimate (nonliving) objects are reversed: it is the animate that endures. This theme is reiterated at the end, when the real nightingale, symbolizing the forces of life, banishes death: in the words of the emperor, "I banished you from my country and empire, and yet you have charmed away the evil forces from my couch, and banished Death from my heart!"[13]

Through this short story Andersen is saying that the difference between humans and automata is simple and straightforward: one represents life and the other death, cold and mechanical. It is the Romantic lament. As the nightingale tells the emperor at the end, "I will sing of those who are happy and of those who suffer. I will sing of good and of evil that remain hidden round about you."[14]

Though Andersen's answer to his question about humans and automata is seemingly an untroubled one, it is really surrounded by ambiguous thoughts and feelings. (Andersen had an unhappy youth and occupied his time in solitude by constructing puppet theaters.) His tale is not calculated to satisfy those who felt, and feel, themselves deeply puzzled and disturbed over the mysteries of life and mechanism.

The artificial nightingale is a clockwork figure. Mary Shelley's *Frankenstein* draws on other sources: it reaches back to the Hermetic tradition, to which it adds the threatening aspect of the legendary golem. Badly written, stilted, a pastiche of styles and inspirations, the book nevertheless exercises an uncanny power over us. An alchemist's brew of ideas, its very formlessness allows us to instill in it all the shapes and forms of our own imagination. Frankenstein's monster looms over our most primordial fears and desires, hulking above our ambivalent feelings toward animals and machines, symbolizing the way in which they take on a "life" of their own.

Mary Shelley had no formal education. Nevertheless, being the daughter of Mary Wollstonecraft and William Godwin, she moved in a circle of advanced thought. Influenced by the enlightenment of her time, she also breathed the air of mysticism and romanticism that emanated from the gothic novels of Walpole and Rutledge or the poetry of Samuel Taylor Coleridge. Her peculiar genius was to connect ancient myths with early nineteenth-century science.

The Hermetic tradition seemingly had blessed human participation in the demiurge and looked benignly on efforts to give life to inanimate statues. In *Frankenstein*, a dark shadow creeps over these efforts: Cornelius Agrippa, Paracelsus, and Albertus Magnus, "canonical" figures in the Hermetic tradition, are all mentioned as the hero's inspirations, but they are seen as Mephistopheles-like figures, leading him to perdition. It is a golem, not the statues of Hermes Trismegistus, that here becomes animated.

Golems may have originated as wooden or clay models of human beings that were placed in graves to act as servants of the dead.[15] In Europe, they take on an especially legendary form in the sixteenth century. The golem, a shapeless mass of clay, could be given form by conjuration, in this case, Jewish cabalism. A rabbi pronounces holy words and writes on the creature's forehead *Emeth*, meaning "truth" in Hebrew, thus endowing it with life. By erasing the *E*, the word becomes *Meth*, which means "death," and the creature disintegrates. (In another version, the rabbi writes *Shem*, the name of God, but the process is the same.)

The golem is supposedly Man's servant. He is to protect his maker. But in the legends, the golem almost always also threatens his master— running out of control, falling on his master, or going berserk—and must finally be destroyed. (The most famous golem is that in the service of Rabbi Loew, in early seventeenth-century Prague.)[16]

Mary Shelley doesn't make overt reference to the golem tales; but they, along with the Hermetic tradition, lie in back of her story. Further influences crowd in. Her rationalist father, William Godwin, had written a book *Lives of the Necromancers*, which, though not published until 1834 (by Mary), reflected earlier conversations between him and his daughter about Agrippa, Paracelsus, Albertus Magnus, the Rosicrucians, and other cabalistic and maguslike sources. Another current of thought—contemporary science, especially chemistry and electricity—came to play about Mary's mind through her husband, Percy Bysshe Shelley.

Though a poet, Percy Bysshe Shelley was fascinated by science. Like Godwin, he had read Paracelsus (who, incidentally, was famous for having claimed that he could create "a little man or homunculus"). As a boy, Shelley had also become intrigued with chemistry, and his rooms at Eton are said to have resembled an alchemist's laboratory. He was also exposed, according to one scholar, "to androids, or mechanical toys that functioned like humans"—a product of the scientific genius of Adam Walker, to whose lectures he had listened.[17]

At Oxford, Shelley also experimented with electrical machines, air pumps, galvanic batteries, and other such paraphernalia. Though Lord Byron probably encouraged Mary Shelley to read Sir Humphry Davy's *Elements of Chemical Philosophy* (1812) at the time she began the composition of *Frankenstein*, it was her husband, Percy, who really served as the lightning rod, connecting the ancient alchemists and the modern genie of science in her thought. Indeed, it was Percy who urged her on with the book, helped her to write it, penned the preface, and secured its publication.

Davy's *Elements*, which hinted at the possibility of discovering a life force—a subtle universal fluid or vital magnetism—dealt with recent researches into galvanism and electricity. Luigi Galvani's work, or what I like to call the "galvanic twitch" (whose movement through nineteenth-century thought has still not been sufficiently traced), had demonstrated the identity of electrical and chemical forces, that is, their interconvertibility. It also suggested that galvanic electricity could bridge the gap between the animate and inanimate; the frog's leg made to twitch seemed to lead to Aldini's experiment in which shock applied to a recently hanged man produced an effect that, as he wrote, "surpassed our most sanguine expectations, and vitality might perhaps have been restored if many circumstances had not rendered it impossible."[18]

Percy Bysshe Shelley was probably also influenced by the climate of opinion embodied in the term *Natürphilosophie*, though it remains something of a will-o'-the-wisp in the history of science except among specialists. An important movement of thought in the early nineteenth century, it has generally been treated with scorn, as befitting a kind of mystical attitude to nature. Though it emphasized vitalism and holism against the dominant materialism and analysis of contemporary Western science (hence, the scorn), both types of philosophy sought to depict the universe as unified and falling under one connecting net of forces and thus laws. In any event, *Natürphilosophie* propagated the idea of the interconvertibility of forces, linking the animate and inanimate through galvanism, magnetism (in the form of mesmerism, it becomes "animal magnetism"), and electricity. Thus animating forces could be made to run between the poles of life and death.

Mary Shelley's knowledge of these developments in science was a

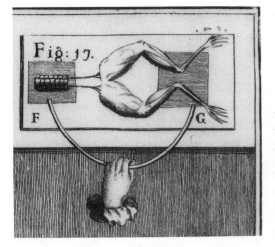

The Galvanic twitch. Twitching frog's legs lead from Galvani to Aldini's experiments, thence to Mary Shelley's *Frankenstein* and the supposed creation of life by means of a spark infused into inanimate materials (Courtesy Burndy Library, Dibner Institute, MIT, Cambridge, Mass.).

hodgepodge; she only dimly and intuitively grasped their meaning. But like the ancient alchemists, she thought she knew enough to attempt their transmutation into the gold of art—and succeeded, creating an immortal work of fiction, *Frankenstein*. In 1816, on the edge of Lake Leman, Geneva, Switzerland, the shreds and tatters of true science were combined with the myths of antiquity.

We can reconstruct *Frankenstein*'s composition. Byron and a friend, Dr. John Polidori, had joined Mary and Percy. Outside their villa a storm rages; the friends amuse and terrify themselves by telling ghost stories. Byron then proposes that each write his or her own. That night, Mary has a nightmare in which, as she tells us, "I saw the hideous phantasm of a man stretched out, and then, on the working of some powerful engine, shows signs of life, and stirs with an uneasy, half vital motion." From this nightmare, *Frankenstein* is born.[19]

I have given some of the background to Mary Shelley's book because to do so illustrates vividly the range of human curiosity, embodied in scientific inquiry and legendary stories, concerning the creation of life from inanimate material. "More, far more will I achieve," exclaims Frankenstein, "treading in the steps already marked, I will pioneer a new way, explore unknown powers, and unfold to the world the deepest mysteries of creation."[20] In penetrating these mysteries, the book resurrects and reclothes a number of humanity's deepest concerns about automata: for example, the servant-machine rising against its master, the fear of the machine reproducing itself (fundamentally a sexual fear, as the example of Caliban in Shakespeare's *Tempest* reminds us, and as we shall see in our further account of Mary Shelley's book), and the terror, finally, of humans realizing that they are at one with the machine-monster.

Such is the fundamental attraction and meaning of *Frankenstein*. But little attention has been given to the actual details of the novel, which has now passed into folklore. For this reason, I will instance material that may be familiar to scholars of the book but not necessarily to the general reader.

First, the name Frankenstein is often given to the monster created, rather than to its creator; yet, in the book, Frankenstein is the name of the scientist, and his abortion has no name. Second, the monster is *not* a machine but a "flesh and blood" product; even a student as informed as the distinguished historian Oscar Handlin makes the typical quick shift when he says, "The monster, however, quickly proves himself the superior. In the confrontation, the machine gives the orders." Third, and last, it is usually forgotten or overlooked that the monster turns to murder *because* his creator, horrified at his production, refuses him human love and kindness. Let us look at a few of the details.

In writing her gothic novel in 1816 to 1817, Mary Shelley gave it the subtitle "The Modern Prometheus." We can see why if we remember that Prometheus defied the gods and gave fire to humankind. Writing from an early nineteenth-century Romantic perspective, Mary Shelley offers Frankenstein as an example of "how dangerous is the acquirement of knowledge"; in this case, specifically, the capability of "bestowing animation upon lifeless matter." In the novel we are told of how, having collected his materials from "the dissecting room and the slaughterhouse," Frankenstein eventually completes his loathsome task when he infuses "a spark of being into the lifeless thing that lay at my feet." Then, as he tells us, "now that I had finished, the beauty of the dream vanished, and breathless horror and disgust filled my heart." Rushing from the room, Frankenstein goes to his bedchamber, where he has a most odd dream concerning the corpse of his dead mother (the whole book as well as this passage cries out for psychoanalytic interpretation) from which he is awakened by "the wretch—the miserable monster whom I had created." Aghast at the countenance of what he has created, Frankenstein escapes from the room and out into the open. Upon finally returning to his room with a friend, he is relieved to find the monster gone.

To understand the myth, we need to recite a few further details of this weird story. Frankenstein's monster eventually finds his way to a hovel attached to a cottage, occupied by a blind father and his son and daughter. Unperceived by them, he learns the elements of social life (the fortuitous way in which this occurs may strain the demanding reader's credulity), even to the point of reading *Paradise Lost*. Resolved to end his unbearable solitude, the monster, convinced that his virtues of the heart will win over the cottagers, makes his presence known. The result is predictable: horrified by his appearance, they duplicate the behavior of his creator and flee. In wrath, the monster turns against the heartless world. He kills, and his first victim, by accident, is Frankenstein's young brother.

Pursued by Frankenstein, the creature eventually confronts its creator. The monster explains his road to murder and, in a torrential address, appeals to Frankenstein:

> I entreat you to hear me, before you give vent to your hatred on my devoted head. Have I not suffered enough that you seek to increase my misery? Life, although it may only be an accumulation of anguish, is dear to me, and I will defend it. Remember, thou hast made me more powerful than thyself; my height is superior to thine; my joints more supple. But I will not be tempted to set myself in opposition to thee. I am thy creature, and I will be even mild and docile to my natural lord and king, if thou wilt also perform thy part, the which thou owest me. Oh, Frankenstein, be not equitable to every other, and trample upon me alone, to whom thy justice, and even thy clemency and affection is most due. Remember, that I am thy creature; I ought to be thy Adam; but I am rather the fallen angel, whom thou drives from joy for no misdeed. Everywhere I see bliss, from which I alone am irrevocably excluded. I was benevolent and good; misery made me a fiend. Make me happy, and I shall again be virtuous.

Eventually, the monster extracts from Frankenstein a promise to create a partner for him "of another sex," with whom he will then retire into the vast wilds of South America, away from the world of humankind. But Frankenstein's "compassion" does not last long. In his laboratory again, Frankenstein indulges in a long soliloquy:

> I was now about to form another being, of whose dispositions I was alike ignorant; she might become ten thousand times more malignant than her mate; and delight, for its own sake, in murder and wretchedness. He had sworn to quit the neighborhood of man, and hide himself in deserts; but she had not; and she, who in all probability was to become a thinking and reasoning animal,

might refuse to comply with a compact made before her creation. They might even hate each other; the creature who already lived loathed his own deformity, and might he not conceive a greater abhorrence for it when it came before his eyes in the female form? She also might quit him, and he be again alone, exasperated by the fresh provocation of being deserted by one of his own species.

Even if they were to leave Europe, and inhabit the deserts of the new world, yet one of the first results of those sympathies for which the demon thirsted would be children, and a race of devils would be propagated upon the earth who might make the very existence of the species of man a condition precarious and full of terror. Had I right, for my own benefit, to inflict this curse upon everlasting generations?

With the monster observing him through the window, Frankenstein destroys the female companion on whom he had been working.

With this, the novel relentlessly winds its way to its end. In despair, the monster revenges himself by killing Frankenstein's best friend, Clerval, and then Frankenstein's new bride, Elizabeth. Fleeing to the frozen north, the monster is tracked down by Frankenstein, who dies, however, before he can destroy his dreadful creation. It does not matter; the monster wishes his own death and promises to place himself on a funeral pyre and thus at last secure the spiritual peace for which he has yearned.

It is important to be acquainted with the myth of Frankenstein *as actually written* by Mary Shelley. For most of us, Frankenstein is Boris Karloff, clumping around stiff, automatic, and threatening: a machine of sorts. (My students tell me this image is hopelessly out-of-date; for them *Frankenstein* is Gene Wilder in Mel Brooks's film *Young Frankenstein*.) We shall have forgotten completely, if ever we knew, that the monster *cum* machine, is evil, or rather becomes evil, only because it is spurned by humans.

Implicit in *Frankenstein* is the question of the fourth discontinuity. If humans insist on their separateness and superiority in regard to machines (as well as other animals), viewing them as a threatening new "species," rather than as a part of their own creation, will they, indeed, bring about the very state of alienation that they fear? Do differences between humans and machines—and I shall deal extensively with them in my last two chapters—add up to a discontinuity? Although Frankenstein's creation is, in fact, a monster, its existence raises the same fundamental "mysteries" as if it were a machine—such are the amorphous connecting powers of myth.[21]

Mary Shelley, of course, was writing about creation before Charles Darwin; her "mysteries" are without the benefit of his great work on what he called the "mystery of mysteries." Another Darwin, however, not Charles, was summoned directly to Mary's assistance: Erasmus Darwin, Charles's grandfather. In the preface to *Frankenstein* (actually written by Percy) the opening lines state that "the event on which this fiction is founded has been supposed by Dr. Darwin, and some of the physiological writers of Germany, as not of impossible occurrence."[22] Later, in her introduction to the 1831 edition, Mary recalls how she, her husband, and Lord Byron discussed "the nature of the principles of life, and whether there was any probability of its ever being discovered and communicated. They talked of the experiments of Dr. [Erasmus] Darwin . . . who preserved a piece of vermicelli in a glass case, till by some extraordinary means it began to move with voluntary motion."

In *Frankenstein*, much ambivalence pervades the scientific quest. "What had been the study and desire of the wisest men since the creation of the world was now within my grasp," we are told by Frankenstein, but it involves him in a loathsome search through "vaults and charnel-houses." When he triumphantly announces that he has become "capable of bestowing animation upon lifeless matter," he must surround it with the disclaimer "I am not recording the vision of a madman."[23] His demurral aside, Frankenstein not only symbolizes the "modern Prometheus" overreaching himself but also has come to epitomize the "mad scientist," whose hubris has removed him from the circle of humanity. If humans are created in God's world, the monster is spawned in the laboratory. Man, the evil scientist, has taken God's place.

Moreover, the scientist has also taken the place of woman. She has been displaced from the acts of conception and birth. It is a man, Frankenstein, who creates sexlessly. In the novel, sexuality is a threatening force. (In Mary's own life, sex meant death: her mother had died giving birth to her, her best friend had died in childbirth, and so forth; thus these biographical details are important to our understanding her fiction.) If the monster is allowed to breed, it will take over from mankind. In aborting the birth of a mate, as we have seen, Frankenstein reveals not only his revulsion from sexuality, but also his racist fears— a "race of devils" is how he describes the potential new species.

Mary's father, William Godwin, had also envisioned the end of sexuality in his *Enquiry Concerning Political Justice*. As he wrote there, "The whole will be a people of men, and not of children [that is, men will live more or less forever]. Generation will not succeed generation."[24] Diminished sensuality would ensure that the end of generations would also mean the end of the act of generation. Thus, Godwin foresaw a timeless, unchanging utopia where creation had taken place once and for all. Indeed, it was against this illusion that Thomas Malthus wrote his essay *Population*, insisting that sex, that is, procreation, was one of the necessary postulates of human existence, the other being the necessity of food. If not prevented by moral restraint, procreation leads in turn to the threat of overpopulation. When we deal with Charles Darwin, we shall note how reading Malthus helped spark into life Charles Darwin's great theory of evolution by natural selection, giving humans a new, scientific account of genesis.

Mary Shelley, however, echoes her father's hopes and fears. She substitutes the test tube for the sexual act in *Frankenstein*. What is more, without a real father and mother, the creature thus conceived is without nurturance and development. "No father had watched my infant days," he laments to Frankenstein, "no mother had blessed me with smiles and caresses." Like a fairer creature, Minerva, from Jove's forehead, the monster has sprung full grown (and larger than a normal human). He is, as a result, because of lack of development, inhuman. Made animate by his scientific creator, he is still like an automaton, ultimately lacking in the qualities that would bridge the discontinuity between him and humans.

In *Frankenstein*, Man, in disgust and fear, rejects his own creation. In doing so, he rejects a part of himself, his "double" (recognized unconsciously by readers who refer to the monster as "Frankenstein"), for both Frankenstein and the monster are destroyed at the book's end. Left behind them, in the shape of the gargoyles of the mad scientist and the golem-automaton run amok, is a new-old commandment: "Thou shalt not create matter in thine own image."

*Frankenstein* still gives rise to a frisson in a modern reader, but it has not put a stop to our mechanical ambitions. In fact, the automaton frequently has been domesticated in the form of the robot and often given a friendly, serving face. One such figure is found in the Oz books for children. He is called Tiktok and first appears in *Ozma of Oz* (1907). In this seemingly simple book, many of the fundamental questions surrounding humans, animals, and machines are dealt with disarmingly.

L. Frank Baum, the author, seems to have had a genial obsession with the idea of human identity.[25] An American Andersen of sorts, he modernized the timeless fairy tale. Though in such tales the threatening characters previously were monsters—the giant in "Jack and the Beanstalk"—they are now often humanized and humorous machines. Harmony reigns in the land of Oz among humans, animals, and machines, and even witches are gently laughed away.

We see these elements at play in all of Baum's Oz books, but especially in *Ozma of Oz*, one of his most delightful excursions into our subject.[26] Dedicated to all boys and girls, it starts with Dorothy Gale of Kansas on a boat, then being washed overboard and clinging to a chicken coop, whose only other occupant is a hen named, by Dorothy, Billina. Unexpectedly, the hen can talk, and when Dorothy says, "I thought hens could only cluck and cackle," the hen replies, "I've clucked and cackled all my life, and never spoken a word before this morning, that I can remember. But when you asked a question, a minute ago, it seemed the most natural thing in the world to answer you. So I spoke, and I seem to keep on speaking, just as you and other human beings do. Strange, isn't it?" Thus, at the beginning of the book, the question of the defining quality of language—humans have language, and hens generally don't—is put before us.

We are, of course, in fairyland (though first the chicken coop must wash ashore in the land of Ev and of Oz). The point of fairyland, however, is to define "real land" by comparison. When Dorothy urges the hen to eat the egg it has laid, because "You don't need to have your food cooked, as I do," the hen indignantly cries, "Do you take me for a cannibal?" When Dorothy, pursuing the subject, says how dreadful her companion's eating habits are—"Why, eating live things, and horrid bugs, and crawly ants. You ought to be *'shamed* of yourself!"—the unflappable hen responds, "Goodness me! . . . Live things are much fresher and more wholesome than dead ones, and you humans eat all sorts of dead creatures." To Dorothy's denial, Billina instances lambs, sheep—and even chickens. Dorothy's triumphant rejoinder is "but we cook 'em." When the hen questions whether there is any difference, the little girl answers, "A good deal . . . I can't just 'splain the diff'rence, but it's there. And, anyhow, we never eat such dreadful things as *bugs!*" The hen's cackling reply leaves Dorothy thoughtful: "But you eat the chickens that eat the bugs . . . So you are just as bad as we chickens are."

We seem to be in the presence of a jovial Claude Lévi-Strauss. Humans are cannibalistic animals that cook their food and feel superior to other animals. Speech, however, allows them to examine their own actions. Baum is helping children grope toward a sense of what it is to be human and different from hens and other animals.

A creature called the Wheeler serves as an intermediary between animals, such as Billina, and machines. "It had the form of a man," we are told, "except that it walked, or rather rolled, upon all fours, and its legs were the same length as its arms, giving them the appearance of the four legs of a beast. Yet it was no beast that Dorothy had discovered, for the person was clothed most gorgeously in embroidered garments of many colors, and wore a straw hat perched jauntily upon the side of its head. But it differed from human beings in this respect, that instead of hands and feet there grew at the end of its arms and legs round wheels." Here, clothes seem to be the defining quality of a human, differentiating it from both a machine and an animal.

It is Tiktok, the Machine Man, however, who occupies the central place in what comes to be a kind of comical Cartesian discourse. Dorothy finds a key that unlocks a door in a rock where she sees "the form of a man—or, at least, it seemed like a man, in the dim light. He was only about as tall as Dorothy herself, and his body was round as a ball and made out of burnished copper. Also his head and limbs were copper . . . 'Don't be frightened,' Billina calls out. 'It isn't alive.' "

Reassured, Dorothy remembers the Tin Man and makes a comparison. "But he [the Tin Man] was as alive as we are, 'cause he was born a real man, and got his tin body a little at a time—first a leg and then a finger and then an ear—for the reason that he had so many accidents with his axe." (Baum does not pursue the question of prosthetic devices, but I shall make it central to chapter 11.) Her conclusion is that, in contrast, the copper man "is not alive at all."

He is a robot. The card around his neck defines him as a "Clock work" that "Thinks, Speaks, Acts" (if you wind him up). He "Does Everything but Live." Everything, that is, except eat, feel either sorrow or joy, be kind (or unkind), or sleep (these, at least, are the specific differences alluded to in the book). When, however, the Scarecrow claims that, unlike Tiktok, he has brains, Tiktok replies, "Oh, yes, I have. I am fit-ted with Smith and Tin-ker's Improved Com-bi-na-tion Steel Brains. They are what make me think." Like the animal Billina, the machine Tiktok has language and brains.

What, then, distinguishes "him" (it?) from humans? The answer seems to reside in the specifics cited, revolving especially around emotions, that is, consciousness of a state of feeling. Also, according to Baum, Tiktok suffers from the defect of always having to be rewound (but this is merely a technicality; after all, humans have to eat).

Another mechanical figure in the book, the Giant with the Hammer, *appears* not to suffer from this latter defect (in fact, he seems to continue until turned *off* by a key), though, unlike Tiktok, he has no thinking or speaking attachment. A gigantic "man" made out of plates

"THIS COPPER MAN IS NOT ALIVE AT ALL"

Tiktok, the Machine Man. Illustration by John R. Neill, from L. Frank Baum, *Ozma of Oz* (1907). Dorothy explores, with the direct naivete of a child's eye, the difference between humans and machines.

of cast iron, he stands astride the only road into the Kingdom of the Nomes, pounding the earth so that all are too scared to go past. But his very strength, his unwearying mechanical regularity, proves his weakness and allows him to be defeated. As the Scarecrow points out, all that the members of Dorothy's party have to do is run under the hammer when it is lifted and pass to the other side before it falls again.

Tiktok himself is an utterly unthreatening robot. He exists only to serve Dorothy, which he does. In the illustrations, he looks like a copper Humpty-Dumpty. Even the Giant with the Hammer is little to be feared, for he can easily be outwitted because of his mechanical qualities. Automata in Oz are domesticated creatures, different from hens and other animals, but no less under human—in fact, a child's—domination.

Robots, however, do not occupy only the sunny fields of Oz in our imagination. They also often take on dark, threatening shapes, such as we have seen in *Frankenstein*. Their more modern incarnation in Karel

Capek's *R.U.R.*—which introduced the term *robot* into popular usage—reflects similar fears.[27]

Like its Shelleyean predecessor, Capek's play *R.U.R.* (1921; performed in America in 1922), is a poorly written hodgepodge of mostly improbable ideas. (Perhaps this is because a crude style matches the crudeness of its creatures, or because gothic is necessarily crude.) In any case, Capek, a Czech, obviously wrote with one eye on the Bolshevik Revolution of 1917, though one cannot be sure of his actual attitude toward that epochal event. Between Act I, which is about the manufacture of robots, and Acts II and III, when they revolt, there is a dichotomy. Yet the play is effective and has come to symbolize much of our feeling about robots.

The play opens when Helena, a beautiful young girl, comes to visit on an island the factory of Rossum's Universal Robots, which is managed by a man, Domin. He immediately falls in love with her and, on her promise not to divulge it, tells her the true story of the invention. (The process itself is secret, preserved in only two copies.) Rossum, he says, was a "great physiologist" who "attempted by chemical synthesis to imitate the living matter known as protoplasm until he suddenly discovered a substance which behaved exactly like living matter." As Domin explains, "This artificial living matter of his has a raging thirst for life. It didn't mind being sewn or mixed together."[28] Thus, old Rossum set about to imitate nature: first, an artificial dog, which took him several years and "resulted in a sort of stunted calf," and then the manufacture of a man.

The dog anticipates or is derivative of Pavlov (see chapter 6); the man reminds us of the creature in *Frankenstein*. Rossum is obviously cast in Frankenstein's image. Domin sardonically calls him "mad . . . the old crank wanted to actually make people." Rossum's "bungling attempt" occupied him for ten years—"It was to have been a man, but it lived for three days only." Then, we are told, "up came young Rossum, an engineer . . . When he saw what a mess of it the old man was making, he said, 'It's absurd to spend ten years making a man. If you can't make him quicker than nature, you might as well shut up shop.'"

Frankenstein-Rossum and his "monstrosities" are pushed aside. Young Rossum is an engineer, not a physiologist, who says to himself: "A man is something that feels happy, plays the piano, likes going for a walk . . . But a working machine must not play the piano, must not feel happy." As Domin concludes, "And to manufacture artificial workers is the same thing as to manufacture . . . motors." (Later, the mechanical metaphor is betrayed when we are told that "there are vats for the preparation of liver, brains . . . and a spinning mill for weaving nerves and veins"; consistency was not Capek's strong point.)

All that the worker need do is to work: hence, a robot (from the Czech *robota,* meaning work). The requirement is to reproduce "the cheapest . . . worker with the minimum amount of requirements." It is as if Young Rossum were answering the desires of the classical economists and their Iron Law of Wages. Only robots are not people. "Mechanically," as Domin defines them, "they are more perfect than we are, they have an enormously developed intelligence, but they have no soul." In fact, we are told that the cost of producing a robot has been brought down within fifteen years from $10,000 to $150!

Young Rossum, Domin goes on, "then proceeded [like his father, though he has repudiated the old man] to play at being God." He tried to make a superrobot. "Regular giants they were. He tried to make them twelve feet tall. But you wouldn't believe what a failure they were." In this area Frankenstein seems to have done better.[29]

The robots are constrained not only by size but by longevity. They have only a twenty-year life span. They do not, however, die—which involves a consciousness of death—but simply "get used up." Though they appear lifelike—the young lady, in an amusing bit, mistakes a robot for a live human being, and a human for a robot—dissection proves they are not. They feel nothing (reminding us of Descartes's views on animal-machines); consequently, one can be accused not of "killing" them but only of destroying a machine, just as wringing the neck of a chicken is not murder. All is well and peaceable in Rossum's factory.

Trouble enters this mechanical paradise when, in Act I, Helena pities the robots and wants to treat them as "brothers" and to "show them a little love"—shades of *Frankenstein!* As befitting a play of 1921, the language is also of "liberating" the robots, that is, the workers.

By Act II, Helena is married to Domin, ten years have gone by, and the robots number millions and millions. One of the other humans in the factory, Dr. Gall, under the influence of Helena, has begun to introduce modifications into the manufacture of some of the robots: pain, ostensibly so that they can withdraw their hands from dangerous operations, irritability, so that they begin to show defiance, and other such human attributes.

Capek's argument is really disingenuous. Humans are depicted as "imperfect" machines. "For example," as an engineer explains, "from a technical point of view, the whole of childhood is a sheer absurdity. So much time lost." Humans obviously also waste time with sex. Their intelligence is less than what it might be. Hence, robots are created that are more intelligent and powerful than humans, have no interest in sex, and are clearly superior. Yet, as soon as this is done, it becomes obvious that Capek considers them *less perfect* than humans because they do not have feelings, such as love and fear.

The contradiction becomes clear as the play unfolds in the last two acts. Owing to Dr. Gall and Helena's meddling, a new species of robot is produced that soon starts to go "mad" and ends up in revolt against humans. As the robot leader declaims to Helena: "You are not as strong as the Robots. You are not as skillful as the Robots." To her words about equality, he responds, "I want to be master. I want to be master over others." He proclaims to his fellow robots: "We command you to kill all mankind. Spare no man. Spare no woman."

The robots take over the island, and all humans are killed except one "last man," Alquist. Indeed, humans have already, as Dr. Gall noted earlier, "become superfluous." The problem is, however, that the robots, too, are about to die out, for they cannot reproduce themselves. (In a moment of humanitarian fervor, Helena had destroyed the copies detailing the secret process of creating the robots, so as to prevent further manufacture and hence exploitation.) In the epilogue, the robots command Alquist to rediscover Rossum's secret. However, much as he wishes to do so, Alquist lacks the scientific ability. He prays, "Lord . . . if there are no human beings left, at least let there be Robots!—At least the shadow of man!"

At this point, a miracle occurs. Two of Gall's newest robots, a male and a female, enter. They are experiencing strange feelings—love, sexual longing, it appears. Also "laughter—timidity—protection." To test them, Alquist proposes to take one of them into the dissecting room. When each is prepared to sacrifice himself or herself to save the other, Alquist knows that a new race has been born. "Go, Adam, go, Eve. The world is yours," he says in the last line of the play.

I find the whole play incredibly muddled. In the last act and the epilogue, Capek is obviously writing as much about the workers' revolution in Russia as about the robots' uprising in Rossum's factory. On one hand, the play is a kind of Luddite-*Frankenstein* protest against human hubris in making machines: Helena's human maid, Nana, exclaims at one point, "All these new-fangled things are an offense to the Lord. It's downright wickedness. Wanting to improve the world after He has made it"; and we are not meant to snicker. On the other hand, it seems to preach a certain idealism, that machines can free Man from toil and thus allow him to reach for perfection. In Domin's proud, and possibly ironic, words, "He [the human] will not be a machine and a device for production. He will be Lord of creation."

Capek's identification of the robots with the workers of the world, led by Bolsheviks, is not without roots. Frankenstein's monster, too, was frequently identified by nineteenth-century readers with the rebellious masses. Thus, in the novel *Mary Barton* (1848), Elizabeth Gaskell writes of how "the actions of the uneducated seem to me typified in those of Frankenstein, that monster of many human qualities" and Sir John Lubbock, a conservative scientist speaking in the House of Commons around 1870 against liberal reform, gave as his reason that he "believed it would be impossible to control the Frankensteins we have ourselves created."[30] (Here they make the typical slip of calling the monster by its maker's name.) Feelings about the right ordering of the social world are thus projected onto the subject of robots.

The social and psychological springs of *R.U.R.* do not mesh smoothly. But even though its theme is unfocused, *R.U.R.* does successfully reflect our primordial feelings about automata, as promise and threat. Capek's final message is ironic and ultimately baffling because he posits that the "new Man" of the future is a robot—but one that is just like a human in its feelings! Thus, Capek provides a null response to both the threat and the promise. But what is memorable about the play, or accounts of it, is that, like Frankenstein's monster, unless they are first destroyed, or at least emasculated, robots will usurp humans.

*R.U.R.* was written before robots were used widely in industry, and by an author who shows no evidence of having thought much about the science and technology animating them. Nevertheless, the play has achieved canonical status. *I, Robot*, by Isaac Asimov, is a much more thoughtful book—actually, a connected series of short stories—by an informed author at a time when the presence of robots is becoming real; yet the book is mainly known only to sci-fi fans. It should be read, however, by anyone interested in probing our contemporary feelings toward robots.

Its protagonist is a woman psychologist, Dr. Susan Calvin (whose name, surely, is to symbolize the Protestant work ethic); with one or two exceptions, she is one of the few females in the book, with all the other humans and the robots apparently male. So much for the sex problem!

The first story, "Robbie," raises the familiar problems. Robbie is a nontalking "nurse-maid" robot for little Gloria. While the child loves "him" and thinks of him as "a *person* just like you and me," her mother is actually jealous of Robbie, fears the machine—"it has no soul, and no one knows what it may be thinking"—and thinks "some little jigger will come loose and the awful thing will go beserk."[31] She insists the robot be removed and a collie dog substituted.

Gloria is inconsolable. Her father arranges for a tour of the premises of U.S. Robots and Mechanical Men, Inc., to show his daughter that Robbie is just a machine. When she breaks away to embrace Robbie, whom she sees on the assembly line, she steps in the path of a huge, lumbering tractor. Her father and the others are unable to act fast enough—"The overseers were only human, and it took time to act"—but Robbie, acting "immediately and with precision," saves his little playmate.[32] All is forgiven, and Gloria has her mechanical friend to take home.

A contrived tearjerker, the story is effective. It introduces us to our own fears, in a homey, humdrum way. We are told that the event occurred in 1998; as the stories continue, by 2002 mobile speaking robots have been invented, and, between 2003 and 2007, most of the world governments, presumably pressured by the mothers of innumerable Glorias, have banned robot use on earth for any purpose other than scientific research.

As further protection, all robots are bound by "The Three Laws of Robotics: 1—A robot may not injure a human being, or, through inaction, allow a human being to come to harm. 2—A robot must obey the orders given it by human beings except where such orders would conflict with the First Law. 3—A robot must protect its own existence as long as such protection does not conflict with the First or Second Law."

The remaining stories explore variations on one or more of these laws, their applications, and possible violations. Asimov is an interesting logician and rings the changes nicely. In the story "Reason," the robot Cutie pursues logic to its Cartesian conclusion, announcing "I, myself, exist, because I think." Hubris overtakes this robot, who announces conversion to the religion of "The Master": "The Master," it tells the two humans who are in charge of it, "created humans first as the lowest type, most easily formed. Gradually, he replaced them by robots, the next higher step, and finally he created me, to take the place of the last humans. From now on, I serve the Master."[33]

The rebellious delusion, however, turns out to be harmless, because Cutie still operates dials and graphs correctly, though claiming it does so in obedience to the Master, and, obedient to the Second Law of Robotics, does not harm humans. As one of its two tenders remarks,

"What's the difference what he believes."[34] The incipient danger has been nicely damped down.

It breaks out again in a story in which a robot lies, against the strictest injunction. Finally detected by Dr. Calvin, using a clever piece of logic, it is destroyed. The dark shadow of the robot, however, has grown more menacing. In another story, a robot faced with conflicting demands behaves just as does a human: it suffers a nervous breakdown. Yet Asimov tries to keep clear the distinction between humans and machines: the machine, he declares, is an *"idiot savante*—it doesn't really understand what it does—it just does it."

The penultimate story, "Evidence," poses the "difference" question most squarely. Is the lawyer Stephen Byerley, running for high political office, a man or a robot who looks exactly like a man? His opponent accuses him of being inhuman and offers as proof that he never is seen eating. Byerley responds that his habit of eating in private is probably neurotic, but not inhuman. The test finally comes in a public debate when a man emerges from the audience, taunts Byerley, and says, "Hit me," pointing out that a robot can't violate the First Law and harm a human. Byerley punches him, thus proving his "humanity," and, of course, wins the election.

Only as it turns out (though Dr. Calvin alone comes to know), Byerley actually is a robot. Created by a crippled human to perform in his place, Byerley has simply struck another robot, cleverly planted in the audience to rise and challenge the original humanoid robot. When Dr. Calvin's colleague is queried about the possibility of such a human-oid robot, he reluctantly admits that "by using human ova and hor-mone control, one can grow human flesh and skin over a skeleton of porous silicone plastics that would defy external examination. The eyes, the hair, the skin would be really human, not humanoid. And if you put a positronic brain, and such other gadgets as you might desire inside, you have a humanoid robot."[35] (Shades of our Chinese automa-ton of two thousand years ago!)

Asimov is not dismayed by this possibility. Like his fictional cre-ation Dr. Calvin, Asimov believes that robots are "a cleaner better breed than we are." They are decent and logical entities, who as civil execu-tives and "World-Co-ordinators" (Byerley, for example) will run the world and bring peace and prosperity to mankind. Whereas "humans are fallible, also corruptible," machines are only subject to mechanical failure, not wrong results (that is, if fed the correct data).

Like everyone writing about robots, however, Asimov is also ambiv-alent. Humans, he seems to be saying, still possess a creativity denied to machines. "The Machine is only a tool after all, which can help humanity progress faster by taking some of the burdens of calculations and interpretations off its back. The task of the human brain remains what it has always been; that of discovering new data to be analyzed, and of devising new concepts to be tested."[36] Yet, on the very last page of *I, Robot*, the machine appears as Providence, superior to humans but clever enough to hide its superiority so as not to injure human pride. (Earlier, we have seen Cutie making an open avowal of superiority—a clear sign of a kind of madness.) The book ends with Asimov's message:

> How do we know what the ultimate good of Humanity will entail? We haven't at *our* disposal the infinite factors that the machine has at *its!* Perhaps, to give you a not unfamiliar example, our entire technical civilization has created more unhappiness and misery than it has removed. Perhaps an agrarian or pastoral civilization, with less culture and less people would be better. If so, the Machines must move in that direction, preferably without telling us, since in our ignorant prejudices we only know that what we are used to, is good—and we would then fight change. Or perhaps a complete urbanization, or a completely caste-ridden society, or complete anarchy, is the answer. We don't know. Only the Machines know, and they are going there and taking us with them.[37]

It is a wishy-washy conclusion to an intriguing group of stories, in which Asimov cleverly explores both our logical and illogical attitudes toward robots. I have not mentioned, for example, his handling of the "Fundamentalists," who would destroy all machines, or his assumption that in the mid-twenty-first century, robots are still under the control of private, capitalistic enterprises, competing unscrupulously with one another (the cost of a robot is, in this book, $30,000). Overall, however, the book is a provocative rehandling, generally optimistic, of the themes we have been pursuing from Andersen's nightingale through Capek's Rossum's robots.

In this chapter I have only touched on the wealth of literature relating to automata. The subject seems to crop up everywhere, in almost everything one reads. Some light on its ubiquity may be shed by "The Uncanny," a strange and difficult paper by Sigmund Freud.[38] Here Freud points to what may be involved, psychologically, in the fear of the inanimate, of automata. Discussing E. T. A. Hoffman's story "The Sandman" (later part of Offenbach's opera *Tales of Hoffman*), Freud argues that the feeling of the uncanny arises where we are in doubt as to whether an apparently animate being—an automaton—is really alive, or not.

We need not follow Freud in his specific and tortuous analysis of the story in terms of castration fears, or in his general analysis of the uncanny in terms of animistic mental activity. For our purposes, we need only be inspired to realize that automata, mechanical dolls, and machines of all sorts awaken special undefined fears in us. Does the machine represent a part of ourselves of which we are afraid? Do we project into it our secret, and most forbidden, desires? A moment's reflection on our feelings toward robots, Pygmalion-like statues, or Frankenstein monsters (though this is, as stressed, in fact a flesh-and-blood creation) will confirm the extent of our emotional involvement, even if not its exact nature.

With this as a psychological context, I can use the examples given in this chapter to make the following general points. What are variously called automata, or androids, or robots, are conceived by humans as originating either at the hands of gods (for example, the Delphic oracles), or by men using magic (for example, the automata or golems of the Hermetic tradition), or by men using science (for example, the clockwork nightingale, Frankenstein's monster, and Capek's and Asimov's robots). (It would be nice to think of this as a chronological progress, but ancient Chinese scientists obviously used clockwork, and the followers of Hermes Trismegistus used magic very early on; what we find, therefore, is a recurring juxtaposition of the animating forces.) The created figures are either primarily biological or mechanical; flesh and blood or clockwork-machines, animated by a spark or wound up.

However created, whatever the material, they all pose the same compulsive question: how do they differ from humans, or, more simply, what is a human? This is the "uncanny" feeling analyzed by Freud. So, too, they all arouse in us the same range of ambivalent reactions: the sense of a perfection and infallibility to which we aspire—the angel in us—and the sense of the destructive and degrading in us—the ape in us.

Something new is now emerging: the robot as an industrial reality. Still, the same feelings seem to attach to it. Thus we are told that when a Japanese worker was crushed in a robotics accident, arising from his being in a restricted area and failing to notice that he was in the automatic path of a transport robot (and no "Robbie" to rescue him!), the incident was reported in the press as "though it had been a robot uprising."[39] Will these feelings change as familiarity breeds boredom?

The fact is that our feelings toward the robot-automaton are caught up anew in our feelings toward its new version, the computer. The robot now becomes the tool—really, the body—by which the computer—a "brain"—can "move" and take on "animated" form. Automata now take the shape of artificial intelligence machines. In that form I shall attempt later in this book to deal further with the questions raised in this chapter.

## **Chapter** Four

Humans, as we have seen, come into the light of history with tools. Tools are the first primitive form of machines. By a tool, we generally mean an instrument, such as a stone chip or a hammer or a saw, worked by hand. By a machine, we generally mean a more complicated apparatus, an assemblage of parts acting together for a common purpose. Karl Marx tried to distinguish between the two on moral grounds: the tool extends our personal power; the machine subjects us to its impersonal organization. Eschewing such an effort to distinguish between the two, I shall treat tool and machine as on a continuum of use and complexity, but both being "artificial" extensions of the human power to interrelate with the environment.[1]

Until now, I have made little or no effort to describe the history of technology. Rather, I have been inquiring into the way humans have tried to define their own nature in relation to machines in terms of philosophical ideas and psychological feelings. In our two previous chapters, we have dealt with these topics by, on one side, the idea of the animal-machine and, on the other, that of the automaton.

In looking closely now at the Industrial Revolution, we shall be working more specifically with technological, economic, and social data, but with the same overall aims in mind: their effect on the human sense of self. I shall be claiming that the time of the Industrial Revolution marks a quantum jump in our story, and especially in the relationship humans have toward both animals and machines.

The Industrial Revolution, of course, is a huge subject, whose own nature and causes and consequences have called forth numerous books.[2] There can be little doubt, however, that it marks a transformation in human evolution as significant as the Agricultural Revolution of about 12,000 years ago.

One way to approach the Industrial Revolution is to see it as a solution (at least up to now) of the Malthusian predicament, itself occasioned to a large extent by the economic expansion of Western Europe by the late eighteenth century. According to Malthus, humankind's evolutionary success (he wouldn't have used that term, of course) was resulting, or could result, in a geometric (exponentially multiplying) expansion of human population that, soon, would necessarily outrun the arithmetic (additive) increase of the food supply, that is, plants and animals. In this light the Industrial Revolution can be seen as a mechanical solution to the latter problem: by mechanizing the production of food and animals, as well as of textiles and furnishings, the dismal outcome predicted by Malthus was averted. A modern agricultural as well as industrial transformation took place, both in terms of mechanization.

The first thing to note is that the transformation first took off in the textile industry in Great Britain. Humans, in distinction to the (other) animals and machines, are the creatures that wear clothes. They take the skins of other animals and put them on, giving them an enormous geographical range and especially tolerance for cold climates, and they also weave fabrics out of plant and animal materials. Clothing of some sort is usually used to hide sexual parts, in an effort to seem less animal-like.

Clothes also play a social role: they mark status differences and therefore can be equated with the display patterns more "naturally" exhibited by birds and other species as they contend for dominance. For Thomas Carlyle, in *Sartor Resartus*, clothes became the symbol for human culture, the artificial skin, if you like, taking the place of natural skin. It was only fitting, then, that the first industry to start the profound continuing change in human culture that we refer to as the Industrial Revolution should have been the textile industry.[3]

The breakthrough came in cotton textiles. Wool had been the staple of the British textile industry from the Middle Ages to the eighteenth century. It came, of course, from an animal, the sheep. Its production had expanded with the enclosures of the time of Saint Thomas More, who lamented that "sheep were eating men," meaning that the animals were using arable land that otherwise would have been devoted to crops that could feed humans and prevent starvation. Silk was also an animal product, being first spun by caterpillars. Cotton was different: it came from a plant whose fiber was vastly more flexible than spiky wool and more spinnable than the exotic silk, and whose production could be more readily expanded. Cheaper than its rivals, it also could be worn in tropical as well as cold climates.

I need not recite the triumphs of invention of Arkwright, Hargreaves, and Crompton. As a result of their combined efforts, machines were substituted for the fingers of those who formerly sat at home spinning on the distaff wheel. The end result was the creation of the textile mill and of the factory, or manufacturing, system.

This system had both supporters and detractors. One of its supportive "philosophers" was Andrew Ure, who sought to capture the meaning of the new factory system in his book *The Philosophy of Manufactures* (1835). His work is revealing, for both its ideological message and its understanding of what was involved in the emerging new mechanical world. "I conceive that this title," he declared, "in its strictest sense, involves the idea of a *vast automaton,* composed of various *mechanical and intellectual organs,* acting in *uninterrupted* concert for the production of a common object, all of them being subordinated to a *self-regulated moving force"* (italics mine).[4] Ure's work is sprinkled with phrases about "self-acting machines," this "mighty revolution," and the system being "an inevitable step in the social progression of the world."

Though many of his contemporaries saw the factory as a dirty, noisome, unhealthy, and dehumanizing setting—a veritable hell—Ure drapped it in admiring prose. He spoke of the factory as "apartments more airy and salubrious than those of the metropolis in which our legislative and fashionable aristocracies assemble," of "those spacious halls [in which] the benignant power of steam summons around him his myriads of willing menials."[5]

If we remove some of the drapery surrounding Ure's use of the technological sublime, we are left with his very perceptive observations that "the principle of the factory system then is, to substitute mechanical science for hand skill . . . on the automatic plan, skilled labour gets progressively superseded, and will, eventually, be replaced by mere overlookers of machines." The word *mere* suggests the possible fate of humans in the "vast automaton" world that was emerging in the early nineteenth century.

The factory system represented the new reality of the Industrial Revolution. Its ramifications were what economists call backward and forward linkages. Backward they led to the cultivation of cotton by slaves (emancipated only in the second half of the nineteenth century) whose pickings were then ginned mechanically by the invention of Eli Whitney. Forward, they led to a developing chemical industry, spurred on by the new requirements of bleaching and dyeing. And on all sides, they led to increased demands for bulk transportation, first provided by the canals, as well as for coal to power the mills and for iron to serve as material to build the machines formerly made out of wood. The interlocking nature of the Industrial Revolution is perhaps its most striking feature.[6]

If textiles were one vital part of that interlock, another was the steam engine. It first was used in the mine, pumping out the water that threatened to block access to tin, copper, and especially coal so essential to the new industrialization. The steam engine then, at the behest of James Watt, learned to consume the coal it was helping to raise out of the earth and powered the mechanical shuttles of the textile factories and later the mechanical beasts of the railroad (the road itself an extension of the tracks, first wooden, then iron, laid down in the mines, and only latterly used for the locomotors).

The steam engine's ability to consume mineral "food" as it supplies unprecedented energy to mankind is singularly important. In our Malthusian perspective, this machine, the steam engine, can be said to increase manyfold the number of animals so essential to human survival, and, paradoxically, to do so in large part by replacing them or making them obsolete (for example, transforming the horse into a beast of pure pleasure).

David Landes states the matter beautifully when he says the key to the steam engine's revolutionary effects was that

> it consumed mineral fuel and thereby made available to industry, for the provision of motive power as against pure heat, a new and apparently boundless source of energy. The early steam-engines were grossly inefficient, delivering less than 1 per cent of the work represented by their thermal imputs. This was a far cry from the performance of organic converters: both animals and man can deliver from 10 to 20 per cent of imputs, depending on conditions. But neither man nor beast can eat coal. And since the supply of organic nourishment was and is limited—as the Malthusian checks of famine and disease abundantly testify—it is this increment of fuel made available by the steam-engine, however wastefully used, that counted.[7]

There is another way to view the subject. As Landes goes on, "In 1870 the capacity of Great Britain's steam-engines was about 4 million horsepower, equivalent to the power that could be generated by 6 million horses or 40 million men. If we assume the same patterns of food consumption as prevailed in the eighteenth century, this many men would have eaten some 320 million bushels of wheat a year—more than three times the annual output of the entire United Kingdom in 1867–71." Landes concludes, "Coal, in short, has been the bread of industry."

As we shall see, bread itself, and not just its substitute, coal (which humans cannot consume), was to be mechanized. But a word more about the steam engine. As with Landes, it can be described in admiring tones and seen as freeing humans from their biological restraints. Others can see it, however, as a despoliation of the environment and a violation of our humanity. Lewis Mumford, for example, though admitting that coal, the steam engine's food, had the advantage of being mineable long in advance and stored up for use independent of seasonal influences and the weather, also noted that "industry was beginning to live for the first time on an accumulation of potential energy, derived from the ferns of the carboniferous period, instead of upon current income."[8] Worse, besides exhausting future resources, it was polluting the present environment. Such pollution was social as well as physical, for the coal-consuming steam engine could bring humans together in overcrowded cities, forcing them to live in dehumanized conditions. Coal and the steam engine, so it was and is argued, blackened souls as well as hands and faces.

We shall come back to this negative reaction a bit later, when we deal with nineteenth-century contemporary responses to the Industrial Revolution. I have said that not only automata but also animals, viewed as animal-machines, were also subject to the influences of mechanization. This took many forms. The most immediate, at the end of the eighteenth century, was domestic breeding. It is frequently asserted (in fact, the matter is complex) that innovators such as Bakewell vastly increased the weight of their cattle, from around 200 pounds to 800, turning them into organic production machines for meat.[9] The way was open, for example, for chickens, confined in laying bins, to be automatically fed and to live only (from the point of view of their owners) to produce an increased number of eggs; to pigs being bred for increased poundage; and eventually to the development of artificial insemination and biotechnology to improve the breeds.

The increased production, for example, of cattle, chicken, and pigs was then further subject to the mechanization process by the time of the mid-nineteenth century. Sigfried Giedion, in his *Mechanization Takes Command*, gives us the gory details of how these organic beasts were placed on an assembly line, skinned, cleaned, and cut into pieces by a standardized procedure, and then packaged for mass consumption.[10] The result is that once again the predictions of Malthus had been defeated.

All of agriculture was subject to the same kind of development. In the late eighteenth century, large-scale enclosures in England increased the arable land devoted to crops. By the middle of the next century, marshy places were drained by steam engines and kept dry by earthenware tubes, creating more land for cultivation. New techniques of sowing and plowing, based on mechanical inventions, increased the yield. By the middle of the nineteenth century, the invention of the McCormick reaper meant soaring grain production. In 1858, Cyrus McCormick manufactured over 4,000 reapers, whose use on the great plains of America and elsewhere provided a cornucopia of bread.

For ages baked at home, bread in the nineteenth century entered the factory. Kneading by hand was replaced by rotary mixers. Soon the baker's oven was scrutinized by Count Rumford and others and improved by indirect heating, allowing for a continuous flow of production. Next came the endless belt from which standardized loaves of bread emerged, untouched by human hand. A most fundamental part of human contact with the organic—procuring the basic food, bread—had become part of an increasingly (for even earlier, humans had "milled" grain) mechanized world.

All of these developments were rooted, if one can use that organic term, in the swelling movement toward mechanization characteristic of the Industrial Revolution. Of course, that revolution drew upon earlier developments, both technical and conceptual. Only the degree and sweep of what happened in the Western world in the period from around 1760 to 1850 justifies the use of the term *revolution*.

To understand better the impact that the Industrial Revolution had upon humans' sense of themselves, as related to the other animals and machines, it is necessary to go back before the 1760s to the Newtonian worldview. In so doing, we are again dealing with the first discontinuity—that between the earth and the rest of the universe, whose overcoming required the discovery of universally applicable physical laws—as well as with the fourth discontinuity, as humans come increasingly to view themselves as living in a mechanical universe.

What Newton did, standing, as he remarked, on the shoulders of giants (that is, Copernicus, Kepler, Galileo, and so forth), was to bring order into the chaos of matter by imposing on it a few additional universal laws of nature. His particular laws were those of gravitation and optics, and they reigned on the moon as well as the earth and, indeed, through all of stellar space.

The favorite Newtonian metaphor for the planetary system was that of an immense clockwork. Nature in the sublunar world was also now similarly seen in clockwork terms. Instead of nature being conceived of as a matter of organic renewal and rebirth, it was increasingly viewed in terms of linear regularity.[11] Days were no longer regulated in a "natural" fashion, that is, by the rising and setting of the sun, but by a mechanism that clocked and watched over time in invariant minutes. Time became Man-made; in an urban environment, artificial illumination could do away with the need for natural light.

In the economic sphere, the results were all-pervasive. In the textile mills, workers "clocked" in and worked in clockwork unity with the spinning machines, whose inner workings had sprung in part from the techniques of earlier clock making. Work "around the clock" became possible with the introduction of gas illumination. Productivity could now be measured in terms of output per unit of time. Ultimately, time and motion studies would become the basis for scientific management.[12] Time had literally become money, with both based on a strictly numerical calculation. It was not by accident that the worker's good behavior was ultimately rewarded, on retirement, by the presentation of a gold watch.

The railroads, of course, were supposed to (and generally did) run according to a rigid schedule. Their timetables symbolized the omnipresent hand of the clock. Business witnessed a change of pace, with deliveries "on time" making the holding of inventories a new and different enterprise. To summarize a complex development, we can say that in and out of the factories, in the whole of social life, mechanical time was imposing a new discipline on humankind.[13] The social world had taken on the same dimensions as the Newtonian physical world. To put it imagistically, Father Time had been transmogrified into a mechanical clock.

Clockwork was clearly one dominant image. Another was "hands"; and not just in terms of the "hands" of a clock. Thomas Carlyle seized upon the essence of his age when he labeled it a Mechanical Age and declared that "Man are grown mechanical in head and heart, as well as hand."

A robotic hand, realizing the age-old dream of endowing machines with humanlike capabilities (Photo by David Lampe).

For Carlyle's contemporaries, the term factory *hand* expressed the way in which a human had been reduced to a part in a large machine. Earlier, Adam Smith had recognized that the increased division of labor was turning humans into specialized parts—a hand—even while making for greater total productivity. (For Smith, humans also became a commodity; but that is another story.) By the time of Karl Marx, this insight had been generalized and conceptualized into the notion of alienation. In Marx's language, "In tearing away from man the object of his production, therefore, estranged labor tears him from his *species life* . . . and transforms his advantage over animals into the disadvantage that his inorganic body, nature, is taken from him."[14]

The impulse to turn humans into hands (with the intention later on of removing them from the production process completely) arose to a large extent from the dissatisfaction with the unregulated and undisciplined nature of the so-called domestic system. In the putting out system, men, women, and children, spinning and weaving in their own homes, worked according to their own rhythms and desires, often stopping when they had secured enough money to satisfy their immediate needs, and just when the entrepreneur needed additional production to satisfy the market. Such workers were not part of an emerging clocklike world. The challenge, then, was to make them into "hands," as regular and mechanical as those on the face of a clock. The solution was to bring them into factories and subordinate them to the new textile machines.

In so doing, head and heart, as Carlyle said, became mechanical along with the hand. This is also Charles Dickens's message, for example, in his novel *Hard Times*. The machine had brought not only hard times in the sense of unemployment and starvation for the workers but also made men such as Gradgrind hard-hearted. Similarly, the liberal, reform-minded Josiah Wedgwood, whose Etruria factory (note the humanist Greek name) was intended to bring well-designed pottery into the homes of the average worker, spoke of how "few hands can be got to paint . . . in the style we want them. I may add, nor any other work we do. *We must make them.* There is no other way. We have stepped forward beyond the other manufacturers & we must be content to train up hands to suit our purpose."[15] His contemporary Jeremy Bentham, designing his infamous Panopticon, paused for a moment to wonder "whether the liberal spirit and energy of a free citizen would not be exchanged for the mechanical discipline of a soldier, or the austerity of a monk? And whether the result of this high-wrought contrivance might not be constructing a set of machines under the similitude of men?" His pause was not for long.

Not only in the textile factories and in the manufacture of steam engines but also in all other branches of industry the new ethos came to prevail. We have already noted Wedgwood's inspiration in his pottery works. Having said that he must make Men anew, he added that his task was "to make such *machines* of the *Men* as cannot err."[16] To accomplish his aims, Wedgwood aimed to tie his workers to the clock and to regulate their existence by rules of punctuality, constant attendance, and fixed hours. Thus, the Man-like machine he had in mind was truly a mere "hand," a mechanical part of the production process, and no longer an autonomous craftsman.

Ironically, the later Communists would take as their symbol the man with a hammer and sickle—hand instruments. (The hammer especially was the traditional symbol of the handicraft worker.) The human hand is, indeed, a wonderful instrument in itself, able to grasp other instruments. A prehensile tool, a grasping mechanism of extraordinary flexibility and articulation, it can seize, hold, pull, and manipulate with great strength or subtlety. What it cannot do, however, as Sigfried Giedion points out, is "continue a movement in endless rotation."[17] This a machine can do. By replacing the human hand by the machine, one is then made vulnerable to being made a "hand," which is no longer a versatile part of a whole human being but a clockwork essence. After the Industrial Revolution, the hammer and sickle are completely anachronistic.

As merely hands, the industrial workers were supposed to be the capitalist solution for the problem of an unruly, undisciplined, and insubordinate labor force. In part, this is what happened. As noted, workers did become subject to the clocklike regularity and discipline of the modern factory, whose final embodiment could take the shape of time and motion studies.

However, as a newly created proletariat, both in actuality and in imagination, the hands posed a new threat. Brought together in factories and cities, they became a mass. Organized in labor unions and movements, they threatened insurrection. In the early nineteenth century, they were seen, as we noted earlier, as Frankenstein's monster, who might rise up against its creator. The hand had become transmogrified into a mechanical monster.

What was threat for the masters was promise for the workers. The hand-as-machine could also be seen by and for them as a form of emancipation. As Jacob Bronowski remarked about the Industrial Revolution, "It forced men in the long run to seek their destiny, and to find their station, not in the hand of God but in their own hands."[18] What had been seen as fate and fixity now was seen as an open future determined by humankind's own hands.

In short, a profound struggle was going on. Humans could be seen as the creators of the machine. They could also be seen as being made into machines by the very mechanisms they had created. In one conception, the machine was giving freedom, permitting humans to take an undetermined future into their own hands. In another conception, humankind was being enslaved to the machine, turned into hands without lives of their own. The struggle in human minds persists in full force till today.

The image of the hand has allowed us to pursue a few themes either manifest or latent in the Industrial Revolution. (Remember our earlier mention of the hand as a mechanical tool in the drawings of Ambroise Paré.) I want now to pursue further the early opposition to the increasing mechanization of life occurring at that time. We need to turn to some of the historical events of the period.

Those who opposed the introduction of machinery are now called Luddites. The name itself goes back to the early nineteenth century, but hostility to machines has a much longer history. For example, as one author points out, "In 1579 the hapless inventor of a weaving machine was ordered strangled by the Council of Danzig, on the ground that his device would reduce many workers to beggary." Closer to our time, "When John Kay invented the flying shuttle in 1733 he was forced to leave England; workers invaded Hargreaves' home in 1768 and destroyed his spinning jennies; and Crompton, who invented the spinning mule in 1799, was forced into hiding as a reward for his work."[19]

As we know, these were isolated episodes in a losing battle; Arkwright, after all, was knighted. What made the Luddite outbreaks more memorable was that, though sporadic and without lasting results, they were organized and recurrent. A wave of such outbreaks occurred in Britain from about 1811 to 1816, when masked men sought to break machine frames, mainly machines used for knitting hosiery. The machines themselves were not new, dating back a couple of centuries, nor was their putting men and women out of work completely novel. But the growing sense of injustice was new, and the sense, not perhaps by the workers themselves but by society at large, that the frames were part of an omnipresent takeover by machines.

The framebreakers of 1811 took their name from a Ned Lud, who, in 1779, broke a couple of frames and was hanged for it. The masked bands of men now swore allegiance to King Ludd (or Captain Ludd as he was also often called), in sarcastic rejection of the traditional British monarchy. The followers of King Ludd, obviously, were Luddites.

As such, they might be viewed as revolutionaries. Lord Byron, who, in his maiden speech in the House of Lords, argued against a proposed bill establishing the death penalty for their activities, wrote a friend comparing them to earlier revolutionaries, calling them "the Lutherans of politics—the reformers." Byron was wrong; they were, historically, counterrevolutionaries, trying to turn back the clock of the Industrial Revolution.[20]

A similar resistance flared up again in 1830, in the great English agricultural uprising of that year. This time the specific enemy was the threshing machine, which put the rural laborers out of work, and the resistance went forward under the command of a pseudonymous Captain Swing. As described by Hobsbawm and Rudé, the rising in 1830 "was the greatest machine-breaking episode in English history."[21] While this may be so, the earlier series of protests, the Luddite breakings, gave its name as a generic term for the opposition to the coming of the machines.

The actual Luddites were formally uneducated rural laborers fighting for their livelihoods and perhaps their way of life. (One account, in fiction, is given in Charlotte Brontë's novel *Shirley* [1849].) The Luddites in spirit who followed them were generally highly educated intellectuals who felt and believed that the machines were dehumanizing, perhaps even demonic, forces. And if not so in themselves, the machines certainly were so as employed by the capitalists, who saw in them mere labor-saving devices.

We can capture the intellectual Luddite reaction in figure after figure, and remark after remark. Many such reactions were hedged by partial or ambivalent admiration for the inventiveness of humans and the emancipatory possibilities in the machine if correctly used. Carlyle, for example, though deploring what he called the Midas effect—in which productivity was turned to gold, which humans could not eat (a modern update of Sir Thomas More's sheep eating men analogy)—nevertheless admired the Arkwrights of this world and their powerful contrivances. Marx, though lamenting the alienation involved in capitalistic use of machines, insisted that even further mechanization was necessary before the coming of communism was possible.

A purer Luddism, as I am using the term, is to be found in Mary Shelley's *Frankenstein*. Here, both the threat and the reaction are dealt with in novelistic, mythical terms, working mostly in the realm of our unconscious. More direct condemnation of the emerging machine world is to be found in writers such as John Ruskin and Henry Adams. The latter's reaction to seeing the dynamos of the Paris Exposition of 1900 is well known; but even thirty-eight years earlier he was writing his brother Charles that "you may think all this nonsense, but I tell you these are great times. Man has mounted science, and is now run away with. I firmly believe that before many centuries more, science will be the master of man. The engines he will have invented will be beyond his strength to control."[22]

The most dire reading of the Industrial Revolution was that it symbolized death. Most immediately, it meant the death by starvation from unemployment, or else by overwork, or by unsanitary conditions of large numbers of workers. More drastically, it meant the self-destruction of the human race. Symbolically voiced by Frankenstein's monster killing his maker's younger brother and then his fiancée, this reaction is given more explicit form in the statement by Henry Adams, which continues the statement we have just read above: "Some day science may have the existence of mankind in its power, and the human race commit suicide by blowing up the world."

The theme of death was a generalized sense of the threat posed by the perceived artificial and lifeless nature of a mechanical world.[23] This theme surfaces early, even before actual industrialization, in the writings of Friedrich Schiller. His general view is that the emerging system of manufactures was destroying human "organic" life, leaving only "an ingenious clockwork, in which out of the piecing together of innumerable but lifeless parts, a mechanical kind of collective life ensued."[24] Coleridge makes it explicit when he speaks about "the philosophy of mechanism, which, in everything that is most worthy of the human intellect, strikes *Death*."

In Carlyle, however, Schiller's most faithful English follower, the fullest identification of mechanization with the death of the spirit, as well as the body, can be seen. In fact, Carlyle is crucial in setting the tone by which so many of his contemporaries as well as people today have responded to industrialization.[25]

Carlyle states his position most importantly in "Signs of the Times" (1829), published in the *Edinburgh Review*, and in *Sartor Resartus* (1833–1834). For Carlyle, the primary "sign" of modern life was the machine, which he characterizes relentlessly as "inanimate," "iron," "resistless," and "opposed to the mysterious springs of Love." As he tells us, "Were we required to characterize this age of ours by a single epithet, we should be tempted to call it, not an Heroical, Devotional, Philosophical, or Moral Age, but, above all others, the Mechanical Age. It is the Age of Machinery, in every outward and inward sense of that word . . . nothing is now done directly, or by hand; all is by rule and calculated contrivance."

The charge is broadened: "Not the external and physical alone is now managed by machinery, but the internal and spiritual also . . . The same habit regulates not our modes of action alone, but our modes of thought and feeling." And then comes the famous phrase: "Men are grown mechanical in head and in heart, as well as in hand."[26]

In *Sartor Resartus*, Carlyle immortalized this mechanical system by coining the term *Industrialism* for its overall manifestation in and as a society. He also talked of Man's relation to Man as being reduced to a "cash-payment," a phrase that was echoed by Karl Marx in *The Communist Manifesto*.[27] Marx, as we know, drawing on additional sources, further developed Carlyle's position into a full-scale analysis of what he called "alienation" (to which we alluded earlier). Carlyle's imagination, however, had helped ignite an important way of viewing humankind's increasing relation, or lack of it, to the machine and its products.

Carlyle's reaction to and personal ambivalences about industrialism were reflected in and reflective of the culture at large. One must not lose sight in this picture, however, of other voices, the yea-sayers, those who embraced the new mechanization of humans and society and saw in it, for example, not death but life. Paradoxically, for them, mechanization meant denying organic decay and, in its most extreme version, giving mankind a secular form of eternal life.[28]

Symbolic of the mixed emotions of fear and hope, ambitions and anxieties, that clustered around the emerging mechanical world was the Great Exhibition of 1851, the Crystal Palace Exhibition. To its supporters, the exhibit was a sign of urban enterprise triumphing over the rural—the census of that year revealed that for the first time more people were living in conditions of city or town life than of country—and of the upward-and-onward nature of capitalist industrialization. To its opponents, it was a monstrous example of bad taste and a monument to the dehumanizing effect of the mechanical civilization that had erected it.

In fact, the idea for an international exhibit arose among a group of reformers who wished to unite fine art with manufacture and, in general, to reform the production system.[29] The leader was Henry Cole, an English civil servant. His Society for the Encouragement of Arts, Manufactures and Commerce enlisted the support of the Prince Consort, Albert, in its plans for a Great Exhibition.

After a number of false starts, the planning committee finally selected Joseph Paxton, the head gardener for the Duke of Devonshire, to design the proposed structure. His design was a great greenhouse, using large amounts of glass (hence the name, Crystal Palace, at first given in derision) and iron. It was immediately attacked by John Ruskin, who had declared that "architecture does not admit iron as a constructive material" and who believed that, as Nikolaus Pevsner paraphrased him, "a railway station [many of which were also glass enclosed] is as alien to architecture as a wasp's nest and a rat hole."[30] Needless to say, Ruskin was infuriated by the Crystal Palace.

Paxton's design, in fact, symbolically incorporated the country in the city, amalgamating the greenhouse and its botanical attributes to the factory and its mechanical features.[31] Indeed, he had been inspired in his design by studying a huge water lily at Kew (brought from New Guinea), on which his daughter had stood, supported by its ribs and cross-ribs, from whose structural principles Paxton learned how to build his Crystal Palace.[32]

Once the Crystal Palace was erected, the exhibition was opened by Prince Albert, who hailed the vast collection as demonstrating Man's power "to conquer Nature to his use—himself a divine instrument."[33] The interior was subsequently photographed by Fox Talbert, who thus used a new device to preserve for posterity the mechanical and material treasures within the exhibit.[34]

In the next two years, among the throng of visitors were two Russians. Chernyshevsky saw it in 1859 and used it in his novel, *What Is to Be Done?* (1863), to envision a future utopia, a modernized world, basically a dream world. Dostoevsky came in 1862 and, as his hero in *Notes from the Underground* (1864) makes clear, saw the Crystal Palace as heralding a nightmarish world of unfeeling mechanisms.[35]

Amid the differing views of the Crystal Palace, one common note persisted: machines were becoming more and more omnipresent, for better or for worse, and perhaps even potentially omnipotent.

A possible forecast of their "evolutionary" nature might be found, and this before Darwin, in the copper coal scoops of Joseph Tylor and Sons, which, as George Stocking, Jr., tells us, "were arranged so as to demonstrate 'the changes in their patterns' and their 'different improvement from 1780 till the present time.'" Stocking speculates that the arrangement might have stimulated the "evolutionary interests" of the young Edward Tylor, future author of *Primitive Culture* (1871).[36] Can one also speculate that it dimly and unconsciously anticipated Samuel Butler's notion of the evolutionary nature of machines?

In any case, it was clear to both sides in the debate over the Crystal Palace that the Industrial Revolution had drastically changed the human condition and that humankind's relation to the world of machines had taken on a new dimension. Once the initial industrialization had taken place, roughly in the period between 1760 and 1850, and especially in England, it was also clear that a new form of (at least temporarily) sustainable development had been introduced, with a dynamic hitherto unknown.

My intention is not to try systematically to trace that continuing development here, that is, not to duplicate for the latter period our more or less detailed look at the early Industrial Revolution, but only to remark on one or two further points particularly illustrative or germane to our inquiry into humanity's relations to the increasingly mechanical environment around it. Flying high above the terrain of history, I will seek to spot a few bends in the river, marking the actual flow of events. In that flow, the current seems increasingly to have shifted to the machine makers and away from the machine breakers, whether Luddite workers or Carlylean intellectuals.[37]

In the event, the new mechanical creations displaced not only humans but animals (animal-machines?) as well. One could argue that what took place, especially for many animals, was a form of emancipation. Dogs for hunting, horses for pulling and riding, oxen for plowing, all became unnecessary. At the same time, ironically, this new "freedom" carried the potentiality for their elimination, or at least a kind of obsolescence; if lucky, some of these animals could survive as pets or be useful in sports, if no longer in productive activity.

As for the machines that were replacing animals and humans, they were also made of replaceable parts. What is more, machines were increasingly used to make their own parts and to make other machines as well: enter the machine lathe and the assembly line.

One example shall speak for many variations on this theme. In building his auto factories, Henry Ford derived part of his blueprint from the meat packing industry (whose mechanization we have already described). As E. L. Doctorow, the novelist, dramatized it, Ford "had gotten his inspiration from a visit to a beef-packing concern where the cows were swung through the plant hanging in slings from overhead cables." As Doctorow continues, Ford "conceived the idea of breaking down the work operations in the assembly of an automobile to their simplest steps, so that any fool could perform them. Instead of having one man learn the hundreds of tasks in the building of one motorcar, walking hither and yon to pick out the parts from a general inventory, why not stand him in one place, have him do just one task over and over, and let the parts come past him on moving belts."

Doctorow sums up the result: "He [Ford] looked at his watch again. . . . Exactly six minutes after the car had rolled down the ramp an identical car appeared at the top of the ramp . . . then rolled down and crashed into the rear of the first one. . . . Now he experienced an ecstasy greater and more intense than that vouchsafed to any American before him, not excepting Thomas Jefferson. He had caused a machine to replicate itself endlessly."[38]

The effects of the auto assembly line on the men tending it have been depicted by Charlie Chaplin in his immortal satire the film *Modern Times*. The frame of the movie that has been reproduced more than any other shows Chaplin desperately hanging on to the hand of a large clock, trying helplessly to stop it. Relentlessly, however, the real assembly line went on turning out cars by the thousands and then millions, as well as also stamping out "mechanical" men. Additionally, the car not only substituted, as already suggested, for horses, donkeys, camels, and other beasts of burden, but also, so to speak, replaced legs for millions of humans as well. In doing so, it can be said to have become a "part" of Man (see chapter 10 for a further development of this theme).

To pursue this idea just a bit, in America alone, in the 1980s, over ten million people had an auto doing the "locomotion" for them. These cars, in the form of the production facilities needed to build them, "ate" about 20 percent of the steel and iron casings, 68 percent of the lead, 65 percent of the rubber, and 5 percent of the plastics used in the United States.

To appreciate the magnitude of what was happening, we also need to look at worldwide figures. Thus, in the late twentieth century, about 30 million vehicles each year were "created," that is, rolled off the world's assembly lines. Such a new "population" was the equivalent of many a moderate-sized country, for example, Poland. They joined an already existing fleet, which was about 300 million vehicles, a population greater than either the United States or the former Soviet Union. Their consumption was about twelve million barrels of oil per day. We must remember David Landes's comments about the steam engine and coal to appreciate the significance of what was happening.

Other "machines," such as the microscope and telescope, are extensions of human capabilities, in their case, sight; the auto extends use of the legs—but with what a "material" difference! The energy expansion, and we have already noted the consumption of "food" that this requires, involved in the auto is simply of a new magnitude.

If we speed up our exposures, like the early silent films, and briefly extend here the sequence of industrial development, we can see how the line that started in the textile mills and steam engines of the early Industrial Revolution moves to the assembly lines of the late nineteenth and early twentieth centuries, turning out automobiles as well as packaged meat.

By 1870 and thereafter, Ure's "factory system" had taken on a much extended shape. Inventions such as the incandescent light, the radio, the gasoline-powered auto, and the airplane, to name just a few, have become part of "total" technological systems: for generating and marketing electric power, for producing and selling cars and getting roads built on which they could run, for setting up telephone and wireless networks. As Thomas Hughes points out, these were the forerunners of even more ambitious projects, such as the Manhattan project and NASA's space program.[39] The machine had become part of a larger machine, the technological-social system.

In the twentieth century, we are now in the presence of a Computer Revolution, cranking out information as well as controlling the production of goods. The replacement of autos by information processing as the centerpiece of modern industrial life is symbolized by the same Charlie Chaplin of *Modern Times* appearing in IBM ads, madly rushing around a store.[40]

The coming linking of computers to robots clearly marks a next stage of this revolution. While I shall deal with that development in detail later (see chapter 11), I want to remark here that the earlier visions of automata-become-robots have been mostly misleading. The effort, for example, to develop a robotic hand, modeled on human rather than on humanlike capabilities, has hampered successful development.

It has now become clear that the machine, in order to take our place, need not be created directly in our image but only given shape in terms of our functions. The bicycle extends our leg power by giving us rotary motion, without imitating our pedal extremities. Similarly, robotic machines can carry out boring jobs, such as patroling warehouses at night, or entering hazardous places, such as radioactive facilities, without looking like human *watchmen* (itself a loaded term).

In sum, as machines have been doing since their first invention, they are extending human faculties at the same time as they are both replacing humans and, as Carlyle had prophesied, making humans more machinelike in head and heart as well as hand. The importance of the Industrial Revolution is that it marked a quantum jump in this evolution, for better or worse, of the human species.

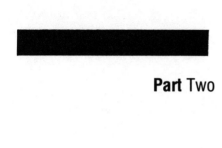

**Part** Two

## **Chapter** Five

In seeking to understand the increasing mechanization of human life and nature, including its manifestation in the Industrial Revolution, it is critically important that we project it against the background of human evolution. Industrialization in the early nineteenth century was a revolutionary speedup of humankind's cultural transformation, itself reaching back to the earliest emergence of humans as tool-making animals some two to three million years ago. I feel it requisite, therefore, to look carefully at the early stages of the development of evolutionary theory, which ended the second discontinuity, even though this may seem at first a diversion from a strictly orderly argument. I do so in order to set the scene properly for the more recent acts in humanity's entanglement with the fourth discontinuity, as well as for the possible "evolution" of a new "species," a mechanical "being."[1]

I will take on this task, neither by a systematic treatment of the history of the theory of evolution, nor of the specialized debates as to the exact nature of that theory (drift, punctuated equilibrium, and so forth)—there are many excellent works on these subjects—but rather by selectively looking at Linnaeus and Darwin and emphasizing their role as early classifiers. (Darwin, of course, was much more than this.) They were reaching toward a genealogical ordering of Man's place in nature. We shall also look at Freud and Pavlov, as epigoni of Darwin, who seek in the light of his theory to define human nature.

In this way I hope to show how the notion

of humans as mechanical beings—animal-machines—was not only explicit in seventeenth-century Cartesianism, but was also implicit in the later effort to classify and understand the place of humans in the biological world. Darwinism as such emphasized the organic aspect of existence; but it had a materialistic bias that led easily again to mechanism.

What is more, though Darwin showed that humans were subject to the laws of (animal) nature, he also pointed out that these laws in the case of humans have led to culture. And though he did not follow this line of reasoning, it in turn leads to machines, that is, as a cultural animal, the human being produces tools and machines. Thus if we are to probe beneath the surface of evolving human nature, we must at least consider these lines of both real and theoretical development.

It is also important, as I have already suggested, to establish the evolutionary context as we seek to assess the future possible development of machines per se. In general, the evolutionary perspective shapes modern humans' whole way of seeing; few informed scientists and even ordinary people contest today that to understand animals, including the human animal, we must view them in the setting of their evolution. Further, this is true for the geological formations of the earth on up through plant life, and the same view extends to the entire planetary system and the universe. Which brings us to the question: must the same now be said of the development of machines? In order better to deal with this problem, I shall once again look selectively, this time at Charles Babbage, T. H. Huxley, and Samuel Butler.

One cannot, of course, merely apply "mechanically" the explanatory mechanism of natural selection to machines. The application of natural selection does not work for the planetary system, and there is no reason to assume automatically that it will work for the "machine world." In an important sense, then, to talk of the "evolution" of machines is perhaps largely a figure of speech; machines do not "adapt" in a "survival of the fittest" manner.[2] What is important, however, is to situate mechanical development in an evolutionary framework and then try to understand the ways in which machines are created and the trajectories possibly available to them in the future. As with humans, machines must be understood in the context of cultural evolution.

Linnaeus is an Enlightenment figure contemporary with La Mettrie whose own life demonstrates the tension in the eighteenth century as the dominant modes of thought moved from the religious to the scientific. His mother had intended him for the priesthood (both his father and his maternal grandfather had been clergymen); he chose science instead. In fact, like La Mettrie, he became a physician (and also studied with Boerhaave), with his medical practice helping to supply both a livelihood and a point of view. In sum, Linnaeus can be described as a rather atypical member of the Enlightenment, ranging his batteries of books on the side of science in its presumed conflict with theology while asserting publicly and privately his faith in a Christian God of justness.[3]

In the self-portraits that Linnaeus began producing at age twenty-seven, he characteristically rejected modesty and claimed that "none before him has reformed so totally an entire science, and created a new epoch. None before him has been a greater botanist or zoologist." In a petition to the Swedish Parliament, he wrote, "I have built anew the whole science of natural history from the ground up, to the point where it is today; I do not know whether anyone now can venture forward without being led by my hand."[4]

These are bold assertions. Yet, Linnaeus's claims to having constructed a new scientific order cannot easily be dismissed. He did establish a novel and powerful classification—an important step in any science—of all flora and fauna (and even of the mineral kingdom). In place, however, of the "Natural" system, where each link in God's chain of being was to be explored in simple empirical terms, Linnaeus substituted his "Artificial" system, based on a sexual classification, to guide such exploration.

This new classification gave humans a place in nature that was more than just a link in a chain; it was potentially an affinity to other animals, with sexuality as the connecting thread. The artificial classificatory system, according to Linnaeus, was to be temporary (as the word *artificial* implied), serving merely as an aid to the mapping of the natural botanical and zoological kingdoms. In the event, though, the artificial system seemed to take on a life of its own. So, too, did Man, though Linnaeus had intended humanity's position to be fixed and static, even in the new classification. This issue I will take up again shortly.

As the builder anew of the whole science of natural history, Linnaeus liked to think of himself as also a new Adam, naming systematically the denizens of what he called his "botanical gardens," which he was pleased to refer to as Edens, or paradises. His critics were less pleased. As one of them, Albrecht von Haller, wrote: "The unbounded dominion which Linnaeus has assumed in the animal kingdom must upon the whole be abhorrent to many. He has considered himself as a second

Adam, and given names to all the animals according to their distinctive features."[5]

Before his work, common names, in all different languages, abounded for plants and animals, overwhelming the memory and affording no sound basis for classification. They expressed little or no relation of animal to animal, or of human to animal, except that of the names given to them. Thus, in the sixteenth century, Conrad Gessner, the most eminent naturalist of his time, in his magisterial work of over 4,000 pages, simply arranged the animals in alphabetical order.[6]

Linnaeus changed all this. In place of the vernacular common names (for example, horse, *cheval, pferd*) he successfully introduced a double name, his binomials, based on Latin or Greek roots: for example, cattle in general received the name *Bos,* and then each species was distinguished by a second name, for example, *Bos domesticus* or *Bos bison.* Paradoxically, then, just at the time when the humanities were moving away from the "universal" language, Latin, to the vernacular, Linnaeus was moving science to Latin exactly because of its generalizing possibilities. Science was to be for everybody (or at least those who knew Latin), not just for the English, the French, or the Germans.

His accomplishment was to bring order out of chaos. In his *Systema Naturae* (the first edition was in 1735, but the tenth edition of 1758–1759 is the classic one), he offered a new nomenclature and classification, his famous "sexual system," establishing the kinship of all plants and animals. Plants, for example, were classified according to their sexual organs, pistils and stamens. In Linnaeus's scheme, the plant genera are grouped into twenty-four classes according to the number of the stamens (together with their relative lengths, and other characteristics). For example, the Monandria have one stamen, the Diandria two stamens, and so on. Within each class the genera are arranged into smaller groups, or orders, according to the number of pistils, the Monogynia having one pistil, the Digynia two, and so on. On this basis, Linnaeus then built his "sexual system."[7]

As an Enlightenment thinker, Linnaeus prided himself on his secular good sense and his refusal to embrace mythical thought. Yet his fervid imagination infused all of his work in botany and zoology. As one reads deeper into his work, one finds that this sober Swede looked at all the plants and animals with an "erotic" eye; he sexualized all of nature. This impulse, in some underground way, informed and vivified his work. It gave order to his great system.

Surely, the reader will now protest, you make too much of Linnaeus's sexual emphasis. It is merely a side issue, an accident or sport that accompanies his deep-thinking, objective approach to nature; or else simply a matter of emphasizing the reproductive capacity, expressed in the language of "sexuality." Indeed, Linnaeus's compulsive sexual interest is presented so naively and directly that scholars have been inclined to pass over or pooh-pooh its importance; after all, if he does not repress it, how can it be so critical? We expect more self-consciousness in our post-Freudian age. Linnaeus was a child in this regard and expressed himself with a child's sexual directness.

The sexual fixation is announced in his university dissertation, when he writes that "in these few pages I treat of the great analogy which is to be found between plants and animals, in that they both increase their families in the same way." Linnaeus lyrically continues: "Every animal feels the sexual urge. Yes, Love comes even to the plants. Males and females, even the hermaphrodites, hold their nuptials (which is the subject that I now propose to discuss), showing by their sexual organs which are males, which are females, which are hermaphrodites."[8]

Plants and animals are given "human" attributes, and a unity of sex life is attributed to all nature. If the sexual life of plants is equated with that of humans, including implications of polygamy, polyandry, and incest, human sexuality is transmuted into the procreation of flowers, a rare form of idealization. Thus in writing to a married woman who was also an amateur botanist, Linnaeus declared that "I have long been trying to smother a passion which proved unquenchable and which now has burst into flame. This is not the first time that I have been fired with love for one of the fair sex, and your husband may well forgive me so long as I do no injury to his honour. Who can look at so fair a flower without falling in love with it, though in all innocence? . . . But should I be so happy as to find my love for you reciprocated, then I ask but one favour of you: that I may be permitted to join with you in the procreation of just one little daughter to bear witness of our love—a little Monsonia, through which your fame would live for ever in the Kingdom of Flora." The tone is jocular and playful, and we must not read the letter with a long face. Still, we can see clearly how Linnaeus lives on a spectrum of sexual feeling that commingles the plants and animals, including humans.

Linnaeus's opponents were quick to sense his infatuation. One of them, Johann Siegesbeck, denounced Linnaeus's "lewd" system with its "loathsome harlotry." "Who," he asked, "would have thought that bluebells, lilies and onions could be up to such immorality?"[9] And an unbiased reader might agree when he sees Linnaeus describing the flower Andromeda in the following terms: "I doubt whether any artist could rival these charms in a portrait of a young girl, or adorn her cheeks with such beauties as are here and to which no cosmetics have lent their aid . . . Her beauty is preserved only so long as she remains a virgin (as often happens with women also)—i.e. until she is fertilized, which will not be long now as she is a bride."

The great Swedish naturalist was in love with nature, and he spoke using a lover's terms.[10] A half century later, Erasmus Darwin wrote a scientific treatise in poetic form, "The Botanic Garden," of which one part was called "The Loves of the Plants."[11] The anthropomorphic note is strong here, too. It is not too fanciful to carry this line of thought to Darwin's grandson Charles, who places procreation, and thus sex, at the center of the evolutionary universe—which is why I have spent so much time on Linnaeus's preparatory sexual proclivities.[12]

In Linneaus's own time, however, his sexual preoccupation made him a subject of mockery. The brilliant but caustic French thinker and doctor Julien Offray de La Mettrie, whom we have discussed earlier, wrote an article "L'Homme plante," in which, as one scholar describes it, "the Linnaean sexual system was parodied and held up to ridicule. In it mankind was classified as *Dioecia* (male and female flowers on different plants), and the male being of the order *Monandria* (one stamen) and the female *Monogynia* (one pistil). The calix was missing, its place being taken by clothes. The petals of the corolla were the limbs, the nectaries the breasts, and so on."[13] This article was included in La Mettrie's *L'Homme-machine,* and a profound issue thereby joined. Man, for La Mettrie, was headed toward the race of mechanical beings and away from vegetative and animal beings.

Linnaeus was moving the other way. In fact, his sexual system denied mechanism and asserted the vital unity of all nature. He was not doing so in an evolutionary sense; his aim was to bring order and fixity out of chaos, not to advocate change and fluidity. He still accepted the framework of the Great Chain of Being and wished only to rename all the creatures who made up its links. Yet, unsuspectingly, he was preparing the way for an evolutionary view of nature that even included Man. Into Linnaeus's rigor mortis—his static classificatory system—a breath of life, sexual in its essence, could and would be introduced, especially by Darwin.

But that was yet to come. Linnaeus and natural organisms stood as fixed as the earth before Copernicus. Emancipated as he was from dogmatic religious doctrines, some lingering scruples compelled Linnaeus to uphold the constancy of species.[14] Nevertheless, as part of his static classification, Linnaeus could not refrain from including Man as a member of the same order—the Primates—as the Apes and Lemurs. At some moments he even went so far as to say that "as a Natural historian I have yet to find any characteristics which enable man to be distinguished on scientific principles from the ape." Yet while observing the apes kept at Drottningholm Castle, and making special mention of the similarity between ape and human behavior, he did not see, as one scholar puts it, "anything more in this than comedy."[15]

In *The Cousins of Man*, which was published long after his death, he spoke of the apes as the "nearest relations of the human race"; and elsewhere he mentions a *Homo troglodytes* although he was unclear whether it was nearer the pygmy or the orangutan.[16] Albrecht von Haller, who as we noted earlier had ridiculed Linnaeus as a second Adam, immediately perceived that his rival (though also sometime friend) could "hardly forbear to make *man a monkey, or the monkey a man.*"[17] Where Thomas Huxley would later praise Linnaeus, "the great lawgiver of systemic zoology," for his courageous insight, a contemporary English naturalist, Thomas Pennant, expressed the general view when he confessed, "My vanity will not suffer me to rank mankind with Apes, Monkies, Maucaucos and Bats."

Vanity aside, there was little good theological reason to object to Linnaeus's classification of Man with the monkeys, as long as it remained a mere matter of naming and placing in an unchanging system. As one scholar, W. T. Stearn, wittily remarks, "Indeed, Linnaeus's methodical disposition and his urge to classify . . . would probably have led to the inclusion of the angels as well had he possessed adequate knowledge based on first hand observation of their characteristics. As things were, he had to stop at man."[18]

Linnaeus did stop, and he stopped any further connection in time, although not on the spaced page, between Man and the other animals. He was not an evolutionist but an encyclopedist. Living in the Encyclopedic age—the eighteenth century—he was characteristic of his time. The word *encyclopedia* comes from the Greek *enkyklios paideia*, meaning instruction in the circle of knowledge. Pliny the Elder had described his great, many-volumed *Natural History* in those words, claiming to encircle or encompass all things known. Linnaeus, as a contemporary of d'Alembert and the other philosophers engaged with the *Encyclopédie*, took his place as one who sought to encompass all of biology by identifying and naming all the known organisms. He also tried to assign Man a place where he would constantly be circling around a fixed spot in an undynamic classificatory scheme.

Even before evolutionary theory, there were intimations from non-biological sources of Man's cousining relation to the other animals. What embryonic evidence would confirm, intuition had already divined, in the form of physiognomic resemblance. Again, as with scientific illustrations, artists were in the forefront of the new perspective. Men were not only described as "strong as a bull" or "courageous as a lion"; they were also perceived to look like these creatures, facially.

To take one example: Charles Le Brun, an artist in the court of Louis XIV, who designed some of the superb Gobelin tapestries, also worked out a supposedly scientific theory to the effect that a person's true character could be known by comparing the person's head and facial features with those of other members of the animal kingdom. In support of his theory, he made numerous engravings, showing, for example, a particular man's resemblance to an ox, where the visual representation carries its own conviction.[19] The eye immediately perceives the resemblance and senses the common bond between the two "animals."

Other artists had glimpsed the same fact. Leonardo da Vinci, for example, had painted a portrait of a mistress of Lodovico Sforza holding in her arms his emblem, a stoat. It is a cruel painting, because Leonardo matches the skull behind the girl's temples with the stoat's, and the bones of her hand with its paw. He lets the viewers see that both are breathtakingly beautiful and sleek—but stupid. In the end the portrait is as much a work of discovery as of likeness—"an emblematic research into anatomy and character together."[20]

William Blake, too, in his strange satire on science, the so-called "An Island in the Moon," fused the artistic and scientific vision when he has one of his characters, Quid, say, "I think your face . . . is like that noble beast the Tyger" to a woman whom he had already induced to agree that his own is "very like a Goat's face." Behind such a statement was a serious belief held by both Blake and his associate in engraving, William Sharp. We are told that Sharp "had some eccentric notions on the subject of physiognomy . . . that every man's countenance had depicted on it the appearance of some bird or beast . . . Thus, in those whose dispositions were generous and courageous he fancied he could discover the likeness of a lion; in those who were fierce, he saw that of tigers or eagles."[21]

Blake and Sharp, in 1789, were engaged in engraving plates for Lavater's *Essay on Physiognomy* and drew confirmation, if not inspiration, from that work. From Lavater's efforts, it was an easy step to phrenology, which may shock us today but was taken seriously in the nineteenth century. Though we laugh at it today, analyzing "bumps on the head" was seen then (and at the time for some good reasons) as a major advance in understanding character. Face and head would tell, character would out in a physical form.[22] And that character would be rooted in humankind's animal nature, as intuited by artists such as Blake and Sharp.

This insight took a strange turn after Darwin. Then humans seemed to see the ape staring at them in the mirror. As T. H. Huxley remarked, "Brought face to face with these blurred copies of himself, the least thoughtful of men is conscious of a certain shock, due perhaps, not so much to disgust at the aspect of what looks like an insulting caricature, as to the awakening of a sudden and profound mistrust of time-honoured theories and strongly-rooted prejudices regarding his own position in nature, and his relations to the under-world of life."[23]

In this other, deeper life, Man's second, or rather earlier, nature might emerge, bestial and primitive: the other side of his divided nature. Again in Huxley's words, "Hoffman's terrible conception of the 'Doppelt-gänger' [sic] is realised by men in this state—who live two lives, in the one of which they may be guilty of the most criminal acts, while, in the other, they are eminently virtuous and respectable. Neither life knows anything of the other." Such a "Doppelt-gänger" are Stevenson's Dr. Jekyll and Mr. Hyde and Oscar Wilde's Dorian Gray, whose physical regression to animality in his portrait recapitulates evolution, but backwards.

The artist's insight as to the physiognomic relationship of humans and the other animals preceded that of the scientist's; indeed, the artists *were* scientists, as in the case of Leonardo. They *saw*, with all the penetration of that deepest power of sight, what the specialized scientists came to *know:* the eye showed the brain which way to go. As we shall see, Charles Darwin's artistic and poetic visions were an integral part of his scientific insight (he was acquainted with the work of both Le Brun and Lavater), even though later he seemed to repudiate his own development as a "seer" when he declared that he had become a "machine for grinding [out] general laws." In saying this, the great biologist was unknowingly also intuiting and embodying the extraordinary double dualism arising in humans, who just as they were becoming conscious in a new way of their human-animal nature were also becoming more acutely aware of their human-machine nature (a term that seems almost to deny and repudiate "nature"). But all this lies both in and beyond Darwin, whom we need now to begin to treat in his own person and work.

Rather than starting with *The Origin of Species* and *The Descent of Man*, I want to jump momentarily to the Charles Darwin who wrote the *Expression of the Emotions in Animals and Man* (1872). This book looked back, in one sense, to the physiognomic school; it, too, saw the hair rising on the head in fright, the snarling lip drawn back in anger, and other facial and bodily expressions of humans as similar to those of the other animals. Where the artist, however, saw mere resemblance, although intuiting a deeper connection, Darwin knew there was evolutionary kinship, understandable in terms of scientific theory.

Darwin had to come to his theory, or rather theories, after a long voyage of life and mind.[24] As is well known, he had to experience a "second birth," as he called it, undertaking a passage of five years around the world, out and away from the sedate university world of Cambridge, England, where he was an undergraduate. Henslow, one of his teachers, recommended him for the post aboard H.M.S. *Beagle*, whose mission was to chart the coasts of South America and other distant lands. The mission was an imperialist one, in fact, part of Britain's industrializing process, and was aimed at widening British trade and maritime power; as a side endeavor, it also intended to serve the cause of science: a naturalist was included in the ship's projected complement.

On the voyage, Darwin took along Milton's *Paradise Lost*. It was a prophetic title, for Darwin was to proclaim a new world in which Man was merely one of the animals rather than their ruler, and in which angels' wings ceased to beat. If at the beginning of the voyage Darwin was a Linnaean, seeing nature as a problem of classification, at its end he conceived of it as a process, first in geology and then in biology.

Darwin's other constant literary companion was Wordsworth. Reading his poems was not a mere pastime. Poetic imagination fused with Darwin's scientific interest; it gave him the vision in which the details of naturalistic observation might fit. We seem to hear the very tones of a Wordsworth (or a Matthew Arnold) when we read the passage in the *Voyage of the Beagle* that tells how

> amidst the din of rushing waters, the noise from the stones, as they rattled one over another, was most distinctly audible, even from a distance. This rattling noise, night and day, may be heard along the whole course of the torrent. The sound spoke elo-

quently to the geologist; the thousands and thousands of stones, which, striking against each other, made the one dull, uniform sound, were all hurrying in one direction. It was like thinking on time, where the minute that now glides past is irrecoverable. So was it with these stones; the ocean is their eternity, and each note of that wild music told of one more step towards their destiny.[25]

The concept of space and time might come from Lyell; the connection of detail and incipient theory was the effect of Darwin's aesthetic sense.

Darwin's interests at this time were extraordinarily wide. His *Journal* records observations not only of flora and fauna, but of economic matters, social customs, ethnographic data, and general mental processes. He obviously saw Man as a being in nature, though he did not yet have the theory to explain how he got there. The Fuegians especially impressed Darwin, and he perceived them as little above the beasts among whom they lived. One description, by another observer, remained vivid in Darwin's memory: a Fuegian father dashing out his "infant-boy's" brain on a rock because the boy had accidentally dropped a basket of sea eggs! Where, Darwin makes us ask with a shudder, does human nature begin and end?

On a previous trip Fitzroy, the captain of the *Beagle,* had collected three Fuegians for exhibit and education in England. Now he was returning them, with civilized clothes and manners, to their primitive brethren. It is a sad story. Jemmy Button, as he had been named, and his two companions were set upon, beaten, and robbed by their former peers and made as naked and destitute as before. The smell of "mankind," just as it marks an animal in captivity, who is then rejected if returned to the wilds, had attached to the unfortunate Fuegian transplants.

Apropos of this episode, Darwin remarks on one of the fundamental characteristics of civilization, as he sees it: "The perfect equality among the individuals composing the Fuegian tribes, must for a long time retard their civilization. As we see those animals, whose instinct compels them to live in society, and obey a chief, are most capable of improvement, so is it with the races of mankind."[26]

Mainly, of course, Darwin observed geological strata, seeing especially through the eyes of Charles Lyell and his *Principles of Geology,* and species distribution. He studied mountain formations and speculated on the upheavals of land and sea that had produced, for example, the majestic range of the Cordillera in present-day Chile. He measured the variations in finches' beaks and pondered over the kinds of turtles found in the Galápagos Islands.[27] Here, indeed, he had a laboratory, a sort of special simulacrum of creation, where species might be studied in a closed setting. By comparing one region with another, Darwin could perform a kind of thought experiment. He could imagine a new Genesis. Still, however, he remained on the edge of his great theory.

It was not until the return of the *Beagle*, and after Darwin had settled down to ordering his notes, that he found a theory by which to link all his observations. He happened, by chance, as he tells us, to have picked up a copy of Malthus's *Essay on Population*. Instantly he realized that if population necessarily increases geometrically and the food supply only arithmetically, a struggle for existence has to take place. Those best fitted to survive, owing to their variations, would win out. Darwin had arrived at his theory of evolution by natural selection.[28]

Before we turn to the details of that theory, a few further words about Malthus are in order. Was the effect of Malthus really that accidental? Much later, in 1858, Alfred Russel Wallace, halfway round the globe in Borneo (where he, too, had been collecting species, but for sale to zoos and not for his private use), in bed recovering from a fever, also picked up a copy of Malthus. At once, Wallace realized that he had in hand the key to how evolution took place by selection from variations. Quickly, he wrote up his thoughts and sent a copy of his article to Darwin. Thus, the Malthusian reading sparked a Doppelgänger effect in biological thought, with Darwin and Wallace the twin theorists.[29]

What in Malthus stimulated the two men in the same fecundating way? Malthus wrote on population because he saw it as a challenge to naive ideas of progress. In fact, population theory, with its emphasis on competition, was a part of economic theory. It came to figure, for example, in Ricardo's Iron Law of Wages: wages raised above the equilibrium point would lead to increased population competing for scarce jobs, which would lower wages and bring about mass starvation until the population equilibrium was restored. Darwin's theory, as we shall see, when it was not a matter of poetic imagination, was a contribution to the "economy of nature." As such, it breathed the atmosphere arising from the Industrial Revolution in Britain, wherein the bourgeoisie was establishing a new dominion—over machines and their attendant workers—and introducing a new social science, economics, to explain its rule.

The other prime factor in Malthus's theory was sex. Population grew because of the sexual impulse. Malthus's contemporaries James Mill and Francis Place knew that the lower impulses of humans' animal nature, that is, sex, threatened to undo humankind's economic gains. Believing from their own experience (Mill had nine and Place fifteen children) that it could not be restrained by moral resolve, they advocated a different sort of check on population growth: birth control by artificial means. Sex, uncontrolled, meant procreation; and it was an easy slide from humans' lascivious nature to the conceptualization of creation in the animal kingdom at large as pivoting on the same force. Linnaeus had sensed this force; Malthus and Darwin after him felt it fully. No wonder that, with covert wonderment and fear of the uncontrollable power of sex in mind, the Victorian Darwin could say of his own theory that "it is the doctrine of Malthus applied with manifold force to the whole of the animal and vegetable kingdoms; for in this case there can be no artificial increase of food, and no prudential restraint from marriage."[30]

In fact, were humans moral beings and thus different from the other animals—able to exercise "prudential restraint"—or was sex the great equalizer? Darwin, unlike Malthus, opted for the latter view, though willing to reintroduce morality after sexual evolution. Sex, so to speak, displaced God as the creative force. Genesis (2:7) speaks of God "breathing" into man's nostrils the spark of life; thus, Man is independently created and animated, as are all other animals. Darwin rejected this view and saw procreation—a sexual act—as a continuing force, with evolutionary implications.

His protégé, T. H. Huxley, would speak about the "question of questions," that is, the question of Man's origins. Darwin used the phrase "mystery of mysteries" and wrote On the Origin of Species in order to solve the mystery. He began with a mundane matter: domestic breeding (the first chapter is entitled "Variation Under Domestication"). Thus he was adding a scientific note to the daily human habit of domesticating the other animals, which goes back perhaps 10,000 to 12,000 years. In Darwin's time, as already noted, concurrent with the Industrial Revolution, an "agricultural revolution," which had started in the eighteenth century, was still under way, in which humans were scientifically breeding cattle and sheep. I have already mentioned the claim that Bakewell, for example, had increased the weight of a cow from 300 to 800 pounds by selective mating. Pigeon fanciers were at work on that species; indeed, the publisher Murray had wanted Darwin to restrict his book to pigeons, for there were ready readers for such a publication!

Darwin had larger aims in mind. He asked, If Man is the mechanism by which variations, which occur naturally, are selected in domestic breeding, leading to new species, what is the mechanism in nature that performs this same function? Who or what in nature acts the role of Man and his mind in domestic breeding? Darwin's answer was that it is a mindless force: the struggle for existence, or, in more neutral terms, natural (and sexual) selection.[31]

As Darwin explained natural selection: "Owing to this struggle, variations, however slight and from whatever cause proceeding, if they be in any degree profitable to the individuals of a species . . . will tend to the preservation of such individuals, and will generally be inherited by the offspring." Actually, Darwin admitted, though he had labeled the principle involved "Natural Selection," the "expression often used by Mr. Herbert Spencer of the Survival of the Fittest is more accurate." The term *natural selection*, however, was more convenient, and Darwin went on to say, "But Natural Selection, as we shall hereafter see, is a power incessantly ready for action, and is as immeasurably superior to man's feeble efforts, as the works of Nature are to those of Art."[32]

The language above is of "profitability" and Spencerian individualism: all are part of mid-nineteenth-century capitalist phraseology. But the theory is of universalizing, scientific import. True, when Darwin spoke of how the struggle was most intense between "the individuals of the same species" he seemed to be laying the foundations of social Darwinism. His language reflected his bourgeois milieu, but that was not his explicit intention: he was observing a fact of nature, independent of humans and their measures, and speculating on its consequences in the world of nature, not commerce.

Similarly, Darwin used the term *economy* as in *economy of nature*, and spoke of the *division of labor*. His usage, however, was peculiar to his evolution theory. He was comparing the "physiological division of labour in the organs of the same individual body" to the larger body of nature, where "the advantage of diversification of structure in the inhabitants of the same region" is the same. "So," he concluded, "in the general economy of any land, the more widely and perfectly the animals and plants are diversified for different habits of life, so will a great number of individuals be capable of there supporting themselves."[33]

Fundamentally, Darwin's economy of nature is an ecology, an interrelatedness of nature. The emphasis is on mutual dependence as well as on struggle; on the species as well as on the individual. When first introducing the term *struggle for existence*, Darwin hastened to add: "I should premise that I use this term in a large and metaphorical sense, including dependence of one being on another, and including (which is more important) not only the life of the individual, but success in leaving progeny."[34]

Darwin spelled out his ecological conviction, tracing the way in which the number of cats, for example, determines the number of flowers. It is a kind of Rube Goldberg contraption operating in nature. Citing a Colonel Newman, Darwin explains: "The number of humble-bees in any district depends in a great measure upon the number of field-mice, which destroy their combs and nests . . . Now the number of mice is largely dependent, as everyone knows, on the number of cats; and Col. Newman says, 'Near the villages and small towns I have found the nests of humble-bees more numerous than elsewhere, which I attribute to the number of cats that destroy the mice.' Hence it is quite credible that the presence of a feline animal in large numbers in a district might determine, through the intervention first of mice and then of bees, the frequency of certain flowers in that district!"[35]

Here we see, dramatically, the checks and balances at play in nature. One species as prey for another, climatic changes, epidemics, these work as checking powers, or brakes, on the consequence of rampant sexual reproduction (a single insect, Darwin noted, could produce twenty million larvae, or potential offspring!).

One result is creation of new species through the subsequent struggle for existence favoring the individuals best adapted to the new conditions. Another result is destruction of species. Darwin's theory offers not only a new genesis, but a new doomsday. As he tells us, we do not need to "invoke cataclysms to desolate the world." Extinction, like creation, is explicable in terms of natural selection.

Sex is a natural force for Darwin, the basis on which natural selection works. It also operates autonomously, as a force for evolution in its own right, though a subordinate force, in the form of sexual selection. As Darwin defines it, "This form of selection depends, not on a struggle for existence in relation to other organic beings or to external conditions, but on a struggle between the individuals of one sex, generally the males, for the possession of the other sex."[36] To the vigorous males belong the females; and the best-horned stag and spurred cock will leave the most offspring. The latter, in turn, will also increase in horn and spur, though there are obviously certain limits. Aesthetic, as well as martial, attributes, such as the peacock's spread, also serve evolutionary purposes. In nature, natural and sexual selection together do the work of Man in domestic breeding.

But humans are also an evolutionary product, the result of the dual selecting forces. They are part of, not outside, the natural world. And most important, their existence seemed to give sanction to the view that evolution moved in the direction of "improvement" and thus of progress. All that was needed was a long stretch of time over which gradual changes could occur. What Darwin actually had in mind was that the evolutionary record suggested a movement toward greater differentiation of parts in the same organ's being and increased specialization of functions. Sometimes, however, he got carried away with Victorian enthusiasm and could write, "And as natural selection works solely by and for the good of each being, all corporeal and mental endowments will tend to progress toward perfection."[37]

The momentary flutter of angels' wings introduced by the word *perfection* should not mislead us. By perfection, Darwin merely meant exquisite adaptation by a species to the niche in the ecology that it had come to occupy. Perfection simply meant survival. And what survived were clearly the fittest, a perfect redundancy. In fact, Darwin knew full well that evolution could work in "reverse," that is, "it is quite possible for natural selection gradually to fit a being to a situation in which several organs would be superfluous or useless: in such cases there would be retrogression in the scale of organization." It did him no good to allow himself the luxury further on in the book of calling such retrogression in organization "degraded."[38] His own theory held survival as the sole value in nature; all else was Man's creation of really irrelevant values, such as progress and retrogression.

Chance, not reason, was at work. Modification, and so evolution, was the result of slight, accidental variations, not of calculated change. And yet a study of the results could be conceived as order—and orders, genera, and species—emerging out of chaos. Linnaeus in his classificatory scheme had shown the way. Darwin gave life to the system by animating the arrangement and showing how it produced new and different species—the offspring need not perpetually be in the image of their parents! This, said Darwin, was the truly "Natural System." And, he added, "Our classifications will come to be, as far as they can be so made, genealogies; and will then truly give what may be called the plan of creation."[39]

Darwin was aware that he had brought about, as he put it, "a revolution in natural history." He had linked all animals to one another through evolution, and to the whole of the natural world. Indeed, as he insisted, "The relation of organism to organism is the most important of all relations . . . and the most important of all causes of organic change."[40] Embryology might confirm the genealogical connection, and fossils unite extinct animals to living ones; the true link, however, was Darwin's creating mind holding together by theory the visible universe with the invisible and lifting humans culturally and morally out of the animal kingdom at the same time as physically it firmly placed them in it.

Darwin knew that his revolution had done for biology what Newton had done for mechanics. At first, he compared his work inferentially, claiming that "the greatest discovery ever made by man, namely, the law of the attraction of gravity" was attacked as irreligious, just as was his own law of evolution by natural selection. Then, boldly, in the very last sentence of the *Origin*, Darwin stepped out and made his claim for a place alongside Newton, though with a nod of deference to the Creator. There is grandeur, he asserted, in the view of life that sees the higher animals as emerging from the "war of nature" and recognizes that "whilst this planet had gone cycling on according to the fixed law of gravity, from so simple a beginning endless forms most beautiful and most wonderful have been, and are being evolved."[41]

A "higher animal" and "grandeur" are prideful words, fitted to make humans (though in the *Origin* Darwin does not yet explicitly include them in evolution) feel of high estate. In having humans implicitly "descend" from other animals—"descending" from "lower" animals suggests the ambivalences and ambiguities involved—Darwin was also claiming, of course, that humans had "ascended" (as Jacob Bronowski recognized in his BBC series, "The Ascent of Man"). Thus humans, as biological beings, were invested with an ambivalent grandeur; they could claim such highness as was available to them in a new plan of creation, where, contrary to the Bible, they had had to fight for their domination over the other animals, a fight that obviously had been successful.

Perhaps this is the moment to pause and to note that I have been presenting a sort of straight-line version of Darwin; and that there is more tension in him than might appear from this study. For example, there are his personal struggles, and especially his prolonged and constant illnesses, which manifest themselves after his return from the voyage of the *Beagle*. The details, and causes, of his "patienthood" have been valiantly debated by doctors and scholars; but all can agree that the life of the Victorian Darwin relates in a complex and perhaps convoluted fashion to his work (he entitled his autobiography *Recollections of the Development of My Mind and Character*).

There is also his shifting, squirming position on religion. As a student at Cambridge, Darwin accepted, apparently without qualms, the orthodox Anglican beliefs. Sometime during the *Beagle* voyage, he began to question. On his return, he tried to keep his opinions private, for he wished neither to give offense to his pious wife nor to cast a shadow on the reception of his emerging theory of evolution. We catch the flavor of Darwin's convictions, however, in a letter of 1860 to Asa Gray, where he confesses that "I cannot see as plainly as others do, and as I should wish to do, evidence of design and beneficence on all sides of us. There seems to me too much misery in the world." Despairingly, he concludes that "the whole subject is too profound for the human intellect."

Despite his reticence, his opponents kept attacking him on religious grounds. As late as 1879, Darwin plaintively wrote a correspondent that "what my own views may be is a question of no consequence to anyone but myself." Then, denying that he was ever an atheist, he adds, ambivalently, "I think that generally (and more and more as I grow older), but not always, that an Agnostic would be the more correct description of my state of mind."[42]

His scientific work shows even more evidence of tension and ambiguity. Fervently declaring his belief in the Baconian method, he habitually brought theory to his observations, his practice thereby differing sharply from his pronouncements. At first, deriding Lamarckism, he introduced more and more elements of the Frenchman's theories into his own work, especially in *The Descent of Man.*

Then there are a host of challenges to Darwin's theory, about which he sometimes waffled and wavered. A Scotsman, Fleeming Jenkin, pointed out that a newly emergent character would be swamped in breeding with the mass of individuals not possessing the favorable trait. Before knowledge of Mendel's work, this was a powerful criticism of Darwin's theory. Not until the sixth edition of the *Origin of Species* did Darwin acknowledge the seriousness of the criticism—without offering any adequate response to it.

Similarly, there was St. George Mivart's attack, his argument that incipient stages, for example, the beginning development of a wing, could have no adaptive value—until it was a fully developed wing. In this case, Darwin counterattacked, arguing that Mivart's position raised even more problems than his own.[43]

In short, a full-scale treatment of Darwin would follow the twists and turns, the temptations and tensions, in his life and work. We should remind ourselves of this more complicated picture as I draw out of

Darwin the lines that appear most relevant to our discussion of his role in regard to our discontinuities.

Implicit in Darwin's *Origin* was the "descent" of Man. Wishing to avoid controversy, however, Darwin at first carefully avoided a plain assertion. That was left, initially, in England, for T. H. Huxley.[44] At the meeting in Oxford of the British Association for the Advancement of Science in 1860, Bishop Wilberforce, "Soapy Sam" as he was known because of his oratory, is reputed to have foolishly baited Huxley with the question whether he was descended from the monkey or ape on his grandmother's or grandfather's side.[45] (Wilberforce, of course, would never have raised such an insulting question with Darwin, who by choice was not there, because of Darwin's upper middle-class family; Huxley, on the other hand, as a man of humble origins, was fair game.)

Huxley, recognizing that "God" (Huxley, in fact, was an atheist, or at least an agnostic) had delivered the bishop into his hands, smote him mightily. Returning the insult, he declared that at least he did not dishonor his parents by such abusive misuse of his mental faculties, and then he proceeded to give a scientific lecture establishing Man's true relations to the other animals. He had become Darwin's "bulldog."

Huxley symbolized the new, tenacious professional: the man of science. Darwin was a gentleman, who, though not merely a naturalist, simply practiced science. William Whewell had coined the term *scientist* in his *Philosophy of the Inductive Sciences* (1840), in contrast to *artist*: "We need very much a name to describe a cultivator of science in general. I should incline to call him a *Scientist*. Thus we might say, that as an Artist is a Musician, Painter, or Poet, a Scientist is a Mathematician, Physicist, or Naturalist."[46] (I might add that *scientist* also replaced the older term *natural philosopher.*) Science was now considered to be a profession, where an individual might spend a lifetime practicing a specialty, and so spending, also earn an income. The scientist was no longer a well-born virtuoso. Huxley, the bulldog, was one of the first of a line that is now well recognized.

Huxley was further unlike Darwin in that whereas the great evolutionist had dropped out of medical school, Huxley went on to obtain his medical degree. The lifelines come closer, however, when we observe that a voyage also figured largely in Huxley's early life: Huxley began his long career of scientific research by sailing as an assistant surgeon on H.M.S. *Rattlesnake* to Australia and New Guinea. Instead of Milton and Wordsworth as his companions, however, Huxley took along Carlyle's critical essays, and especially *Sartor Resartus*. In *Sartor*, Carlyle had experienced a new birth, creating out of the depths of depression an affirmative self, a hero of the "Everlasting Yea." Huxley, too, had suffered in his youth from deep moods of melancholia; in Carlyle, he found the "agent" of his redemption and inspiration for his desire to be a hero of the new science.

At this point the two men diverged. Carlyle, as we have seen, had prophesied a new society aborning, "industrial society," about which he was highly ambivalent, worrying that it was unduly mechanizing Man's emotions as well as mind. Huxley was less concerned.

In fact, Huxley was something of an antivitalist. I shall pursue this aspect of Huxley in more detail later, but a brief comment is here in order. In one of his vivisections, he performed an experiment, connecting a special apparatus to the open, beating heart of a living frog, to show that the force keeping the heart beating "must be regarded as of the same order with other physical forces." As he concluded, "The mechanician has proved that the living body obeys the mechanical laws of living matter."[47]

While the meaning of mechanical here may not be precisely that embodied in the word *machine*, there is nevertheless something very un-Darwinian in Huxley's spirit. He is going in a new direction. We can see how far in his comment that "I protest that if some great Power would agree to make me always think what is true and do what is right, on condition of being turned into a sort of clock and wound up every morning before I got out of bed, I should instantly close with the offer."[48] In other words, Huxley was willing to become a machine in order to be free of erring—do we remember that "to err is human"?— and all this in the name of morality! It is a strange morality, in which moral choice is eliminated. We are on the way to *Brave New World*, as envisioned and satirized by Thomas's grandson Aldous Huxley.

But this line of thought is peripheral to Huxley's role as Darwin's spokesman. On the "question of questions," Huxley was an orthodox Darwinian (though for reasons in some ways different from Darwin's, as we shall see further in chapter 7), adding a new testament in his *Evidence as to Man's Place in Nature* (1863).[49] Here he drew the obvious conclusion from Darwin's *Origin* and boldly declared that humans were animals directly linked to the other animals by evolutionary chains. There was, for example, no "cerebral barrier between man and the apes." As Huxley pointed out, "The difference in weight of brain between the highest and the lowest men is far greater, both relatively and absolutely, than that between the lowest man and the highest ape."[50] The discovery of a Neanderthal skull in 1856, and the language of links and chains, led, naturally, to a search for a "missing link" between humans and the apes, but Huxley knew that the language was misleading and that both had come from a common ancestor. More fitting was Darwin's image of a "tree of life," with diverging branches.

As both Darwin and Huxley saw, however, humans were animals, but of a very special sort. Though not specially created, they had special attributes that raised them above the rest of the animal kingdom. Man is the evolutionary result, as Huxley put it, of "Nature's great progression, from the formless to the formed—from the inorganic to the organic—from blind force to conscious intellect and will." His descent has also entailed an ascent of powers. Implicitly contradicting his statement, quoted earlier, Huxley now continues, "The power of knowledge, the conscience of good and evil—the pitiful tenderness of human affections, raise us out of all real fellowship with the brutes, however closely they may seem to approximate us."[51] While there may be no "cerebral barrier" as such between us and the apes, there is a spiritual barrier that is insurmountable: morality and knowledge make us, uniquely, "the only consciously intelligent denizen of this world."

In this way Huxley sought to resolve a logical problem that he only dimly perceived. Nature was no longer a benevolent anthropomorphized power, but a cold, impersonal system of mechanical forces moving in an evolutionary direction—whether progressive or regressive. If humans are a product of such a mechanical system—and nature's laws were Newton's, hence Huxley's temptation to the mechanical—why are humans, in turn, to be regarded as anything more than a comparable amoral, mechanical entity? This would become the new "question of questions" (which I shall pursue further in regard to Huxley in chapter 7).

Darwin, in the *Origin*, had used the word *nature* as if it meant a personified being working through natural selection. He was aware, however, that it was merely a "metaphorical expression" and, to avoid difficulties, firmly declared that "I mean by Nature, only the aggregate action and product of many natural laws, and by laws the sequence of events as ascertained by us."[52] Such a nature was Newtonian-like, but by not dealing with Man in the 1859 work, Darwin avoided the question of Man's possibly having a mechanical nature. Huxley could not avoid it but dealt with the problem finally by elevating Man to a special moral status (as Darwin was to do, too, in the *Descent*).

By the time of *Evolution and Ethics* (1893), Huxley had turned completely against "Mother" nature. In opposition to it he posited civilization, that is, human creation, which permits opposition to its "Creator." Humans now, to be human, had to rebel against their "Maker." Civilization, Huxley declared, was an attempt by Man "to escape from his place in the animal kingdom . . . to establish a kingdom of Man, governed upon the principle of moral evolution."[53] The wheel of Man's relation to other animals has come all the way around. Removed from the heights where he had been placed in Genesis by God, with dominion over all creatures, he had now fought his way, against nature (even if by its very natural laws), back onto the heights. From there, once again, he could still look down at the other animals and take comfort that he was lifted above his own, instinctual animal nature.

Darwin's own views on what I am calling evolving human nature are to be found in two key works, *The Descent of Man* and *The Expression of the Emotions in Man and Animals*. Huxley, as we have noted, in 1863 had already spoken for Darwin, extrapolating evolution to Man in his *Evidence as to Man's Place in Nature;* in 1871, Darwin spoke for himself. The full title of his book is *The Descent of Man and Selection in Relation to Sex*. The origin of one species, Man, is examined in detail. More than half the book, Parts II and III, is devoted to the sexual theme, that is, sexual selection. Male against male in combat, male for female by aesthetic lure, these are the means by which struggle for the procreational imperative takes form and substance. Thus, Linnaeus's preoccupation with sex is further developed.

In Darwin's hands, sex also becomes the basis of a racial theory. "During many years," as he informs us, "it had seemed to me highly probable that sexual selection has played an important part in differentiating the races of man." Indeed, one of the three objects of the *Descent* is to consider "the value of the differences between the so-called races of man."[54] Darwin thought there *was* a value difference, that is, that some "races" were more advanced than others. Painful as it is to admit, Darwin was a racist of sorts, in the pleasant, self-assured manner of an upper-class Englishman of the nineteenth century. He was, of course, antislavery, but that was on moral grounds.

Darwin's scientific theory, an authentic one in itself, led him in strange directions and allowed him to be a contributor to racial theory, the great nineteenth-century ideological alternative to Marx and his class struggle (whose result was expected to be equality rather than diversification). Domestic breeding showed Darwin that mental, as well as physical, qualities were transmitted "in our dogs, horses, and other domestic animals." Inheritance, Darwin insisted, worked in the same fashion for humans. After all, were they not simply another animal? "Special tastes and habits, general intelligence, courage, bad and good temper, etc., are certainly transmitted" in humans, he announced. Then, he added, "and we now know, through the admirable labours of Mr. Galton, that genius which implies a wonderfully complex combination of high faculties, tends to be inherited; and, on the other hand, it is too certain that insanity and deteriorated mental powers likewise run in families."[55]

Francis Galton was Darwin's cousin. Involved, as he put it, in "a purely ethnological inquiry, into the mental peculiarities of different races," he stumbled onto "the theory that genius was hereditary." One result was his book *Hereditary Genius* (1869), wherein he satisfied himself that his theory was statistically supported. Though an unconvincing work, it elicited from Darwin the comment in a letter to his cousin that "I do not think I ever in all my life read anything more interesting and original."[56] The *Descent* simply made public Darwin's approval and interest.

Eugenics was the name Galton gave to his new science. For Darwin, as well as Galton, it represented the principles of domestic breeding, extended to human beings. In nature, sexual selection had established the different races. It was a "natural" step, therefore, to see humans take conscious control of their destiny and "upgrade" the race by rational, selective breeding. Darwin did not himself particularly develop the idea and certainly did not pursue it to its logical conclusions. It simply followed, or so it seemed, from his having established humans as animals among other animals. "It is only our natural prejudice," Darwin reminds us, "and that arrogance which made our forefathers declare that they were descended from demi-gods, which leads us to demur to this conclusion."[57]

Out of this matrix of theory have come all the contentions revolving around racial theory, eugenics, IQ tests, and on up to sociobiology. Aside from the latter, to be taken up later, these are none of our business here. All we need to know is that they are, for better or worse, part of the great "revolution in natural history" brought about by Darwin's evolutionary view of Man, the emergent animal, and serve as a shadowy context for "racial" fears about machines and their possible future domination.

Darwin himself stayed closer to his original theory. He repeated that humankind was subject to the Malthusian principle, just as were the other animals. "The early progenitors of man must also have tended, like all other animals, to have increased beyond their means of subsistence; they must, therefore, occasionally have been exposed to a struggle for existence, and consequently to the rigid law of natural selection." As one moves up the evolutionary tree, however, sexual selection plays an increasingly important role. Exhaustively, Darwin examines the insects, fishes, amphibians, reptiles, birds, and other mammals in these terms. His conclusion is that "in the lower divisions of the animal kingdom, sexual selection seems to have done nothing: such animals are often affixed for life to the same spot, or have the sexes combined in the individual, or what is still more important, their perceptive and intellectual faculties are not sufficiently advanced to allow of the feelings of love and jealousy, or of the exertion of choice. When, however, we come to the Arthropoda and Vertebrata, even to the lowest classes in these two great Sub-Kingdoms, sexual selection has effected much."[58]

The emphasis is on advanced perceptive and intellectual faculties and, oddly, on love and jealousy. But Darwin always thought in terms of a spectrum, not of sharp discontinuities. He believed, for example, "that there is no fundamental difference between man and the higher mammals in their mental faculties." The lower animals, too, feel pleasure and pain, happiness and misery. They even have vivid dreams, Darwin insists, and possess some power of imagination. Are all other animals without tools? Darwin will not have it so and remarks that "it has often been said that no animal uses any tool; but the chimpanzee in a state of nature cracks a native fruit, somewhat like a walnut, with a stone."[59]

Is language, then, the sharp divide? Again, Darwin contends that it is merely a matter of degree and adds that "the lower animals differ from man solely in his almost infinitely larger power of associating together the most diversified sounds and ideas; and this obviously depends on the high development of his mental powers."[60]

The most fundamental difference between humans and the other animals, in Darwin's view, is that humans possess a developed moral sense, or conscience, and religion. These are the significant "mental powers" that set mankind apart. Neither is innate. Religion, for example, can be explained on naturalistic grounds. Savages, starting with a belief in unseen spiritual agencies, according to Darwin, progressed through the stages of fetishism, polytheism, and ultimately monotheism. Nothing comparable can be found even in their most proximate primate relations.

Similarly, Man's moral sense evolved, for there is no "natural goodness" in the savage state. Unlike Rousseau, Darwin had actually seen

Fuegians and knew whereof he spoke. In Darwin's view, morality is rooted in what he calls the "social instinct" and also in our capacity to feel sympathy. As social beings, humans are able, besides acting instinctively, to reflect on their actions and motives and to sacrifice themselves, if necessary, for the group. Other animals do this instinctively, but Darwin seems to be saying that humans do it also out of conscience. The discussion is rather confused and meandering, with pauses for comparison to the behavior of dogs, baboons, and birds that Darwin has either observed or heard about.

When talking of the social instinct, Darwin also makes a particularly interesting point in the light of future Freudian theory. "The feeling of pleasure from society," he tells us, "is probably an extension of the parental or filial affections, since the social instinct seems to be developed by the young remaining for a long time with their parents; and this extension may be attributed in part to habit, but chiefly to natural selection. With those animals which were benefited by living in close association, the individuals which took the greatest pleasure in society would best escape various dangers, whilst those that cared least for their comrades, and lived solitary, would perish in greater numbers." His next observation contains a hint of the forthcoming Oedipus complex. As Darwin continues, "With respect to the origin of the parental and filial affections, which apparently lie at the base of the social instincts, we know not the steps by which they have been gained; but we may infer that it has been to a large extent through natural selection. So it has almost certainly been with the unusual and opposite feeling of hatred between the nearest relations, as with the worker-bees which kill their brother drones, and with the queen-bees which kill their daughter-queens; the desire to destroy their nearest relations having been in this case of service to the community."[61] It is not an idea, however, that Darwin himself developed further.

Very much aware of utilitarian philosophy, Darwin allowed himself to get into a somewhat muddled discussion of the difference between the general good and general happiness. The general good he defines as rearing the greatest number of individuals fit to survive, and the social instincts of the lower animals have solely this end in view. Man seems more complicated and also aims at general happiness; but Darwin is aware that he is floundering about on his definition and leaves the matter where it is, unresolved.

Quoting Spencer, however, Darwin has no doubt that virtuous tendencies—such as "chastity, temperance, humanity to animals"—can be inherited. In fact, Darwin is sanguine about humanity's future moral development, exactly because of the law of inheritance, whereby moral traits, as his cousin Francis Galton had supposedly shown, are transmitted, both by individuals and by races. "Looking to future generations," he concludes, "there is no cause to fear that the social instincts will grow weaker, and we may expect that virtuous habits will grow stronger, becoming perhaps fixed by inheritance. In this case the struggle between our higher and lower impulses will be less severe, and virtue will be triumphant."[62]

Neither as moral philosophy nor as science is Darwin's discussion of morality particularly cogent or convincing. It is, however, enormously suggestive. Darwin's intuition, his imaginative powers, ran far ahead of the subject matter that was ready for his analytic abilities in this area. He had established, scientifically, that humans are animals like other animals. There is no break, no discontinuity between them. Yet there is a difference, if only in degree. Darwin fumbled his way toward understanding it. Dimly he saw, rather than knew, that culture, in which morality and religion figure so largely, plays a key role. Necessarily, he spoke in terms of natural and sexual selection. He was aware, subconsciously, however, that the tensions generated between Man's "lower nature"—his link to the other animals—and his aspirations to a "higher nature"—to be a "cultured" being—had opened a new chapter in evolution.[63]

At best, Darwin was able to contribute a paragraph to that new chapter. It was originally to have been an "essay on the expression of the various emotions by man and the lower animals," forming part of *The Descent of Man*.[64] That book, however, was already too large, and Darwin published his "essay" as a separate work, *The Expression of the Emotions in Man and Animals* (1872). He had been taking notes on the subject, he tells us, since 1838; thus it connects to the *Origin of Species* and Darwin's Malthusian cogitations as well.

In his *Expression of the Emotions*, Darwin begins by citing the work on physiognomy of Le Brun and Lavater, whom we have mentioned earlier.[65] The true forerunner of scientific work on expression, rather than physiognomy, however, in Darwin's view, was Sir Charles Bell, an illustrious physiologist. Indeed, Darwin was somewhat skeptical of physiognomy and remarked that "whatever the amount of truth the so-called science of physiognomy may contain, appears to depend, as Haller long ago remarked, on different persons bringing into frequent use different facial muscles, according to their dispositions."[66]

Darwin based his speculations on observations made on infants—

his own, for example—and on the insane, both of whom show little restraint of their emotions. He also used a series of photographs, of old men weeping and of children crying, and included many of these in his book.[67] Last, Darwin availed himself of a wide range of comparative data, the result of anthropological observations.

On the basis of all this evidence, Darwin concluded that "the same state of mind is expressed throughout the world with remarkable uniformity; and this fact is in itself interesting as evidence of the close similarity in bodily structure and mental disposition of all the races of mankind."[68] In short, the expression of emotions is a common, universal trait, rooted in Man's evolutionary nature.

Three principles, in Darwin's view, account for the expressions and gestures observed. In the simplest terms, the first principle states that they are serviceable, that is, "in order to relieve or gratify certain sensations, desires, etc.," which are otherwise being "partially repressed through the will"; the second, that they are antithetical, that is, "when a directly opposite state of mind is induced, there is a strong and involuntary tendency to the performance of movements of a directly opposite nature"; and the third, that they arise out of the direct action of the nervous system, that is, "when the sensorium is strongly excited, nerve-force is generated in excess, and is transmitted in certain definite directions, depending on the connection of the nerve-cells, and partly on habit: or the supply of nerve-force may, as it appears, be interrupted."[69]

Clearly, these principles are complicated and even vague. They are also enormously suggestive. In one direction, most immediately, they reach out to Pavlov and his theory of the conditioned reflex (in the other direction, to Freud and psychoanalysis). As Darwin remarks, it is the power of association that is involved, where "actions readily become associated with other actions, and with various states of the mind." Darwin was fully aware that he was not original in this idea—it was the commonplace of the reigning associational psychology—and he quotes Alexander Bain to the effect that "actions, sensations and states of feeling, occurring together or in close succession, tend to grow together, or cohere, in such a way that when any one of them is afterwards presented to the mind, the others are apt to be brought up in idea."[70]

The largest part of Darwin's book is devoted to exemplification of his principles and to illustrations of the expressions and emotions subject to them. The list is long: suffering and weeping, anxiety, grief, dejection, despair, joy, high spirits, love, devotion, hatred and anger, disdain, contempt, disgust, guilt, affirmation, and on and on. Dogs and cats are especially brought in as witnesses, but swans and chimpanzees, snakes and rhinos, cows and sows are also ranged alongside the infants and the insane of humankind.

Blushing is one of the expressions of emotion to which Darwin gives especial attention. It is, he says, "the most peculiar and the mos human of all expressions." (Its peculiar importance for Darwin may lie in its connection with stammering, an affliction of his early years.) It also reveals where Darwin's thought is heading. The physiological cause of blushing is the filling of the small vessels of the face with blood. The triggering of the physiological cause, however, is the "emotion of shame." As Darwin remarks, "Under a keen sense of shame there is a strong desire for concealment. We turn away the whole body, more especially the face, which we endeavour in some manner to hide."[71]

In one grand moment of intuition and imagination, Darwin realized that humans not only reacted physiologically, on the basis of inherited characteristics, in expressing their emotions, but did so for psychological reasons as well, for example, from emotions of shame and guilt possibly peculiar to the species. A footnote confirms for us that Darwin had indeed glimpsed the power of the human mind—a mental cause—in producing organic changes. It is a long footnote, but must be given whole:

> Dr. J. Crichton Browne, from his observations on the insane, is convinced that attention directed for a prolonged period on any part or organ may ultimately influence its capillary circulation and nutrition. He has given me some extraordinary cases; one of these, which cannot here be related in full refers to a married woman fifty years of age, who laboured under the firm and long-continued delusion that she was pregnant. When the expected period arrived, she acted precisely as if she had been really delivered of a child, and seemed to suffer extreme pain, so that the perspiration broke out on her forehead. The result was that a state of things returned, continuing for three days, which had ceased during the six previous years. Mr. Braid gives, in his "Magic, Hypnotism," &c., 1852, p. 95 and in his other works analogous cases, as well as other facts showing the great influence of the will on the mammary glands, even on one breast alone.[72]

The mention of James Braid, an early discoverer and proponent of hypnosis, considered by many in the nineteenth century as a charlatan, but not by Darwin, alerts us to the thread leading through the maze of the great evolutionist's thought to Freud. When Darwin remarked that "few points are more interesting in our present subject than the extraordinarily complex chain of events which lead to certain expressive movements,"[73] he was pointing in a direction that would be pursued by his Viennese disciple.

Sigmund Freud, inspired by his reading of Darwin to enter science, took as his life work the understanding of the mind-body relation. For him, the royal road to that understanding was dream interpretation. In dreams, according to Freud, humans retraced their past, personal and collective. Freud's implied claim was that, upon awakening from such dreams, humans would have a new view of themselves as evolutionary animals. They would have become psychological creatures. Such is one unexpected conclusion of Darwin's "materialistic" evolutionary biology.[74] Another, even larger conclusion is that as we seek to understand evolving human nature and its relation to machines, the line of "descent" stretching from Darwin must serve as the critical inspiration for our developing theses.

## Chapter Six

With Charles Darwin and his theory of natural selection, humans became evolutionary animals. They were now creatures of chance, rather than creations of God. Instead of their lineaments being found in a book, the Bible, where they could see themselves in their Maker's image, now they had to be sought for in painstaking observations of nature. Humans' nature now became a matter of science, not of revelation.

The search for an understanding of the nature of humans, as well as for a greater understanding of the evolutionary world of which they were a part, enlisted many Darwinian disciples. I have already mentioned T. H. Huxley. In this chapter, I want to concentrate on two perhaps less obvious disciples of Darwinian science: Sigmund Freud and Ivan Pavlov. Between them, they staked out major positions in psychology, each developing important strands in Darwin's own work; and these, as we shall see (especially in chapters 10 and 11), remain central to any present consideration of human (animal)-machine relations— the fourth discontinuity—and the question of human nature itself.

Freud's was unquestionably a Darwinian universe. He took it for granted; hence he had little occasion to mention Darwin's name, any more than a person who breathes naturally has cause to mention air or breathing. I underline the fact that not to understand this about Freud is to miss a fundamental dimension surrounding him and his work.[1] In breaching the third discontinuity—between the rational and the irrational—Freud was following on Darwin's closing of the second discontinuity—between humans and other animals. In so doing, he also pointed to a definition of the human—what *is* Man's "nature"?—that should inform any examination of the human-machine boundaries.

Freud took as his starting point Man's Darwinian animal nature. Darwin (along with Goethe) had inspired Freud's choice of career: as he remarks in his autobiography, "The theories of Darwin, which were then of topical interest, strongly attracted me, for they held out hopes of an extraordinary advance in our understanding of the world."[2] In his first year as a medical student at the University of Vienna, Freud elected to take Professor Carl Claus's course on general biology and Darwinism, and then under his and Ernst von Brücke's guidance, to work in physiology.[3] In addition, Freud was influenced not only by the *Origin* and the *Descent*, but especially by reading and rereading the *Expression of the Emotions*.

Freud's route to the resumption of Darwin's inquiries concerning Man's uniqueness as a cultural, not merely physical, animal was, as he himself admitted, a "circuitous" one. Darwin provided a general inspiration, an imaginative vision. Brücke and others, such as Helmholtz and Du Bois-Reymond, offered a narrower, more intensely physicalistic view of nature. As the latter summarized their position in a letter of 1842: "Brücke and I pledged a solemn oath to put into power this truth: no other forces than the common physical-chemical ones are active within the organism. In those cases which cannot at the time be explained by these forces one has either to find the specific way or form of their action by means of the physical-mathematical method, or to assume new forces equal in dignity to the chemical-physical forces inherent in matter, reducible to the force of attraction and repulsion."[4]

In this spirit, Freud happily labored away on the neuroanatomy of Ammocoetes (*Petromyzon planeri*), a primitive form of fish, and on the gonadal structure of the eel. His task in the latter enterprise was, as he wrote in his paper, that "no one has ever found a mature male eel—no one has yet seen the testes of the eel, in spite of innumerable efforts throughout the centuries."[5] After dissecting some four hundred eels, Freud's results were still inconclusive, though they generally supported the findings of another researcher, who had located the missing testes in a small lobed organ.

Freud also worked on a study of the nerve cells of the crayfish, and here T. H. Huxley had preceded him. Huxley's *The Crayfish* (1879) impressed Freud greatly—his own work was being done in 1882—and he clearly admired both the older man's specific contribution and his general physicalistic-physiological view of the subject. Thus, initially, it was the Huxley line of Darwinian development, with all its ambivalences toward vitalism and antivitalism, as we have noted, in which Freud sought to place himself.

According to Freud, he would have been content to spend the rest of his days in such laboratory research if it had not been for the accident of his "father's generous improvidence."[6] Under the spur of financial necessity—Freud wanted to marry his beloved Martha—and the good advice of Brücke, the aspiring scientist abandoned his "theoretical career" and entered upon the practice of medicine. Moving from the study of the eel and the crayfish, he directed his attention to the human central nervous system.

Though a momentous shift, it was carried out at first in a Helmholtzian spirit. Man was simply a more complicated physical-chemical system. When Freud moved from studying the human nervous system per se to studying the psyche, he stili employed the same terms for a long time. He tended to regard the psyche as a closed energy system, and in his "Project for a Scientific Psychology" of 1895 (though intimations of deeper insights peep through), treated it more like a steam engine, subject to the Second Law of Thermodynamics (the conservation of energy), than like a mental construct.

Freud announced his intention in the first lines of the project's introduction: "to furnish a psychology that shall be a natural science: that is, to represent psychical processes as quantitatively determinate states of specifiable material particles."[7] In pursuit of this aim, Freud worked out in tortuous detail what he called "the most fundamental attributes of the psychical mechanism (the law of constancy)," that is, the tendency of the mental apparatus to maintain a constant tension.[8] He never abandoned his image of the psychical mechanism as an energy system, nor his use of electrical metaphors, as in the statement, "The expenditure of force on the part of the physician was evidently the measure of a *resistance* on the part of the patient."[9] Indeed, at the end of his life, Freud still looked forward to the establishment of an acceptable connection between psychological and biochemical processes, and for the translation of his strange psychological terms into physiological and physical language.[10]

Nevertheless, hesitantly, Freud moved along his journey from physiology to psychoanalysis, more and more under the inspiration of Darwin rather than of mechanistic science. It is not my purpose here to trace that development in detail. Eels, the human nervous system, hot baths, electric shock, hypnosis, catharsis, free association, case histories—they are all landmarks on that extraordinary voyage of Freud's mind.[11]

Instead, in our effort to understand what is human nature (and how it might differ from a machine), I shall focus only on a few key features of Freud's new science. In his expanding clinical practice, and his theorizing on its cases, Freud came to an overwhelming insight: in humans, sex was not "natural." To give an example (although one that is not his), a male puppy, as soon as it can, seeks to mount its mother. Neither it nor the bitch feels shame or guilt: their sexual behavior is natural. For humans, it has become "unnatural," a matter of loathing and disgust, to be cordoned off by the incest taboo. If the anthropologists can be believed, the incest taboo, though different objects may be tabooed, is a constant for all societies. The roots of human sexuality are unconscious, stretching back into the dimness of the human evolutionary past. But once the human becomes human, conscious and unconscious motives and impulses clash, leaving an ambivalent and neurotic creature: psychological Man.

Psychological Man is the divided being, split along the "fault" of consciousness, half-beast, half-god, separate from the other animals. Freud, with his passion for Egyptology, shared Hegel's fascination with the sphinx, as a symbol, for it is the sphinx that stops Oedipus on the road to Thebes and poses to him the riddle of human nature. As is well known, for Freud the Oedipus complex is the nuclear complex, the basic building block of psychological Man, whereby a man wishes, unconsciously, to act like the puppy with his bitch but fears the retribution that may come in the form of castration.[12]

In *Totem and Taboo*, Freud acknowledges his debt to Darwin's idea of the "primal horde," as the "historical" source of the oedipal feeling, and builds his evolutionary picture of morality and religion around it. The result is one of the great myths—which Freud justified as a "scientific myth"—of human origin.[13]

There is another connection to Darwin, however, that Freud does not overtly explore, though it surely underlies his whole conception of the Oedipus complex. It is developed by Alex Comfort, best known for his *The Joy of Sex*—happy title!—but also a noted researcher in biology. Freud had resorted to racial memory to explain castration fear; Comfort speculates on what an evolutionary explanation would look like. He guesses that young males, to avoid being killed or driven away by their fathers, developed oedipal feelings. As Comfort puts it in his fascinating and curious article "Darwin and Freud":

It would call for a major adaptation in behaviour to maintain the family-pattern, if young males had to love their mother in order to stay with her, but avoid her as a sex object, so as not to be chased off the territory. Avoidance of the sexually displaying female as a "castration threat," and mixed feelings toward the adult male in which his genitalia served as a dominance-signal, could serve to keep young males out of the competitive situation while still maternally dependent. . . . We cannot confirm it by direct observation in animals, for none of Man's direct ancestors are available for study, and modern apes may differ from us precisely in their failure to evolve such a mechanism. On the other hand if this guess is wrong, I strongly suspect that something very like it is right.[14]

What we do know is that the human animal alone seems to have what the psychologist G. Stanley Hall called a "second birth"; that is, an infantile sexuality around the ages of four to six that can serve no reproduction purpose, and then a rebirth of that sexuality, in puberty, that can. Humans are dependent animals for a long time, and because they are psychological ones as well, suffer consciously the pangs of attachment and separation feelings (admittedly, they may not be alone among the animals in this). On top of these, they experience the vicissitudes of infantile sexuality, and then puberty.

On the Freudian model, humans undergo a psycho-sexual development, moving naturally, if all is well, through the famous oral, anal, phallic, and eventual genital stages. Whatever fun we have with this idea, it does serve (suitably modified) to make sense out of much of the human's "plastic" sexual nature.[15]

Freud's ideas are also directly related to the fact that humans, along with their subhuman primate relation, the gibbon, appear to be the animal who most significantly exhibits year-round heterosexual behavior: "obsessive" in comparison to other mammals, for example, who have set periods of heat and arousal. Man *is* the sexy animal— equally so whether sexual impulses are expressed or repressed. Year-round sex appears to have the function of binding the male to the female, with her need to care for and nourish her young for an extended period; it also serves as the basis for sociability, the formation of a social group.

The omnipresent sexual interest, however, though it serves to bring humans together, in families and societies, and thus provides the structure within which cultures can arise—and it is culture that most distinctly separates humans from the other sexy subhuman primate, the gibbon—serves also to divide person from person. Sexual rivalry, that is, Darwin's sexual selection, is a source of discord, threatening to tear the group apart. Hence the need for an Oedipus complex, and for the whole array of taboos and prohibitions—"Thou shall not covet thy neighbor's wife"—for the moralities and religions, that keep men from one another's throats and from their women.

Freud posited two basic drives in humans: the aggressive as well as the sexual. Nevertheless, he tended to neglect the aggressive drive in his analyses, perhaps because it could not be particularly located in body parts, perhaps because it was a less taboo subject in his culture, thus requiring less daring on the part of an investigator. In any event, Darwinian theory, with its interest in sexual selection, seemed to lend itself more readily to Freud's emphasis on aggression as sexual aggression.

Freud's views on human sexuality are occasionally simple-minded (especially in regard to the psychology of women, where Freud exhibits, as noted, his weakest and most limited side); mostly, however, they are complicated and subtle—and always bold and suggestive. Our task is neither to go into these details here, nor to undertake the discussion as to their validity that a thorough account would entail. It is simply to note the way in which Freud, following Darwin, has changed the way humans, or many human beings, can view their nature in relation to the other animals. Humans become now self-conscious beings, psychological creatures, whose psychology, according to Freud, emerges from their evolutionary sexual nature.

But once possessed of this insight, how was Freud to develop it? How to turn it into a "science"?[16] We have already seen that Freud started off in a physicalistic, or mechanical, direction, where the mind was an energy system, with "impulses" and "resistances"; one almost expects to hear of amps and watts. In his mechanistic mood, as described, Freud seems to reduce Man to a machine of special sorts: in this case, a sex machine. We hear echoes of this in Aldous Huxley's *Brave New World*, where the phrase "Our Ford" and similar oaths invoking Freud's name are intended to suggest an amalgamation of Freud and Ford, producing in assembly-line fashion a race of test-tube babies, subsequently conditioned according to the psychoanalytic model.

Aldous Huxley may have been parodying Freud, as well as his grandfather Thomas; but the grain of truth remains. With his compulsions and phobias, the Freudian Man in this view did tremble on the brink of becoming a mechanical Man. More suggestively, Freud realized that some of his patients identified with machines, or felt themselves possessed by a machine-god.[17] What is more, as we have noted, Freud analyzed the feeling of the "uncanny" that humans have in the presence of automata.

It was mainly out of his mechanistic-physicalistic-chemical crucible that Freud originally distilled his conception of how the unconscious operated. He then set about to explain the "dynamics" of the unconscious, not merely to state that they existed; he wished to make his insight operational. He spoke of the various methods of defense used by the ego: regression, repression, reaction-formation, isolation, undoing, projection, introjection, reversal, sublimation, and displacement. These sound very different from his mechanical metaphors, but the initial inspiration, the overarching conception, behind them is the same.

What had been gradually changing was Freud's growing awareness that at the center of human mental life was not just mechanics but meaning. The firing neurons carried messages, not just energy. And the messages, nonorganic in nature, could have organic consequences, as in hysterical paralysis. It was a profound and piercing insight that Freud, grudgingly, came to concede to himself. It meant that scientific analysis now became interpretation, that is, the science of psychoanalysis.

It is the "interpretation," for example, of dreams that is important. They have meaning. They are not merely somatic events. And the meaning is, of course, for Freud, largely rooted in human sexual life. Buried, as in an archaeological dig, the sexual life is layered, going back to our earliest childhood memories, waiting only for the analyst's pickaxe to be brought to light again. Shards and fragments emerge in errors, are thrown up in profusion in neuroses, but are mostly strewn about, above and below the surface, in our omnipresent dreams. Thus Freud called dreams the "royal road" to the unconscious, leading to the underground caverns of the mind. He took as his task to measure these caverns, to establish their geological and archaeological formations, and to expose them to the light.

The pickaxe, or tool, by which to uncover these depths was talk. The earliest psychoanalytic patient, Anna O., showed the way, first to Josef Breuer, Freud's early medical colleague, and then to Freud. In what she labeled her "chimney sweepings," Anna O. talked her way back to the original traumatic events that lay in back of her hysterical paralysis. Developed by Freud, her talking cure became the method of free association. Free association, of course, according to Freud, is utterly deterministic. Words and associations are linked in an unbreakable chain. They are "free" only in the sense that they are no longer repressed, no longer under the constraint of social convention.

Humans, then, are the animals that free associate. Other animals also have language, if not talk. But language is not only demotive for human beings, as it is for other creatures, but also emotive in the particular way found in free association. Human language is filled with ambiguity and ambivalence. Thus, words can hurt, as we acknowledge when we refer to a "cutting remark" or "biting satire," and they can cure, as in Freudian therapy.

The cure is effected by our following words back to our earliest memories and their attendant feelings, and doing so if possible with the aid of the analyst's empathy and our transferences to him or her.[18] That is "meaning" in the Freudian sense. Within narrow Freudian orthodoxy, such meaning is simply sexual in origin (indeed, Freud thought that language probably originated in sexual cries and utterances), though it clearly need not be so limited.

*In this sense,* then, language is, for Freud, a distinctive attribute of humans, separating them from the other animals—and probably as well from all future machines (see chapter 10 for a continuation of this argument). It also becomes the basis for continuing human society and for culture. Freud is less concerned, however, with language as the carrier of information from one generation to another, its storing effect, so to speak, than as a means of conveying "meaning," as I have defined it.

I have been stressing up to now the Darwinian as well as the mechanistic basis of Freudian psychoanalysis. Why, then, can an acute observer declare that "practically all later changes in psychoanalytic theory have one common denominator *they move away from Darwinian thinking*"—a move actually initiated by Freud himself.[19] The move has been so great that some critics have declared psychoanalysis a strictly linguistic or hermeneutic study (for some of the reasons given in previous paragraphs). After all, as we have seen, the analyst deals with "words," and at its extreme, psychoanalysis therefore appears to fall under the domain of literature, rather than science. Thus, if we wish truly to understand Freud, we must add literary studies to biology and mechanistic science as formative influences.

Literature has always considered the dreamlike, the childlike, and the abnormal, whether in myths and fairy tales or in plays and stories. And before the institutionalization of psychology as a science in the late nineteenth century, psychology too paid attention to such matters, being more a philosophical or literary inquiry than a laboratory one. As Wolf Lepenies reminds us in a suggestive article, psychology was only becoming a respected academic discipline when Wilhelm Wundt, its founding father—having taught a course at Heidelberg, psychology as a natural science (reminding us thereby of Freud's "Project"), starting in 1862—published his *Principles of Physiological Psychology* in 1873 and established the first psychological institute, at Leipzig, in 1879.[20]

Wundt and his followers dismissed the childlike and the abnormal from psychological study and insisted that only the matter of consciousness was worthy of attention; psychopathology was solely about "the events of the diseased conscious." As we know, Freud restored these subjects to psychology and took the unconscious as the focus of his inquiry into mental processes. His genius was to attempt to make a rational science, admittedly of a very peculiar nature, out of the "irrational" materials found in literature as well as in the dreams, the symptoms, and even the everyday slips of normal as well as abnormal human beings.

Ultimately therefore by holding the two parts—biology and hermeneutics—in creative tension, not reducing the human to either one, Freud was able to work toward his new science. Yet in the end the form his scientific reports took tipped far more to the hermeneutic than to the biological research paper.

Psychoanalytic discoveries are conveyed to others in the "case history," which at first dismayed Freud. As he explained in *Studies on Hysteria*, "I have not always been a psychotherapist. Like other neuropathologists, I was trained to employ local diagnoses and electroprognosis, and it still strikes me myself as strange that the case histories I write should read like short stories and that, as one might say, they lack the serious stamp of science."

How then could he justify his "case histories"? As he goes on, "I must console myself with the reflection *that the nature of the subject is evidently responsible for this*. . . . The fact is that local diagnosis and electrical reactions lead nowhere in the study of hysteria, whereas a detailed description of mental processes *such as we are accustomed to find in the works of imaginative writers* enables me, *with the use of a few psychological formulas*, to obtain at least some kind of insight into the course of that affection" (my italics). What Freud then discovers is "an intimate connection between the story of the patient's sufferings and the symptoms of his illness."[21]

For Freud, drawing his inspirations from Darwin and Brücke, all science is an effort to establish lawlike connections among phenomena. Yet in psychoanalysis he is forced to conclude that the "connection" explaining a symptom is a narrative one, a "story," which is then written up as a "case history" (described by one critic, who had Kipling in mind, as a "Just So" story).

In fact, for Freud the case history is not just one narrative but the culmination of hundreds or even thousands of narratives told during the course of an analysis. He would maintain that although the final written case history appears to be about an individual, and idiosyncratically so, it is also about the species, common humanity. For Freud believed that the commonality of the human experience on which each analysis depends is based in biology and stems from the evolutionary human inheritance. An example might be the Oedipus complex: a constant relation exists, based on a Comfort-like biological explanation, with the subjects involved being different, each requiring her or his own "story" to be invoked as explanation.

We can see from Freud's letters how he was dream-walking his way to his new scientific analyses and reports. As early as 1883, in a long letter to his fiancée, Martha Bernays, he tried to understand and explain the suicide of one of his close friends who was outwardly successful. But as Freud writes, "His death was by no means an accident, rather it was a logical outcome of his temperament; his good and bad qualities had combined to bring about his downfall; his life was as though composed by a writer of fiction, and his catastrophe the inevitable end." As Freud concludes, "He all but screams for the novelist to preserve him for human memory."[22]

We are still far from the case history. The novelist may preserve a character for "human memory," but the psychoanalyst must use memories, the patient's, to construct a psychological science, though using the same device of narrative. The contrast with Freud's friend Arthur Schnitzler may help us to understand the difference. Like Freud, a medical student, who served as an assistant in the clinic of Freud's teacher Theodore Meynert, and who also employed hypnosis in clinical situations, Schnitzler explored what Carl Schorske has called "the compulsiveness of Eros" (that is, the power of instinct), but he did so in plays and novels. So penetrating were his insights that Freud hailed him as a "colleague" in the inquiry into the "underestimated and much-maligned erotic." Indeed, as Schorske tells us, "so strongly did Freud feel his affinity to Schnitzler that he consciously avoided the writer as his 'double' (Doppelganger)."[23]

However, affinity is not the same as true similarity. What was lacking in Schnitzler, and in all the other novelists of psychological intuition, was the Darwinian inspiration to science. Another doctor, this time a fictional one, can give us the hint we need. He is Lydgate, the flawed hero of George Eliot's *Middlemarch* (incidentally, one of Freud's favorite novels). In Eliot's words,

> He [Lydgate] had tossed away all cheap inventions where ignorance finds itself able and at ease; *he was enamored of that arduous invention which is the very eye of research, provisionally framing its object and correcting it to more and more exactness of relation;* he wanted to pierce the obscurity of those minute processes which prepared human misery and joy, those invisible thoroughfares where are the first lurking-places of anguish, mania, and crime, that delicate poise and transition which determine the growth of happy or unhappy consciousness [my italics].[24]

The fictional Lydgate became the real Freud. From the hazy intuitions of his letter of 1883, Freud moved to the beginnings of psychoanalytic science in the studies on hysteria of 1895. Thus, in retrospect, the appearance of the "Project for a Scientific Psychology" in that same year seems an anachronism, and perhaps a paradox. In between, the youthful nervous specialist had learned hypnosis and studied its use, under Charcot, on hysterics. Such a technique and such a study taught him to believe in the power as well as in the existence of the unconscious (and not just Lydgate's consciousness). It also showed him that the line between the abnormal and the normal was porous, with neurotic symptoms (and a little later, dreams and parapraxes) having the same mechanisms as normal mental life. It allowed him, in the end, to use novelistic techniques and form to convey these notions in the service of psychological science.

Freud's new science also allowed him to identify what I have been calling the third discontinuity. Moreover, by his circuitous route, Freud had returned to Darwin's quest for an understanding of humans as animals evolving not merely physically but mentally—and mentality meant culture. In works such as *Totem and Taboo, Group Psychology and the Analysis of the Ego,* and *Moses and Monotheism,* Freud tried to connect his observations on individual psychology to that of the group—and thus culture. (In my view, he was not very successful.)

Freud may have been more successful in showing that the dynamics of the mind were universal at least within the human species; that underneath the different cultural formations lay general, timeless laws.

As we have seen, Psychological Man was a parlous combination of the mechanical and the hermeneutic. Freud's model for the uniform laws that applied to this creature could well have been Lyell's geology, as well as Darwin's evolutionary biology.

Like Darwin's "bulldog," T. H. Huxley, Freud was troubled by the way Man's nature, that is, his animality, ran counter to the direction of evolution, that is, civilization. In *Civilization and Its Discontents,* another of his efforts at a kind of metapsychological, group analysis, Freud wrestled with the dilemma. Civilization, he argued, was based on the repression of human instincts, the sexual impulses. Sublimation was vital to the erection of culture (replacing thereby, to be crude, another sort of erection). The resulting culture, or civilization, however, also made humans "sick." This entire process for Freud defines the "human condition," in which humankind yearns for the "oceanic feeling" of complete merger with the world, or for the paradisical Garden of Eden, where they existed in a state without knowledge of good and evil and the resultant unhappiness of civilized life.

For Freud, the only cure for this diseasing knowledge is—more knowledge, that is, science. We must give up, he tells us, the childish illusions of religion, with all its cradling comforts, and resolutely face the reality of our condition. We must practice a scientific stoicism. We must transcend the third discontinuity and accept the blow to our ego involved in recognizing that we are not the mostly rational, and potentially totally happy, creatures we have prided ourselves on being.

Paradoxically, however, we must continue seeking to claim what rationality we can from our psychological, that is, emotional, nature. We must recognize that we are on a spectrum that runs from child to adult, primitive to civilized, normal to abnormal, and seek to establish ourselves on one end of the continuum while remaining aware that we may always slide back to the other. In short, we must come to terms with the third discontinuity.

Such is Man's "animal" (and mechanical) nature, according to Freud. Darwinian in inspiration, Freud's science speaks not of Darwin's variations over time, but of varying character types: the hysterical, the compulsive, the narcissistic personality, and so forth. Man becomes the pseudonymous creature of the Freudian case studies: the Little Hans, the Anna O., the Dora, emerging from—or encased in?—a dream world.

We are, in the end, the "sick" animal-machine, with both terms newly defined: that is our "nature." Darwin had seen in procreation— sex—the force propelling evolution, creating Man physically. He also sensed that the force had changed, been transmuted into a moral, cultural one, with evolution now in terms of civilizations, that is, complex and evolving social entities of a new kind. Freud also saw in procreation, in sex, the force behind the evolution of Man and his civilization. With magnificent audacity, he went further than Darwin, however, and sought to depict the taxonomy, the embryology, and the developmental etiology of the new species: psychological Man. Rooted as the human being is in a physical animal nature—and thus with potentially mechanistic features—humans had evolved, on this schema, into the uniquely cultural, neurotic, and sometimes psychotic animal of the civilized world.

Darwin had thought of Herbert Spencer as his intellectual descendant, carrying evolution theory into the field of psychology. "Psychology," Darwin declared, "will be securely based on the foundation already well laid by Mr. Herbert Spencer, that of the necessary acquirement of each mental power and capacity by gradation."[25] In light of this quotation, Freud can be thought of as an unexpected mutation.

In contrast, the Russian scientist Ivan Petrovich Pavlov could claim to be more in the direct line of mainstream Darwinian theory. Operating as a physiologist, who then applied his findings on unconditioned and conditioned reflexes to psychology, Pavlov saw himself as remaining true to Darwin's fundamental insight that Man was an animal. Like Freud, whose conception of Man shifted from his being a physiological (and possibly mechanical) to a psychological creature, Pavlov came to accept Man as a psychological creature; but, even then, Pavlov insisted on Man's essentially physiological and, as we shall see, mechanical nature.

Born in 1849, Pavlov grew up in a religious atmosphere—his father was a poor parish priest—and his early education was in a local theological seminary; soon he exchanged the religious vocation for a scientific one. To science he seems to have brought an almost religious dedication. The influence of the "revolutionary" literature of the sixties, as he tells us, and especially of the nihilist writer Pisarev, turned him toward natural science. Moreover, reading an article by Pisarev, Pavlov first became acquainted with the theories and examples of Darwin; they became his lasting inspiration.

So inspired, Pavlov enrolled at Petersburg University, majoring in animal physiology. From then on, he pursued a long circuitous route, like Freud, to his ultimate work in psychology cum physiology. After obtaining a degree in natural science, Pavlov began medical training. His aim, however, was not to practice medicine but to do research in physiology. Gradually entering further into laboratory work, he did his doctoral thesis on cardiac nerves. Here he investigated, in a dog, the way in which the nerves of the heart might augment as well as retard heartbeats. A scholarship for study abroad allowed him to work in Germany with Brücke's counterpart, Carl Ludwig. (Freud, on a comparable scholarship, went to Paris to study with Charcot.) On his return, Pavlov began his research into digestion.

For about twelve years, Pavlov concentrated on this research, culminating in his book *The Work of the Digestive Glands* (1897), which led to the winning of a Nobel prize in 1904. Before then, however, around 1900, he had begun his investigations into the conditioned reflexes, for which he is best known. This work he quickly connected to the study of brain functioning. Only quite a bit later, however, did he turn his attention to human psychology; indeed, he was over seventy-five years old when he first began to study psychiatry, visiting hospitals for disturbed patients in order better to understand how the experimental neuroses he had learned to stimulate in dogs correlated with those to be found in humans.

To Pavlov's scientific eye, there was little or no difference. Put in the bluntest terms, and ignoring any qualifications, Pavlov saw humans and dogs as both being machines, and therefore equal. It is the inheritance of T. H. Huxley, which Freud had reluctantly put aside, now brought to its culmination. Pavlov and his work symbolize the way in which humans are mechanized, not through their culture and the tools they devise, but through their own physiological, animal nature. Paradoxically, by becoming most animal-like humans become most mechanical. To understand both how this is a result of Pavlov's work and the consequences for Man's view of his own nature, we must go further into the nature of Pavlov's work.

Pavlov was not only a physiologist. He was a master surgeon who operated with incredible speed. His teacher, Ilya Cyon, a brilliant lecturer, had introduced demonstrations on warm-blooded animals into his classroom presentations.[26] Pavlov carried on in the tradition of his teacher. In studying digestion, Pavlov realized that the process could be precisely measured and therefore understood in terms of the amount of saliva secreted by the animal. Wishing a window, so to speak, into the digestive system, Pavlov created what is called Pavlov's Pouch, where the gastric secretions could be directly observed. Nineteen dogs died on the operating table before Pavlov succeeded, but his persistence and skill finally brought him success.[27]

Another Russian scientist, Ivan Mikhaylovich Sechenov, influenced

Pavlov even more than did Cyon. (Sechenov, incidentally, refused to do experiments on warm-blooded animals.) In his *Reflexes of the Brain* (1863), Sechenov treated reflexes, not as a mere special case, but as the fundamental form of all forms of behavior, no matter how complex. His idea was also profoundly Darwinian: the reflex, such as salivation, is built into the species by natural selection. For Pavlov, the reflex became an idée fixe. He pursued it monomaniacally. Nothing stood removed from its power. With infinite skill and patience, Pavlov traced its manifestations and set them down in exquisite detail.

Aware that anesthetics distorted the reflex action of his dogs' nervous systems, Pavlov used a punishment-reward system to keep them still. Observing that the dogs salivated, not only when food entered their mouths, but when they saw him approaching with food, Pavlov moved to the idea of a conditioned, as well as unconditioned, reflex. The dog could be trained to salivate, say, at the ringing of a bell thirty seconds before the arrival of the actual food. Once so trained, Pavlov could experiment with what happened if the routine were varied so that the food arrived only half the time after the bell, or one fourth, and so forth; if the bell were made louder or softer on a scale, and so forth; if the dog were more or less hungry, anxious, and so forth.

Pavlov's laboratory reduced the phenomenal world to "unconditioned stimulus," "conditioned stimulus," "unconditioned reflex," and "conditioned reflex." The abbreviations spell out the difference between Pavlov and Freud. For the former, UCS meant "unconditioned stimulus," and CS, "conditioned stimulus"; for the latter, UCS meant the "unconscious," and CS, "consciousness"!

With the powerful tool of the conditioned reflex, Pavlov probed the brain as well as the salivary glands. As the CR showed, the nervous system controlled the dog's physiological behavior. There was, therefore, no real divide between psychological and physiological processes; and vice versa. Moreover, Pavlov quickly discovered that his dogs varied in personality; and that "strong" and "weak" dogs responded differently to the stimuli presented to them. By taking puppies and dividing them into two classes—one raised solely in the kennel, and the other allowed to roam outside—Pavlov was able to show that the first group turned out to be "cowardly and susceptible to inhibition given the slightest changes in the surroundings; in the animals of the second group nothing of the kind was observed."[28] Acknowledging that the Greeks, and especially Hippocrates, had preceded him with their theory of the four temperaments—choleric, phlegmatic, sanguine, and melancholic, based on the amount of bile—Pavlov updated the theory in terms of his own four basic types: "the strong and impetuous type, the strong equilibrated and quiet type, the strong equilibrated and lively type, and the weak type."[29]

Such a typology not only harked back to the Greeks but also was in the tradition of nosology, or mere classification, so prevalent in nineteenth- and twentieth-century psychiatry before Freud. Kretschmer's system, for example, was representative, and Pavlov merely sought to extend and refine it.[30] The problem, however, was to analyze the dynamics involved in mental life and not merely to label externalities. To attack this problem, Pavlov attempted to apply his single-minded theory of the CR by creating what he called "experimental neurosis." By mixing up his stimuli, by applying electrical shock, Pavlov found he could drive his dogs mad. Even the strongest type could be reduced to a howling body of quivering nerves.

By studying and experimenting on canines, Pavlov believed he was also studying humanity. He had a special sense of the dog's unique— and yet general—relation to humans. "Although it is not at the top of the zoological ladder," Pavlov remarked, "(the monkey occupies a higher place), it [the dog] is closer to man than any other animal and has been his companion since pre-historic times . . . 'it is the dog that helped man to become what he is.' "[31]

Dogs, like humans, had different personalities, as we have seen; and Pavlov personalized them further by giving them names indicative of their personalities—"Gunshot" a "lively" beast, and "Milord" a "calm" one—and working with the same dog, carefully keeping it alive, for several years.[32] If humans are like dogs, then dogs are like humans, and should be treated as such.[33]

Pavlov believed that science could only study external behavior, not imaginary inner states of mind. In part, this conviction allowed him to numb any apprehension he might have had about operating on—torturing?—his dogs: "We endeavored not to concern ourselves with the imaginary mental state of the animal."[34] In Pavlov's view, animals could not talk, and there is, therefore, no way of confirming any hypotheses we might make as to their supposed subjective mental states. Introspection was out, and only behavior (in America, Pavlov's scientific compatriots, such as John Watson, proudly took the name "behaviorists" and, so inspired, preferred to work on rats rather than dogs) could be a proper subject of *scientific* study.[35] And this was the case for humans as much as for dogs. "Is not the eternal sorrow of life," Pavlov asked, "the fact that in most cases human beings do not understand each other and cannot enter into the inner state of the other? And then, where is the knowledge, where is the power of knowledge that might enable us correctly to comprehend the state of another human being?"[36]

At only one moment, in a seemingly unconscious slip, did Pavlov appear to deviate from his conviction that humans and dogs, mutatis mutandis, were alike. Pavlov, we are told by his intimate biographer, B. P. Babkin, rated independence "higher than any other human attribute."[37] He refused ever to grovel before authority. Complimenting Babkin on maintaining his integrity and refusing to return to Soviet Russia, Pavlov wrote in 1924: "I am amazed at the absence of this feeling of integrity in those around me. A person is thrown once, twice, three times into jail, *chained like a dog* [my italics], but he soon forgets this and seems to be unaware that he has been insulted." Uncharacteristically, Pavlov here, in a personal moment, appears to expect humans to behave unlike dogs.

Much more characteristically, as we have seen, Pavlov equated the two, human and dog. The reason, quite simply, is that Pavlov considered both to be mere machines. How, then, logically could they be different, except in degree of complexity? But surely not of behavior! Both were living organisms, and Pavlov early and late announced that in his work "the living organism showed itself to be merely a machine—a very complicated one, of course, but just as submissive and obedient as any other machine."[38] In his earliest work on the digestive system he had already chosen his images carefully, comparing it to:

a chemical factory, where the raw materials—the foodstuffs—are submitted to an essentially chemical process. In this factory the foods are brought into a condition in which they are capable of being absorbed into the body fluids and made use of for the maintenance of the processes of life. The factory consists of a series of compartments, in each of which the food, according to its properties, is either retained for a time or at once sent on to the next; and each single compartment is provided with suitable reagents. These reagents are either prepared in adjoining little workshops, burrowed into the walls of the laboratory itself, or else in distant and separate organs, connected, as in other large chemical factories, with the main workshop by a system of transmitting tubes.[39]

He was never to abandon such imagery. In 1932, he asked, rhetorically, "A system (machine) on the one hand, and man with all his ideals, aspirations and achievements on the other—what a terribly discordant comparison this seems at first glance. But is this really so?" His answer is quick and ready. "Man . . . is a system (roughly speaking, a machine), and like every other system in nature is governed by the inevitable laws common to all nature."[40] These laws, of course, were the laws of the reflex. One needed only to apply them equally to Man, dog, and any other living organism—for they were all equally machines. In dealing with them, one need only be a technician, applying scientific law. "The mechanic," Pavlov declared, "completes his apprenticeship by passing a test which consists in assembling the mixed-up parts of the dismantled machine. This should hold for the physiologist too."[41]

Pavlov was aware that he might be charged with reductionism and defended himself. For example, did language make Man unique, separate from the other animals? "Of course," he wrote in 1927, "a word is for man as much a real conditioned stimulus as are other stimuli common to men and animals, yet at the same time it is so all-comprehending that it allows no quantitative or qualitative comparisons with conditioned stimuli in animals." But by treating speech as merely a second signal system, that is, as signals of signals, Pavlov could incorporate it in his general theory of the reflex. "In man there comes to be . . . another system of signalization, a signalization of the first system . . . a new principle of neural action is [thus] introduced."[42] Language acquisition, for Pavlov, therefore, is simply a complicated evolutionary development of earlier reflex action. It could be explained by the one general mechanical law of the reflex, and, indeed, Pavlov was convinced that "the time will come, be it ever so distant, when mathematical analysis, based on natural science, will include in majestic formulae all these equilibrations and, finally, itself."[43]

In considering Man a machine, reducible in principle to mathematical analysis, Pavlov was in a tradition of thought stemming actively from around the seventeenth century, and especially from Descartes, whom we have already studied. Indeed, as we have noted, René Descartes first used the term *reflex*, in the sense of reflection (as in a mirror). As we have also seen, La Mettrie was the culmination of this tradition; one scholar sums up La Mettrie's view: "the brain secretes thought as the stomach secretes digestive juices."[44]

On another side, Pavlov drew upon the tradition of associational psychology. Its roots were in Hobbes and Locke, who, rejecting Descartes's innate ideas, found the contents of the mind arising from the experience of the senses. But how was sense experience connected to ideas, and ideas to one another? By "association" was the answer, and associationalists such as Hume, Hartley, and both Mills (James and John Stuart), sought to spell out the laws of contiguity in space and time, of

repetition, and so forth, that underlay the theory. It was all very spec-
ulative. What Pavlov did was to give an experimental underpinning to
the theory and transmute the vague notion of association into the
precise measurements involved in the conditioned reflex.

In short, Pavlov saw himself, and rightly so, as turning philosophy into science (and psychology into physiology). Science, for Pavlov, meant the facts speaking for themselves: "There is nothing excep-
tional in my work," Pavlov announced, "it is all based on facts from
which logical conclusions were drawn. That's all."[45] The word he constantly uses about science is *objective,* by which he meant measurable
facts. As he defined the reflex, "a certain external phenomenon causes
strictly definite changes in the organism."

The scientist, on such a view, is merely a machine, both as subject
and as object. The professional scientist is, of course, a specialized
machine who dedicates an entire life to science. Ironically, Pavlov
allowed for passion *in* science only as a passion *for* science. Advising
young people who wished to dedicate themselves to science, he recommended consistency, modesty, and then "passion." "Remember, science requires your whole life and even if you had two lives to give they
would not be enough. Science demands of man the utmost effort and
supreme passion."[46] It was advice he had taken to heart for himself. So
dedicated was he to the pursuit of "pure" science that, in the early
phases of his career, rather than enter medicine and make enough
money to support his wife, he preferred to live apart from her, while
working in the laboratory, until the award of a Chair of Pharmacy
rescued both of them from his penury.

In fact, however, Pavlov was hardly the impersonal, "mechanical"
scientist of his ideal persona. He was easily irritated, given to outbursts
against his assistants, and an egoist, as his friend Babkin admitted,
before excusing these traits as unimportant in the case of a man of
genius.[47]

Perhaps a comparison with Freud can highlight aspects of Pavlov's
belief system. We see how much Pavlov and Freud differed on the question of human nature, animal and/or machine, when we realize that
Pavlov almost never uses the word *sex,* and then only in an unimportant
sense. Freud, as we know, matched Pavlov's obsessive concern with the
conditioned reflex with his own obsession regarding sex. For Freud, as
we have noted, evolution pivoted on Man's procreational nature; for
Pavlov, on his mechanical nature, as a creature of unconditioned and
conditioned reflexes. Where the later Freud sees the mind as a competing arena, wherein ego and superego wrestle with id, Pavlov sees it as a

mechanical system, with neurons firing in response to stimuli.[48] For Freud, therapy consists of the "talk cure," psychoanalysis; for Pavlov, of bromide and reconditioning. The two men appear worlds apart, with a completely different Man inhabiting the two worlds.

They actually shared significant common beliefs. Pavlov, though he made nothing further of the insight, recognized the phenomenon of repression, so essential to Freud's schema: "Does not," Pavlov asks, "the development of our personality consist in the fact that under the influence of education and religion, social and civic requirements, we gradually learn to inhibit, to repress that which is not admitted, which is prohibited by the factors just mentioned."[49] Both Pavlov and Freud accepted the crucial role of determinism, so central to the physical sciences of the late nineteenth century. Where Pavlov remarked that "the theory of reflex activity is based . . . in the first place [on] the principle of determinism, i.e., an impulse, an impetus, or a cause for every given action or effect," Freud commented that "if anyone makes a breach . . . in the determinism of natural events at a single point, it means that he has thrown overboard the whole *Weltanschauung* of science."[50] And, even more revealingly, and perhaps surprisingly, Freud agreed with Pavlov that psychical phenomena would eventually be reducible to a physio-chemical explanation. However, whereas this was a working principle for Pavlov, not even to be temporarily suspended, for Freud it was an ultimate goal, though he resorted to more introspective methods in the present state of Man's possible knowledge.

The really fundamental difference, however, between the two men, and their respective views of human nature, is probably best illustrated by their divergent attitudes to learning and to perfectibility. Pavlov saw Man as perfectible. In what sounds like a typical nineteenth-century fit of scientific hubris, Pavlov declared that "I am deeply and irrevocably convinced that along this path [of conditioned reflexes] will be found the final triumph of the human mind over its uttermost and supreme problem—the knowledge of the mechanism and laws of human nature. Only thus may come a full, true, and permanent happiness."[51] The alternative is that the "human creature, led by dark powers to wars and revolutions and their horrors, produces for itself incalculable material losses and inexpressible pain and reverts to bestial conditions." Salvation lies "only [in] science, exact science about human nature itself."

Freud saw Man as imperfectible, ineluctably led by "dark powers." This was the human condition, and one had stoically to accept it. Terms such as *final triumph* and *permanent happiness* were alien to Freud. His was not, however, a counsel of despair, but of realism, or so he felt. Man, as a "civilized" animal, was also necessarily a "discontented" and "sick" animal. His discontent, however, could be ameliorated by science, and Freud felt powerfully committed to the therapeutic function of psychoanalysis. Analysis was a kind of reeducation, a relearning of the emotions, guided by the intellect. As Freud put it, the "work of overcoming resistance is the essential function of analytic treatment; the patient has to accomplish it and the doctor makes this possible for him with the help of suggestion operating in an *educative* sense. For that reason psychoanalytic treatment has justly been described as a kind of *after-education*."[52]

There is a world of difference between this view of what science can do, and Pavlov's. For Pavlov, "learning" or "education" meant "conditioning." It is a form of what is involved in animal training. For Pavlov, it also carried evolution a step further, placing it under the control of Man, and leading to the state of "final" and "permanent" happiness. Unconditioned reflexes were the adaptive responses built into the organism over a long time. Such reflexes were inherited. Now Pavlov proposed to induce conditioned reflexes in his subjects, whether dogs or humans. In this form of learning—"unnatural," as opposed to "natural"—with the scientist as pedagogue, "conditioning" would be used to alter and thus improve the "human condition."

Pavlov and his followers felt that they were fulfilling a long-held dream of humankind. Whether in the classic form of Pavlov's CR, or Watson's behaviorism, or B. F. Skinner's "operant" or "instrumental" conditioning (where behavior is rewarded, not merely stimulated, as when a rat is given food for running a maze correctly), scientific control over erring behavior was being made available to humans. For those who oppose the Pavlovian school, such teachings are a nightmare, and the control involved an insidious tool of elitist tyranny. The use, or misuse, of "thought control" methods by the Communists, as in the famous Cardinal Mindszenty case, is seen as evidence of the correctness of such fears; and Orwell's *1984* is built around the realization of these fears.

Pavlov might answer that the misuse of science is a hangover from the human fraility he was seeking to eliminate. Whatever the correct judgment in this regard, there can be no doubt as to the view of human nature resulting from the work of Pavlov and his disciples. Humans are that animal, heir to the unconditioned reflex, which, along with the other animals, has thus become "mechanical"; and which, as a machine, can be "conditioned." This is, for Pavlov, the logical conclusion of Darwinian science. If for Freud psychological Man is a neurotic animal, for Pavlov he is a perfectible machine, whose operating principles are those of what might be called inner-mindless physiology. For Pavlov, Man's evolutionary destiny is to be a perfected machine, permanently content and happy.

# **Chapter** Seven

In the two previous chapters, using Linnaeus and Darwin as reference points, I have been trying to establish the context of evolutionary theory surrounding the human-machine question. With Freud and Pavlov, I tried to explore further the human-machine question while focusing especially on the implications of Darwinian theory for our view of human nature. Now I wish to pursue both these inquiries via three thinkers in the nineteenth century who grappled strenuously and originally with them: Charles Babbage, T. H. Huxley, and Samuel Butler.

The man who is at the juncture where the age-old thoughts and feelings about the mechanical take on a new, modern life is Charles Babbage. Though the calculating machine, or computer, rethought by Babbage in the early nineteenth century, was at first obscured by the development of a lesser order of machines—the "brute" iron and steel artifacts of the Industrial Revolution—it has proliferated exponentially in the twentieth century, posing in the most challenging form the question of human identity vis-à-vis machines. Babbage is the prototypic figure in that development.

One way to start our consideration of Babbage is by a brief comparison with one of his contemporaries whom we have already mentioned: Thomas Carlyle. In "Signs of the Times" (1829), that most brilliant statement on the cultural implications of the Industrial Revolution, Thomas Carlyle announced, as we have seen, that "men are grown mechanical in head and in heart, as well as in hand."

He followed up this statement by quoting, scathingly, the French ideologue Dr. Cabanis to the effect that "as the liver secretes bile, so does the brain secrete thought." Earlier, as we noted, the great sixteenth-century French physician Ambroise Paré had depicted the human hand as a system of levers, and Julien La Mettrie, his eighteenth-century successor, had declared Man to be "L'Homme-machine." Carlyle was now saying that Man is not a machine by nature, but can be made so by culture. Having invented clocks and steam engines, Man is becoming like them.

Seer that he was, Carlyle also unknowingly intuited the future connection of humans and computers, which is the advanced form of the machine of the future. Evoking the names of the great mathematicians Legrange and Laplace he remarks "that their calculus, differential and integral, is little else than a more cunningly-constructed arithmetical mill; where the factors being put in, are, as it were, ground into the true product, under cover, and without other effort on our part than steady turning of the handle." A few years later, in *Sartor Resartus* (1833), he noted that science, "destroying Wonder" in its progress, was proceeding to a state in which the human mind became an "Arithmetical Mill."[1]

Did Carlyle have knowledge of any specific development at the time, tending to an "arithmetical mill"? The chances are, as we shall see, that he did. Did he go further and foresee that the arithmetical mill would raise not only the question as to humans being machines, but the further question as to whether the machine could possess human powers of thought, that is, do more than just add, logically, one number to another? Understandably, Carlyle's vision faltered and did not reach to this transformation of the basic question concerning human nature.

In fact, an arithmetical mill was being constructed at the time Carlyle wrote; and its basic concepts had been thought out by Charles Babbage, a man whom Carlyle knew.[2] In 1822, at age thirty, Babbage read a paper to the Royal Astronomical Society, announcing that he was engaged in the construction of a calculating machine. By 1832 such a full-scale machine existed.

Babbage's machine is variously called a Calculating Engine, or, in its two incarnations, a Difference Engine or an Analytic Engine. It is, I am arguing, a product of the Industrial Revolution and cannot really be conceived separate from that great transformation.

Babbage came upon the idea when he and his friend John Herschel were asked in 1820 to 1821 to prepare improved astronomical tables. The purpose was to serve British commercial shipping, in short, imperialism, which in turn served the needs of British industrialization. (The

Babbage's Difference Engine—an "arithmetical mill" or, as Babbage referred to it in another image, an "Engine eating its own tail" (Courtesy International Business Machines Corporation).

same purpose was behind the voyage of the *Beagle,* on which Charles Darwin went as naturalist.) While Babbage and Herschel were tediously verifying the calculations brought to them by various human computors, Charles is reported to have exclaimed: "I wish to God these calculations had been executed by steam."[3]

Soon, Babbage conceptualized and then constructed a model of what he called the Difference Engine (and it is this work he reported on in 1822).[4] Babbage's was a mechanical engine and depended on the existence and further development of the machine tools so critical to the Industrial Revolution.[5]

The other image surrounding Babbage's calculator was that of an "arithmetical mill." The mill is, of course, the symbol of the textile factories at the heart of Britain's Industrial Revolution—identified

The Jacquard loom. As Lady Lovelace remarked, "[Babbage's] analytical engine wove algebraical patterns, just as the Jacquard loom wove flowers and leaves" (Courtesy International Business Machines Corporation).

with Blake's "dark satanic mills"—as well as of the heavens. (The mill is also the hub of the mechanical trade, that is, of the millwrights—such as James Brindley—who constructed the water and threshing mills and became the mechanical engineers, constructing the canals and factories of the early nineteenth century.) The arithmetical mill, in short, was a kind of factory that could grind out calculations.

Another, similar image, specifically the textile one, emerges from Babbage's calculator by his employment of punched cards, derived from their use in the Jacquard weaving loom, invented in 1801 by the Frenchman Joseph-Marie Jacquard. As Babbage's assistant and friend, Lady Lovelace, a gifted mathematician and, incidentally, the daughter of Lord Byron, observed appropriately: "It could be said most aptly that the analytical engine wove algebraical patterns, just as the Jacquard loom wove flowers and leaves."[6]

Engine or mill, grinding or weaving, Babbage's machine, in its calculated way, was to have what is truly an incalculable effect on our civilization. It would take almost a century and a half for it to begin to show its effects, but the future was already laid down in the convoluted lines of Babbage's brain and made evident in his designs. Still Babbage was aware, as he wrote Sir Humphry Davy, that his mechanical schemes "may perhaps be viewed as something more than Utopian." Then he added, "of the extent to which the machinery whose nature I have described may be carried, opinions will necessary fluctuate."[7]

The present-day computer, derived from Babbage's conceptualizations, is hardly utopian, or nowhere; it is, in fact, everywhere. It is shaping us and our civilization anew, just as the mills and steam engines of the Industrial Revolution at the beginning of the nineteenth century. Drawing on the long tradition of the "uncanny," this new automaton also is raising once again, with great urgency, the debate over human and machine and conjuring up before us the specter of a "new species," which may be the servant but perhaps, instead, may become the supplanter of humans, as we have hitherto known them.

Babbage himself was a strange individual. He was aware that even many of his friends, as he tells us in his autobiography, "thought that my intellect was beginning to become deranged."[8] But though he was quite eccentric, he was eminently sane. Fortunately, Babbage's monomaniacal and compulsive mind turned early to mathematics and machines. Babbage's mother, apparently, first took him as a child to "several exhibitions of machinery." One especially was memorable. The exhibitor, fittingly named Merlin, noticing the boy's rapt interest, proposed taking him and his mother to his workshop, "where I should see still more wonderful automata."[9]

In the workshop, Babbage saw two nude female figures of silver, about twelve inches high. As he described them,

> One of these walked or rather glided along a space of about four feet, when she turned round and went back to her original place. She used an eye-glass occasionally, and bowed frequently, as if recognizing her acquaintances. The motions of her limbs were singularly graceful. . . .
>
> One other silver figure was an admirable *danseuse*, with a bird on the fore finger of her right hand, which wagged its tail, flapped its wings, and opened its beak. This lady attitudinized in a most fascinating manner. Her eyes were full of imagination, and irresistible.

We can recognize these irresistible figures as stretching from Hero of Greece to Vaucanson and Droz in the eighteenth century, and now to Babbage.

The statues came to be a kind of leitmotif in Babbage's life. In later years, he came upon the statues again at an auction. Purchasing them, he tells us that "I proceeded to take to pieces the whole of the mechanism, and found a multitude of small holes which had been stopped up as not having fulfilled their intended object. In fact, it appeared tolerably certain that scarcely any drawings could have been prepared for the automaton, but that the beautiful result arose from a system of continual trials." The automata, which, once repaired, were placed in Babbage's drawing room for the edification of his friends (he loved to give Saturday night banquets), were inspirations leading him to the calculating engine. We see the quantum jump forward, however, when we note that what, until Babbage, was a matter of craftsmanship— making automata by trial and error—became, in his hands and mind, a matter of preconceptualized design: modern science.

The line, however, is continuous, for Babbage contrived it so that his machine, like earlier automata, could play games of skill, such as ticktacktoe, checkers, and even chess. Anticipating the modern computer chess player, Babbage wrote, "Allowing one hundred moves on each side for the longest game at chess, I found that the combinations involved in the Analytical Engine enormously surpassed any required, even by the game of chess."[10] So, too, he noted that clock, automata, and mechanical toys all operated on the same principle of "winding up," a labor of at most half a minute, which labor then, by the aid of a few wheels, spread out over the whole twenty-four hours. Babbage's Calculating Engines, which were mechanical rather than present-day electronic devices, operated on more or less the same kind of clockwork action.

The Difference Engine was so-called because it operated with the mathematical concept of differences, which, in turn, allowed for a process of simple addition. My purpose is not to go into the technical details but to try to understand their implications. The Difference Engine, though a great mechanical leap forward requiring for its construction new machine tools well beyond earlier clockwork mechanisms, was still quite primitive. All it could really do was add, the other three processes of arithmetic being reduced to a series of additions.

Even in its primitive state, however, it could compute astronomical tables more efficiently and more reliably than humans. Equipped with a printout attachment, it realized in its tables what Babbage had designed first in his mind and then in drawings. Still, if left in that primitive shape, the Difference Engine would have been merely a mechanical version of the abacus.

But Babbage's teeming mind would not let him rest. To the dismay of the British government, which had already advanced a significant sum of money for the Difference Engine and wished nothing more than its astronomical and nautical tables, Babbage proposed to replace it before it was totally finished and operative with a more advanced engine. He called his new machine the Analytic Engine because, as Lady Lovelace explained, it "was to the difference engine as analysis was to arithmetic."[11] It could execute all four processes—addition, subtraction, multiplication, or division—each autonomously, and as Lady Lovelace went on, "could tabulate or develop. No finite line of demarcation limited the powers of the analytical engine."

Her words were prophetic. Babbage himself spoke of his machine as the "engine eating its own tail," by which he meant that the results in one table could affect the other columns, thus changing the instructions under which the machine was operating. The machine also had a "library," where logarithms or similar tabular numbers could be stored, and a "memory," where it could hold intermediate results until the program called for their use. Babbage claimed that it possessed the ability to operate along lines not specifically laid down in the machine's instructions beforehand.[12]

Did this mean that it possessed the power of original thought? Lady Lovelace opposed such an exaggerated claim. The Analytical Engine, she declared, "has no pretensions whatever to *originate* anything. It can do whatever *we know how to order* it to perform. It can *follow* analysis; but it has no power of *anticipating* any analytical relations or truths. Its province is to assist us in making *available* what we are already acquainted with." A more modern scientist, Philip Morrison, seems to take a different view when he writes, "It could make judgements by comparing numbers and then act upon the result of its comparison— thus proceeding upon lines not uniquely specified in advance by the machine's instructions."[13] Babbage's own way of putting the matter was that "nothing but teaching the Engine to foresee and then to act upon that foresight could ever lead me to the object I desired."[14] As we shall see, the debate as to the computer's "originality of mind" persists in these same terms to this day.

As one of his friends, Dr. Dionysius Lardner, put it, Babbage considered his engine "a real manufactory of figures."[15] The word *manufactory*, as I have been insisting, is not accidental. The Analytical Engine was, for Babbage, like the steam engine, part and parcel of the mechanizing impulse of the Industrial Revolution. Babbage did not offer a general philosophy of manufactures, as did his contemporary Andrew

Ure, but he did write a book *On Economy of Machinery and Manufactures* (1832), which exhibited what I shall call a "taxonomy" of machines, of which one example was the calculating engine.

In the preface, Babbage begins by saying, "The present volume may be considered as one of the consequences that have [sic] resulted from the Calculating-Engine."[16] Having visited workshops and factories all over Europe to acquaint himself with the extant state of the mechanical art, he tells us that he "was insensibly led to apply to them those principles of generalization to which my other pursuits had naturally given rise." The result, besides what I am calling a "taxonomy of machines," which can be viewed as a kind of mechanical version of Linnaeus's *Systema Naturae*, was the creation of what has come to be called operations research.[17]

The way to the generalizing *Economy of Machinery* was prepared, I shall argue, by Babbage's invention of a system of signs, which he called his mechanical notation. Through this notation, "the drawings, the times of action, and the trains for the transmission of force" of machinery could be explained "in a language at once simple and concise."[18] The notation was generally applicable to all machinery. It even extended, in the hands of an eminent French surgeon, or so it was claimed, to expressing the structure, operation, and circulation of the animal system.

> Not only the mechanical connection of the solid members of the bodies of men and animals, but likewise the structure and operation of the softer parts, including the muscles, integuements, membranes, &c.; the nature, motion, and circulation of the various fluids, their reciprocal effects, the changes through which they pass, the deposits which they leave in various parts of the system; the functions of respiration, digestion, and assimilation—all would find appropriate symbols and representatives in the notation, even as it now stands, without those additions of which, however, it is easily susceptible.

From thence, the notation could jump to operations research:

> Another of the uses which the slightest attention to the details of this notation irresistibly forces upon our notice, is to exhibit, in the form of a connected plan or map, the organization of an extensive factory, or any great public institution, in which a vast number of individuals are employed, and their duties regulated (as they generally are or ought to be) by a consistent and well-digested

system. The mechanical notation is admirably adapted, not only to express such an organized connection of human agents, but even to suggest the improvements of which such organization is susceptible—to betray its weak and defective points, and to disclose, at a glance, the origin of any fault which may, from time to time, be observed in the working of the system.[19]

No wonder Babbage thought well of his system of signs and is reported to have claimed that it was "of even a more general nature than the calculating machinery itself, and pregnant with results probably of higher importance." Specifically, the mechanist, or inventor,

is able, by moving his finger along a certain line, to follow out the motion of every piece from effect to cause, until he arrives at the prime mover. The same sign which thus indicates the *source* of motion indicates likewise the *species* of motion whether it be continuous or reciprocating, circular or progressive, &c. The same system of signs further indicates the nature of the mechanical connections between the mover and the thing moved, whether it be permanent and invariable (as between the two arms of a lever), or whether the mover and the moved are separate and independent pieces."[20]

When Babbage classified machines according to general principles, we seem to hear the same language as his notation. He arranges his machines according to how they accumulate and regulate power, increase and diminish velocity, extend the time of action of forces (for example, as I noted earlier, winding up a clock for twenty-four hours), save time in human operations, and so forth. Thus Babbage's taxonomy is based on the machine's operating principles, rather than on its appearance, or, so to speak, on its skeleton.

For Babbage, mechanical principles, and the machines that embody them, are of no utility unless put into application. *Economy* is the key word in his title, and he emphasizes the difference between merely conceptualizing a machine, or even making a single article by it, and the act of manufacturing articles, that is, producing them in numbers for sale. The manufacturer, Babbage pointed out, must produce at as small a cost as possible, in a competitive market.

Thus, Adam Smith's division of labor takes on a new life in Babbage's *Economy*, and we suddenly realize that it leads by a fresh trail to the Analytical Engine. Babbage was aware of the central role that the idea of division of labor played in Smith's *Wealth of Nations*. He also realized its fecund effect on Gaspard François de Prony, a Frenchman who, during the time of Napoleon, had been instructed to prepare a new set of logarithmic and trigonometric tables. Faced with the monumental task of calculating, for example, the logarithms of the numbers from 1 to 200,000, de Prony chanced on a secondhand copy of the *Wealth of Nations*. Inspired by the chapter on the division of labor, he set up three groups of calculators: the first, a single individual, did not do the actual numerical work, but devised a set of formulae; the second, consisting of seven or eight persons, converted the formulae into numbers, which they delivered to the third; the third group, of from sixty to eighty persons, using nothing more than simple addition and subtraction, worked up these numbers into finished tables.

Babbage's Calculating Engine was simply a substitute for the entire third group. Babbage himself was the first group, and his engineers, such as Clement, constructing the machinery he had designed, were the second group. In Babbage's mind, "the possibility of performing arithmetical calculations by machinery . . . is connected with the subject of the *division of labor*"[21]—and is intrinsically so. It is why he conceived of his "engine" as a "mill" to produce figures in large numbers, in other words, to manufacture them.

For Adam Smith, the division of labor was the source of the "immense multiplication of the production of all the different arts," which led, in turn, to a "universal opulence" that extended to all ranks.[22] In Smith's judgment, the benign effects of the division of labor were owing to three different circumstances: increased dexterity of each workman; saving of time otherwise lost in shifting from one activity to another; and "last of all, to the invention of innumerable machines, which facilitate labour and enable one workman to do the business of many." Smith was writing before the Industrial Revolution and saw machines as a facilitating, but not necessary, part of the division of labor.

Babbage, in contrast, placed the machine at the heart of the industrial process, which he conceptualized in terms of operations research. For Smith and other predecessors of Babbage, the machine meant a substitute for the workman's physical powers. Babbage's great achievement was to devise an engine that could substitute for human mental powers. However, he never was able to build a full-scale Analytical Engine; the realization of his thoughts had to wait until the twentieth century.

How would his contemporaries have reacted if he had succeeded? The Luddite movement of the early nineteenth century gives us some hints. The first Luddites, as we have seen, wished to prevent the mechanization of manual work in the textile industry; they tried to do so by breaking frames. Thus, just as Babbage was completing his Difference Engine in the early 1830s, the last gasp of the machine-breaking movement was occurring under the aegis of Captain Swing. The implications of Babbage's machine, however, evoked no such protests at the time, though later these Frankenstein-like implications were taken up in Samuel Butler's *Erewhon*.

Babbage did not see himself as a Frankenstein usurping God's powers. In fact, he wrote *The Ninth Bridgewater Treatise, A Fragment,* in 1837, in which he set out the scientific arguments for miracles. His calculating machine—and he evidently saw his own role as a programmer as being analogous to God's—could be so regulated that, as Moseley summarizes the argument, "at definite periods, known only to its maker, a certain lever might become moveable during the calculations then making. The consequence of moving it might be to cause the then existing law to be violated for one or more times, after which the original law would resume its reign."[23] Thus, Babbage sought to establish the possibility of a world moving by orderly natural laws, punctuated by so-called miracles, and all alike under the hand of God.

God as a Great Calculator: the idea probably brought little comfort to Babbage's contemporaries. They generally found sacrilegious his effort to reduce all of life to computations. Babbage, by contrast, put mathematics at the center of human as well as divine thought. Indeed, he was instrumental in establishing in 1834 the Statistical Society of London; in applying statistics to life insurance; and even to applying his work on probability theory to gambling. He was thoroughly in tune with the calculating spirit of his age when he exclaimed, "It is the same science which is now preparing its fetters for the minutest atoms that nature has created: already it has nearly chained the ethereal fluid, and bound in one harmonious system all the intricate and splendid phenomena of light. It is the science of *calculation,*—which becomes continually more necessary at each step of our progress, and which must ultimately govern the whole of the applications of science to the arts of life."[24]

He was far ahead of his time in creating a machine that appeared to think by calculation, just as did a human being. True the machine operated mechanically, by wheels and racks and columns, instead of by neurons, as in the brain, but the effect seemed to be the same. As Babbage remarked, "The analogy between these acts [of the calculating engine] and the operations of mind almost forced upon me the figurative employment of the same terms"; thus, he used such phrases as "The engine Knows . . .".

Had Babbage come upon a mere figure of speech or a profound reality of identity? In the twentieth century, with the substitution of electronic for mechanical calculators, which we now call computers, the question has become what I like to call the "galvanic twitch" of our epoch. In his time, Babbage, having first posed the question in truly modern fashion, figures only as a disturbing eccentric, a shooting star, whose ideas momentarily lit up a new landscape of the mind, and then fizzled out, leaving the humans-machines question to be argued about in the old, animalic terms. Only after Darwin, and then the evolutionary development of the computer, could one return to the question and seek to deal with it in newly conceived biological and mechanical terms.

In an earlier chapter, I sketched the way in which T. H. Huxley became agitated over Man as a mechanical and a moral being. For one who prided himself on logical consistency, Huxley seems to have taken up a number of contradictory stances. In fact, he is constantly squirming over the issues of vitalism and mechanism, with Descartes as his touchstone. Though Babbage was Huxley's older contemporary, with both men members of the British Association for the Advancement of Science, Babbage's Calculating Engine seemed to have had no overt impact on Huxley's thought as he picked up the animal-machine argument.

Why, then, do I take up Huxley again here? He is, I would answer, the Darwinian way station to the vision of machines as an evolutionary development after Man. Outwardly and loyally a supporter, Huxley unintentionally weakened Darwin's organic perspective by transmuting biology into a mechanical science of sorts. (Though Darwin himself was a philosophical materialist whose materialism, unrealized by him, may be said to have an affinity with mechanism.)

Indeed, as Huxley confessed in his *Autobiography*, his original desire was "to be a mechanical engineer." He cared little for the profession, medicine, that he finally entered. In medicine, the only part that truly interested him was physiology, which he considered the "mechanical engineering of living machines." As he summarized his career, "I am not sure that I have not, all along, been a sort of mechanical engineer *in partibus infidelium.*"[25] I find myself agreeing with him.

Mechanical minded, Huxley was also basically a materialist, though of a very sophisticated sort. He was prepared, in his writings, to go as far as saying, "I repudiate, as philosophical error, the doctrine of Material-ism,"[26] because it claimed to see nothing in the universe besides matter and force, while he wished to leave room for problems of free will, morality, and so forth. Yet, characteristically, Huxley could also write, "I can discover no logical halting-place [short of admitting that] all vital action may . . . be said to be the result of the molecular forces of the protoplasm which displays it."[27] In the end, I agree with Cyril Bibby's comment that "his impartiality between idealism and materialism was largely formal and that in fact he habitually thought in materialist terms."[28]

Stretched to its utmost, Huxley's mechanical and materialist lean-ings carried him to a strict determinism, in fact, a teleology that seemed to allow little room for free will. Thus he could follow Laplace and write that "a sufficient intelligence could, from a knowledge of the properties of the molecules of that vapour [molecules of which the primitive nebulosity of the universe is composed], have predicted, say the state of the Fauna of Britain in 1869, with as much certainty as one can say what will happen to the vapour of the breath in a cold winter's day."[29]

Only at the end of his life, in writing *Evolution and Ethics* (1893–1894), while still precluding chance from evolution, did Huxley seek to free humans from the necessities of nature and the Darwinian struggle for survival. He did so in two ways, first by setting humanity in opposi-tion to the laws of nature through the creation of human, that is, altruistic, ethics. The second was through human intervention in na-ture, especially in the form of machines, which created an "artificial" world. As Huxley explained, "We call these things artificial, term them works of art, or artifice, by way of distinguishing them from the prod-ucts of the cosmic process, working outside man, which we call natu-ral, or works of nature."[30]

Man and his society as artificial creations appear to be the products of mechanization, materialism, and determinism and yet they tran-scend these conditions. In the end, however, Huxley himself seemed unable to transcend the terms of his own logic and comes across as something of a distressed and tortured soul, whose logic is necessarily tortured as well. His personal solution was a kind of stoicism and an acceptance of the ambivalent nature of his subject and his arguments. It is a solution that humanity may not be able to transcend.

We can best follow Huxley's struggles over the nature of Man by looking closely at his 1874 paper, "On the Hypothesis That Animals Are Automata, and Its History" (for which chapter 3, on Automata, has helped to prepare us). (The other important paper in this regard is "On Descartes' 'Discourse Touching the Method of Using One's Reason Rightly and of Seeking Scientific Truth'" [1870].) In his paper on automata, Huxley affirms the notion that brutes are nothing more than "a superior race of marionettes."[31] Though his argument is convoluted and unclear (at least to me), Huxley is saying that animals lack true consciousness and are dominated solely by reflex actions (which in the earlier essay on Descartes he had referred to as "the mechanical representatives of volition"). Proof is found in anatomical studies, and Huxley describes two cases, one, based on his own work, of a frog, and the other based on the account by a military doctor of a French soldier.

According to Huxley, it is "highly probable" that consciousness in Man is based on the integrity of the anterior division of the brain, and that consciousness can not arise in any segment of the spinal cord and brain not connected to the anterior division. Thus, if a man is injured, for example, has his spinal cord divided, he will not be conscious of pain in his lower limbs. Yet, stimulated, his limbs will jerk involuntarily and unconsciously, by reflex action. Vivisection can be carried out on the frog to prove the general point, for the frog with its spinal cord cut is "a subject parallel to the injured man, on which experiments can be made without remorse."[32]

The story of the French soldier is a curious one. Wounded during a battle "by a ball which fractured his left parietal bone," this soldier ran his bayonet through his opponent, immediately experienced his right arm as paralyzed, had his right leg similarly affected after walking a few hundred yards, and then lost his senses. He did not recover them for three weeks, and when he did, the right half of his body was completely paralyzed, remaining so for a year, after which the symptom almost completely disappeared. However, periodic disturbances of the functions of the brain arose and persisted; the disturbances, occurring at intervals of fifteen to thirty days, lasted from fifteen to thirty hours.

In his periods of normal life, as Huxley describes it, the ex-soldier's health is perfect. In the abnormal, into which he slides suddenly, he feels a sense of weight about the forehead, his pupils dilate, and, though he eats, drinks, smokes, and so forth, in normal fashion, "pins may be run into his body, or strong electric shocks sent through it, without causing the least indication of pain." Is consciousness utterly absent, Huxley asks, "the man being reduced to an insensible mechanism?" Direct evidence is unavailable; the experiment with the frog, however, suggests an affirmative answer: "in the abnormal state, the man is a mere insensible machine."[33]

Yet Huxley is aware of some disturbing features in the case history. Dr. Mesnet, the physician treating the soldier, reports how, in the abnormal state, the soldier seems to reenact the trauma of the original battle. "Did the man," Huxley inquires, "dream that he was skirmishing? or was he in the condition of one of Vaucanson's automata—a senseless mechanism worked by molecular changes in his nervous system?" Huxley's work on the frog seems to support for him the "senseless mechanism" conclusion. Other evidence (for the doctor performs a series of harmless experiments on the soldier, such as hiding his tobacco pouch) raises the question of how to account for the peculiar form of his actions, if they arise purely from an organic cause. Huxley deals forthrightly with this challenge in a preemptory footnote:

> Those who have had occasion to become acquainted with the phenomena of somnambulism and of mesmerism, will be struck with the close parallel which they present to the proceedings of F. in his abnormal state. But the great value of Dr. Mesnet's observations lies in the fact that the abnormal condition is traceable to a definite injury to the brain, and that the circumstances are such as to keep us clear of the cloud of voluntary and involuntary fictions in which the truth is too often smothered in such cases.[34]

(We have seen that Darwin was a little more tolerant of mesmerism and open to the possibility that mental states could affect physical ones.)

Yet Huxley is still troubled. As he continues in the footnote, the soldier's case

> is singularly instructive, for though, in his normal state he is a perfectly honest man, in his abnormal condition he is an inveterate thief, stealing and hiding away whatever he can lay hands on, with much dexterity, and with an absurd indifference as to whether the property is his own or not. Hoffman's terrible conception of the "Doppelt-gänger" is realised by men in this state— who live two lives, in the one of which they may be guilty of the most criminal acts, while, in the other, they are eminently virtuous and respectable. Neither life knows anything of the other.

The theme of the divided self—first made prominent in the confusion of Frankenstein and his "other half," the monster, and given classic form shortly after Huxley's essay in Robert Louis Stevenson's "Dr. Jekyll and Mr. Hyde" (1886)—lay just below the surface of Victorian feelings about humans and their "animal" nature. Huxley, without conscious awareness, is now extending that "terrible conception" to the machine: our "other half" can commit immoral actions because it is "mechanical" as well as "bestial."

As Huxley has been suggesting, humans are machines, and, in the abnormal state, insensible ones. Humans differ from other animal-machines only by having, in some vague sense, consciousness. Implicitly, a potential gap between humans and the other animals appears to be opening up, or so it seems, but at this point Huxley suddenly shifts his emphasis and, instead of discontinuity, advances "the Doctrine of Continuity." Complex phenomena, such as consciousness, he tells us, must appear gradually. As he explains, "The brutes, though they may not possess our intensity of consciousness, and though, from the absence of language, they can have no trains of thoughts, but only trains of feelings, yet have a consciousness which, more or less distinctly, foreshadows our own."[35] Alas, says Huxley, he wishes it were otherwise; the struggle for existence entails much pain, and as semiconscious beings the other animals must therefore experience suffering (he draws no inferences in regard to vivisection). In such a situation, he tells us, we must treat domestic animals as "weaker brethren," and Huxley quotes Hartley to the effect that "we seem to be in the place of God to them."

At this point, having established the continuity, Huxley begins to pull it apart again. Descartes was right that animals are automata, only he didn't realize that they are "more or less conscious, sensitive, automata." Huxley appears next to argue that animals have consciousness, but not reason, that is, " 'ideagenous molecules' which are the physical basis of memory"; and have free will (for example, nothing prevents a dog from chasing a rabbit), but not reasoned volition.[36] He leaves open the question whether other animals do or do not have souls, for Huxley is at pains to state that he is an agnostic, not an atheist, an idealist as much as a materialist.[37]

Can we extract any final position from him on the question of Man as machine? In the 1874 essay, we can see him hesitating over the issue, yet I think his inclination is clear. Having canvassed various arguments or evidence, as we have seen, he concludes by saying, "We are conscious automata, endowed with free will in the only intelligible sense of that much-abused term—inasmuch as in many respects we are able to do as we like—but none the less parts of the great series of causes and effects which, in unbroken continuity, composes that, which is, and has been, and shall be—the sum of existence."[38] Then follows a long quotation from the Swiss naturalist Charles Bonnet, which Huxley claims to support his conclusion.

In the final analysis, with all his agitation (and, as I have suggested, there is plenty of it in *Evolution and Ethics*), Huxley has ended up with Man as fundamentally a mechanism, though of a very special sort. Humans are fully explicable in physico-chemical terms. Moreover, as Descartes and Bonnet have argued, humans are automatons; true, Descartes also gave them souls, but this, as Huxley argues, simply means that they have consciousness. For Huxley, however, unlike Descartes, consciousness is material, in the sense of being rooted in the organic structure of the body.[39] What is more, consciousness is an evolutionary development, with a continuous line leading from the lower animals to Man.

Though fudged, Huxley's message comes through as follows. Animals, with Man as one of them, are mechanisms that have evolved. Reason, or consciousness, is a physico-chemical process, obedient to deterministic laws. We may then ask: can further, more developed, thinking mechanisms be expected to evolve? Should Babbage's Analytical Engine cause us to think seriously about such a possibility? Huxley took up neither question. Though he supplied an evolutionary perspective to the animal-machine problem, he did not grapple with the possibility of thinking machines. Though "mechanical" in his inclinations, he was still too "biological," that is, physiological, I suspect, to advance on the path Babbage had opened up. His evolutionary perspective on mechanisms, however, was taken up by an unlikely candidate: a novelist with an amateur's interest in evolutionary theory.

Samuel Butler was a curious, somewhat bittersweet, and rather eccentric Victorian. He thought of himself primarily as a painter, was a middling musician, and achieved fame as a novelist.[40] His upbringing, in an Evangelical Protestant family, scarred him for life, producing in him divided, or schizoid, characteristics. I would argue that he turned to scientific discourse in an effort to deal with his family and religious stigmata. As a result, he wrote a number of tracts and books on religious and scientific subjects, specifically, on evolution, that are now largely neglected. His novels *Erewhon* and *The Way of All Flesh*, however, remain classics. And, in *Erewhon*, Butler gave persistent form to the view that machines might represent an advanced stage of evolution.

In 1859, the same year of the *Origin of Species*, after attending Cambridge University, Butler emigrated to New Zealand, to raise sheep. Darwin's book had a powerful effect on him, just at a time when Butler was wrestling with religious doubts. Admittedly ignorant of any actual science—as he confessed "not as knowing anything whatsoever of natural history"[41]—Butler nonetheless took it upon himself to write a dialogue, explaining and supposedly espousing the Darwinian theories. I say "supposedly" for although Butler so represented it later to Darwin, the dialogue is a satirical, ambiguous piece, whose final position is by no means clear. Indeed, the fictitious Darwinian protagonist claims belief in both Christianity and Darwinism, though admitting that they appear irreconcilable. (The dialogue, in fact, makes no effort at reconciliation.)

The dialogue, published in *The Press*, a new New Zealand publication, occasioned a reply, from an author subsequently identified by Butler as the Bishop of Wellington. In the exchange that followed, the bishop caught Butler up short on his knowledge of natural history, challenging him to show that the work of Charles Darwin was anything more than a rehash of theories brought forth in the previous century by his grandfather Erasmus Darwin, Joseph Priestley, and Lord Monboddo. Butler seems to have had the worst of the exchange, indulged in self-satire, and then wisely concluded that the truth of Darwin's theory of evolution "can be decided only among naturalists themselves." It was not advice he would later follow.

It is surprising that, somehow, the dialogue fell into Charles Darwin's hands and caused him to write the young author. Was Darwin desperate for allies and welcomed recognition from as far away as New Zealand, and even by an author who hardly represented his doctrines knowledgeably?[42] In any case, a correspondence sprang up between Butler and Darwin, and Butler, having published in 1865 a pamphlet, "The Evidence for the Resurrection of Jesus Christ . . . ," sent a copy to Darwin. Butler's conflation of evolutionary and religious enthusiasm is clear. Darwin expressed polite interest, urging Butler to write "a work descriptive of a colonist's life in New Zealand." In an unexpected sense, *Erewhon* was Butler's response to Darwin's suggestion.

Before that, however, Butler, under the pseudonym Cellarius, wrote an essay "Darwin Among the Machines," which appeared in *The Press* on 13 June 1863 and dramatically announced the theme of the machine as an advanced evolutionary species. Here, the purely satirical, scientific side of Butler, without religious concerns, appears. By an extraordinary, if ambiguous, leap of intuition, Butler foresees a possible future. Aware that his probe may humble human pride, Butler asks,

> If we revert to the earliest primordial types of mechanical life, to the lever, the wedge, the inclined plane, the screw, and the pulley . . . and if we then examine the machinery of the *Great East-*

*ern*, we find ourselves almost awestruck at the vast development of the mechanical world, at the gigantic strides with which it has advanced in comparison with the slow progress of the animal and vegetable kingdom. We shall find it impossible to refrain from asking ourselves what the end of this mighty movement is to be? In what direction is it tending? What will be its upshot?

At a quick stroke, Butler draws a map of his proposed inquiry, admitting his own limitations to undertake it.

> We regret deeply that our knowledge both of natural history and of machinery is too small to enable us to undertake the gigantic task of classifying machines into the genera and sub-genera, species, varieties and sub-varieties, and so forth, of tracing the connecting links between machines of widely different characters, of pointing out how subservience to the use of man has played that part among machines which natural selection has performed in the animal and vegetable kingdoms, of pointing out rudimentary organs which exist in some few machines, feebly developed and perfectly useless, yet serving to mark descent from some ancestral type which has either perished or been modified into some new phase of mechanical existence.[43]

The suggested classification of machines reminds us of Babbage's taxonomy (and before that, Linnaeus's); only Butler is proposing to "animate" his schema, just as Darwin did with Linnaeus's static system. Further, in place of natural selection, Butler is urging human selection as the means by which machine "breeding," just as in animal breeding, takes place. It is an audacious analogy.

The rest of the short essay spells out a few details. As in animal evolution, Vertebrata of great size, for example, dinosaurs, gave way to smaller, so we may expect miniaturization (my word) among the machines. "The day may come when clocks . . . may be entirely superseded by the universal use of watches, in which case clocks will become extinct like the earlier saurians." Although Babbage is not mentioned (and apparently not thought about), Butler foresees machines acquiring "by all sorts of ingenious contrivances that self-regulating, self-acting power which will be to them what intellect has been to the human race."[44]

This evolutionary development raises the prospect of the machine becoming superior to humans. ("We shall find ourselves the inferior race," is how Butler puts it.) We will have to "feed" them (Landes's passage on coal as inorganic food for machines seems to be an echo of Butler's notion), Butler suggests, and in doing so will become unto them a kind of "slave." True, just as we take care of our domestic animals, the machines will take care of us; after all, we are useful to them. Put simply, machines will have dominion over Man.

In our infatuation with machines, Butler continues, we even "desire . . . to see a fertile union between two steam engines," and instruct our machinery in "begetting" other machinery. In short, we are creating the means of our own inferiority and enslavement. Aghast at this vision, Butler has his presumed author, Cellarius, exclaim, "war to the death should be instantly proclaimed" against every machine.[45] With this trumpet call, the author ends his piece.

Two years later, Butler returned to his subject in another essay, "Lucubratio Ebria," published in *The Press* (29 July 1865). The tone is now positive. Machines are, in fact, merely extracorporeal limbs added to the members of the human body: a lever is an extension of the arm, microscopes and telescopes of the eyes, and so forth. Such body changes, that is, extensions, entailed mind changes as well, and Butler suggests, Man comes to *be* his civilization.

"It is a mistake," therefore, Butler says, satirizing his earlier letter, "to take the view adopted by a previous correspondent of this paper, to consider the machines as identities, to animalize them and to anticipate their final triumph over mankind." The machine simply makes for a difference in degree from human to human—the new limbs are preserved by natural selection (Butler gives no details as to how this occurs), descend with modifications into society and thus mark the difference between our ancestors and ourselves. What is more, within an advanced society itself, the command over these new limbs—for example, the seven-leagued foot we call a railroad train—is a matter of class. "He alone," declares Butler, "possesses the full complement of limbs who stands at the summit of opulence." A Rothschild is a "most astonishing" organism and "may be reckoned by his horse-power, by the number of foot-pounds which he has money enough to set in motion." As Butler concludes, "Who, then, will deny that a man whose will represents the motive power of a thousand horses is a being very different from the one who is equivalent but to the power of a single one?"[46]

Adam Smith, in his labor theory of value, had spoken of opulence as meaning command over labor; Butler has now broadened the concept to mean command over energy, and mechanized it by specifying energy from nonliving sources. He is also aware that what separates the races of humans is their level of culture, or civilization, which means their command over "extracorporaneous limbs." In a spirit that Benjamin Franklin and Karl Marx, both of whom called Man "the tool-making animal," would approve, Butler labeled the human being a "vertebrate machinate mammal."[47] In "Darwin Among the Machines," the "limbs" are feared as taking on a life of their own; here they are benignly subordinated to humans.

Yet, ambiguity and ambivalence still press down on Butler. In another essay, "The Mechanical Creation," written after "Lucubratio Ebria" but published shortly before it (in *The Reasoner*, 1 July 1865), his divided feelings reappear. Now we are told that though Butler does not wish to "throw ridicule on Darwin's magnificent work," further thinking suggests the possibility of "an eventual development of mechanical life, far superior to, and widely differing from, any yet known."[48]

The process is Darwinian, but the end result is the replacement of the organic by the machinate. Was this a satiric reductio ad absurdum of Darwin's work? Why not conceive "of a life which in another ten or twenty million years shall be to us as we to the vegetable?" In "Lucubratio," Butler had looked at machines as mere extracorporaneous limbs, hardly threatening to us; now he returns to the prospect of their supplanting us. A spade is simply an extension of our forearm. We must look at a steam engine to see the evolutionary direction. I quote Butler at length, for his working out of the analogy is impressive:

> It [the steam engine] eats its own food for itself; it consumes it by inhaling the very air which we ourselves breathe; it rejects what it cannot digest as man rejects it; it has a very considerable power of self-regulation and adaptability to contingency. It cannot be said to be conscious. It is employed in the manufacture of machinery, and though steam engines are as the angels in heaven, with respect to matrimony, yet in their reproduction of machinery we seem to catch a glimpse of the extraordinary vicarious arrangement whereby it is not impossible that the reproductive system of the mechanical world will be always carried on. It must be borne in mind that we are not thinking so much of what the steam engine is at present, as of what it may become. The steam engine of to-day is to the mechanical prodigies which are to come as the spade to the steam engine, as the ovum to the human being.[49]

The agency of this mechanical evolution is "natural selection and the struggle for existence" in the form of human's exercising self-interest—shades of Adam Smith! Pursuing a competitive advantage, they invent new machines, which then eliminate or exterminate the older, inferior ones. (Butler speaks of guns actually fighting one another for survival.) In the process, the machines "evolve," threatening eventually to become superior to humans.

Can humans halt this process? In "Darwin Among the Machines" Butler called for just such a halt. Here, in "The Mechanical Creation," he tells us that "man is committed hopelessly to the machines."[50] So dependent are we now that, even if we wished, we cannot live without them—and here Butler anticipates the voice of H. G. Wells in his story of the time machine. The dependency, however, will be mutual: the machines are not likely to want us as a delicacy on their table, and we shall be as serviceable to them as they to us.

In three short articles Butler explored, even if in mixed-up fashion and with tongue-in-cheek, the prospect of extending Darwin's theory of evolution to machines. On one side, he has taken up Ambroise Paré's hand as a prosthetic device and extended it to the idea of extracorporaneous limbs, developed in an evolutionary manner, in the service of human survival. On another side, Butler has taken up the Frankenstein-like fears of the monster as machine, now evolving, and threatening our own survival, or at least our dominion over species.

These are powerful premonitions. What did Darwin think of these offspring of *On the Origin of Species*? We have no hint of his reception of Butler's extension of evolutionary theory.

In fact, Butler's three pieces, two of them in an obscure New Zealand journal, awakened little attention. Only when included, slightly revised, in his novel *Erewhon* did Butler's provocative ideas reach the general public. Originally published anonymously in March 1872, the book enjoyed a relatively vigorous sale at first because the public thought it to be a sequel to Lord Lytton's *The Coming Race* (1871). Butler hastily issued a second edition in July, under his own name, and this and seven further editions during his lifetime continued to have a modest sale.[51] It was, therefore, in the book version, rather than the shorter, more self-contained essays, that Butler's views on the evolution of machines came to enjoy popular and critical regard.

Does *Erewhon* add anything to Butler's earlier conception or argument? Let us first look at the book as a whole, serving as it does for the context of "The Book of the Machines." Erewhon, spelled backward (with the *wh* left as is), is "Nowhere," or utopia (thus nicely symbolizing the opposite of Babbage's concept of a "utopia" based on computing machines). It is cast in the form of an imaginary explorer's tale—the hero wanders over a mountain range in New Zealand into the land of the Erewhonians. The opening chapters, with their John Buchan-like tone and air of excitement and adventure, lead us on into the book.

Once in Erewhon, however, we find ourselves engaged in a more serious exploration as we enter into another culture. Butler's purpose is similar to Descartes's in his *Discourse*, or Montesquieu's in his *Persian Letters:* to examine and satirize his own culture by comparing it to a fictitious one abroad. Descartes remarked that customs are obviously uncertain, being different on one side of a mountain from the other. Over the mountain, Butler finds everything different from his own Western, that is, English, customs.

To make his point, Butler inverts everything he can.[52] First, names: for example, the girl with whom the hero falls in love is Yram (Mary), and we have already noted Erewhon. Next, customs: in Erewhon, physical illness is thought criminal and immoral, but crimes such as embezzlement are considered to be a mental disease, to be cured by "straiteners"; unreasoning and colleges of Unreason are preferred to reasoning and Colleges of Reason; the young inflict corporal punishment on the old, for otherwise the latter would be incorrigible (in fact, Butler as a boy had been repeatedly flogged by his parents);[53] progress is a bad word; and so forth.

It is in this world turned upside down that Butler presents what he has to say on machines and their evolution. The subject surfaces when the Erewhonians exhibit displeasure, rather than awe, at the sight of the hero's watch. The concern moves to center stage when the hero is taken through a museum, in which, in addition to stuffed birds and animals, there are rooms filled with broken machinery. Here he is told the following history: that some 400 to 500 years ago, the state of mechanical knowledge being so advanced and threatening, a learned professor wrote an extraordinary book, calling for the extinction of all machinery not in use for over 271 years. In the massive outbreak of Luddism that this professor's book inspired, machinists and antimachinists engaged in a violent civil war for many years, in which half the population perished. Finally, the antis won and, with unparalleled severity, eliminated every trace of opposition. The Industrial Revolution had been made subject to regression.[54]

Aside from this dramatic suggestion, it is the arguments of the professor, in his "Book of the Machines" (purported to be translated by the hero), that are of interest. Mainly, they are a restatement of Butler's earlier essays, as I have outlined them. However, a few points, developed significantly further, or in more powerful form, are worth quoting at some length. Thus, on the subject of consciousness, Butler has his professor say:

> "There is no security"—to quote his own words—"against the ultimate development of mechanical consciousness, in the fact of machines possessing little consciousness now. A mollusc has not much consciousness. Reflect upon the extraordinary advance which machines have made during the last few hundred years, and note how slowly the animal and vegetable kingdoms are advancing. The more highly organized machines are creatures not so much of yesterday as of the last five minutes, so to speak, in comparison with past time. Assume for the sake of argument that conscious beings have existed for some twenty million years: see what strides machines have made in the last thousand!"

Then, continuing on the subject of consciousness, but adding a further thought, the author adds,

> "But who can say that the vapour-engine has not a kind of consciousness? Where does consciousness begin, and where end? Who can draw the line? Is not machinery linked with animal life in an infinite variety of ways? The shell of a hen's egg is made of a delicate white ware and is a machine as much as an egg-cup is; the shell is a device for holding the egg as much as the egg-cup for holding the shell: both are phases of the same function; the hen makes the shell in her inside, but it is pure pottery. She makes her nest outside of herself for convenience' sake, but the nest is not more of a machine than the egg-shell is. A 'machine' is only a 'device.'"

There is no limit, however, to the development of these "devices," with their consciousness. Answering the argument that the machine, even when more fully developed, is merely a servant to humans, the writer contends:

> But the servant glides by imperceptible approaches into the master; and we have come to such a pass that, even now, man must suffer terribly on ceasing to benefit the machines . . . Man's very soul is due to the machines; it is a machine-made thing; he thinks as he thinks, and feels as he feels, through the work that machines have wrought upon him, and their existence is quite as much a *sine qua non* for his, as his for theirs. This fact precludes us from proposing the complete annihilation of machinery, but surely

it indicates that we should destroy as many of them as we can dispense with, lest they should tyrannize over us even more completely.

And, finally, the author deals with the latent sexual, that is, reproductive, threat.

> It is said by some with whom I have conversed upon this subject, that the machines can never be developed into animate or quasi-animate existences, inasmuch as they have no reproductive systems, nor seem ever likely to possess one. If this be taken to mean that they cannot marry, and that we are never likely to see a fertile union between two vapour-engines with the young ones playing about the door of the shed, however greatly we might desire to do so, I will readily grant it. But the objection is not a very profound one. No one expects that all the features of the now existing organizations will be absolutely repeated in an entirely new class of life. The reproductive system of animals differs widely from that of plants, but both are reproductive systems. Has nature exhausted her phases of this power?[55]

Inspired by fears such as these, which sound like our present actualities, the Erewhonians rise up and destroy almost all their machines.

In a letter to Charles Darwin, Butler referred to "the obviously absurd theory" that he had developed in the chapter upon machines.[56] Butler was too quick to dismiss his own theory; it deserved, and deserves, a full hearing. I suspect, in fact, that Butler was satirizing his own satire, in the same deprecating manner we have encountered in his earlier exchange with the Bishop of Wellington.

Most of *Erewhon* is not about machines. It is about what Butler in *The Way of All Flesh* referred to as the "question of the day . . . marriage and the family system."[57] To this question of questions for Butler we must add religion: the hero of *Erewhon* thinks of converting the Erewhonians to Christianity, yet spends much of his time implicitly satirizing Christianity by comparisons to the strange religious customs and beliefs of the local inhabitants. Similarly, the hero satirizes Victorian marriage and the family system by the same device of inversion. The satire on machinery and progress fits into the general picture. It can, however, be taken out of this frame and left to stand on its own, as it does in the earlier essays, as a profound statement about humans, machines, and evolution.

Whatever the intentions behind Butler's venturesome speculations and however oddly arrived at, the result is a shocking challenge to our ideas about the continuity or discontinuity existing between humans and machines. The essence of that challenge is as follows. If one takes Darwin seriously and accepts that the human is in an evolutionary relation to the other animals; adds to this the idea, advocated by Huxley (building on Descartes), that the animals are animal-machines and humans therefore the same (allowing for whatever differences in consciousness exist); admits that humans then create machines, including Babbage-like computers, which are merely consciously contrived versions of the animal-machine (again only differing in degree); then one can conclude that we are on an evolutionary continuum, with machines as a new, and possibly advanced, species.

What this conclusion actually entails, in the detail of evolutionary science, is not yet clear. What is clear is that Butler's view can not merely be laughed out of court. No matter how satirically worked up, for example, in the "Book of the Machines," Butler's is a serious perspective on the evolving world.

In my view, however, the problem remains that Butler confuses the way in which cultural and physical evolution takes place. In the cultural evolution of mankind, intelligence and will can and do enter into the process of "selection." We consciously create machines, art, and civilization (just as we breed domestic animals).[58]

In his discussion of these matters, Butler ostensibly ignored Huxley's views while accepting Darwin's general theory of evolution (though not its means). In fact, without the view on automata enunciated by his hated contemporary, Huxley, and others like him, Butler could not have pushed on to his own speculations. In some moods, Butler might disown his prophecies about machines and evolution; but they remain like Frankenstein monsters casting their shadows before them. Himself a divided soul, Butler mirrors our own ambivalent feelings on the subject.

Seemingly, Butler's lucubrations on machines have disappeared as a serious subject for discussion. I believe, however, that, viewed in terms of the continuity among humans, animals, and machines, which this book is attempting to examine, a revival *of sorts* of this thesis is in order.

A further confession: I do not much like Butler, the man. Nevertheless, unlikely vessel though Butler is, his intuitions are important and far-reaching. Darwin was right: it is as a novelist of ideas, satiric and paradoxical, that Butler imaginatively extends the continuing discourse on humans and machines.

# Part Three

## **Chapter** Eight

I have tried to give some idea of the ways (Western) Man has thought and felt about the machine (and animal) question in the past. What I have presented is a kind of seedbed, where ideas have germinated and given rise to other ideas about humans, animals, and machines. I have been selective as to what went into the seedbed; but I would argue that my selection—ranging from philosophical debates about the animal-machine to construction of automata and industrialized society, from the theories of scientists to the criticisms of literary persons—has been representative of the profound concerns that have shaped, and must shape, any discussion of what I have been calling the fourth discontinuity.

Now, in this third and last part, I want to concentrate on our contemporary situation. First, with Darwin and the second discontinuity, and then with Pavlov especially in mind, I will look at what can be called the biogenetic revolution of our time. In this latest version of the biological as it hovers on the edge of becoming mechanized, we will see how older hopes and anxieties take new form.

The same is true for the chapter on the computer-brain revolution. Babbage's brainchild seems to have taken on a thinking power of its own, at least in the eyes of some computer enthusiasts, bringing us right to the edge of one part of the fourth discontinuity. In dealing with the fourth discontinuity as such, however, I have stressed that there are two parts to it: the first involves human evolutionary development as being inextricably intertwined with tools and machines, and the second focuses on the development of one such machine, the computer, as inevitably making us take seriously the question whether the same conceptual schemes that apply to the "thinking" machine apply equally to the brain.

Such reflections and speculations about the fourth discontinuity lead us directly to our further inquiry concerning evolving human nature. I will try to summarize my thoughts on this subject, in the light of all that has gone before, in a penultimate chapter. Unusual as it may be to have two concluding chapters, I needed yet another chapter to deal separately with the question as to the future development of machines, viewed in an evolutionary perspective.

In fact, of course, as I have tried to show throughout this book, all these subjects—the fourth discontinuity, evolving human nature, and the future of the machine—are intimately connected, each one throwing light on the other.

The view that there is nothing new under the sun is, depending on how one defines the phrase, almost literally true in the evolutionary sense that from the original interstellar gas and the formation of the sun, from which energy available for photosynthesis is derived, all further "forms" have emerged. In terms of life itself, there seems to be a spectrum in which, to put it in hyperbolic terms, almost everything conceivable, no matter how weird, has appeared.

What human being would, a priori, have conceived of a species in which the female gives birth to numerous young who then eat out her stomach as well as to a species in which the male, impregnating the female, has its penis wrenched out by her grasp, causing his death? Or an animal that hops around with its young in its pouch, or one that hangs from its tail? These seem creatures from science fiction, but they are, of course, mundane species on a real earth. Moreover, what has not been created by reality has often been created by human imagination, whether in the form of mythical beasts, human metamorphosis into other animals, feral or wild men, and so forth.

On the other side, coexistent since the beginning with the origin of species, has been the extinction of species; and humans have sometimes (increasingly so in the present) imagined the extinction of all species, their own included.

It is against this background of seemingly infinitely possible even if improbable creation and extinction that we can best discuss the present state of biogenetics, its relation to mechanical development (bearing in mind constantly the earlier animal-machine debate, even if no explicit reference is made in what follows), and its implications for humans' sense of their own nature. I shall be arguing that from artificial or domestic breeding (as highlighted by Darwin) to gene splicing we are on a continuum. What is new, presumably, is not the mechanical principle but the degree and the ethics as, on our own, we proceed further down this road. Are humans taking into their own hands a qualitatively as well as quantitatively different sort of breeding power?

The canvas of what I am calling biogenetics is crowded with many different colors and divergent lines adding up to a varied number of themes. Developments abound each day, and the literature on the subject seems to be expanding exponentially; any expedition through it is daunting. Basically, and perhaps necessarily too boldly, we shall be exploring the furthest reaches of Man's relation to the other animals as a prelude to further understanding humans' relation to machines.

My first thesis, already adumbrated, is that biogenetics is the latest step in the attempt to turn animals into machines, this time in actuality rather than, as with the seventeenth-century animal-machine, in imagination. Such a tendency connects with the latest development of the machine itself, that is, the computer, with research into the brain going hand in hand with research into artificial intelligence.

Yet, in the end I shall take the position that biogenetic developments carry fewer implications for the evolutionary future of humans (as distinguished, perhaps, from humankind's contemporary economic and future medical life) than do machine developments; or rather that the most potent implications of the former are mediated through the more or less independent development of the latter. The reason, to anticipate a fuller exposition, is that modification of the *environment* is more significant than modification of the *genes*, although in evolution the two must interact, and that the evolutionary nature of humans, differing profoundly in degree from any other animal's, has for a long time led them to shape external nature in the image of their own imaging and imagining mind.

I want to return to the fear that Man is exceeding nature, and his own nature, by taking up first the explosive and widespread feeling that he is unnaturally extinguishing existing species.

Extinction is the other side of the face of creation in the process of evolution by natural selection. Thus, at the time of the Permian extinction, about 225 million years ago, it is estimated that about one quarter of then existing species disappeared; in the Cretaceous era, about 65 million years ago, the dinosaurs vanished, leaving humans eventually to take over supremacy. To take an even longer view, as Eibl-Eibesfeldt reminds us, "out of all the animal species alive during the Paleozoic Era only a small percentage have descendants living today. The majority have died out."[1]

In the popular imagination, such extinction is seen as resulting from, so to speak, claw to claw combat: brontosaurs combating triceratops (in the modern version, Godzilla versus Gadzooks). In fact, much if not most of it is due to climatic changes, that is, changes in the environment. The Ice Age, rather than individual animate representatives of "nature red in tooth and claw"—the interspecies and intraspecies struggle—has both massively eliminated and called into being species.[2] In fact, most new species have appeared in the past at times when the environment was changing rapidly and ecological niches were opening up. Thus, in spite of mass disappearances, as in the Cretaceous era, more species are alive today than at any time in the past.

The estimates as to the existing number of species vary widely. They go from a low of two million to a high of twenty million, with about ten million as the most likely figure. New species come into our purview, not only because they are newly created—new species of beetles, for example, constantly arise—but also because humans have newly discovered them. Thus, it has been estimated that more than 1.2 million species have by now been identified, in comparison to the 4,406 known in 1758, when Linnaeus first classified the animal kingdom. Between 1900 and 1950, it is claimed, a peak of 12,100 newly identified species per year was reached, leveling off in the second half of the twentieth century to about 5,200 discoveries per year.[3] (It should be noted, incidentally, that of all animal species, 70 percent are estimated to be insects.)

What, in fact, is a species? One definition, by Ernst Mayr, is "groups of interbreeding natural populations that are reproductively isolated from other such groups." Another, by George Gaylord Simpson, defines species as "a lineage evolving separately from others with its own unitary evolutionary role and tendencies."[4] The key element of the definition is clearly the ability to interbreed.

There are problems with the concept of species. It may be more a human artifact, an artificial means of classification, than a reality in nature. From the very beginning, with its significant introduction by Linnaeus, its validity has been challenged. Thus the French scientist Robinet wrote in 1768, "Only the individual exists. The species of a naturalist is nothing but an illusion."[5] Darwin, too, was skeptical of the idea of species. He was aware that a finch in one territory could breed with those slightly different from it in an adjacent territory, and that

that second finch could breed with its next-door neighbor, and so on until at some farther remove, the original finch could not breed with its $n$th neighbor. Thus, what we really have is a continuous spectrum, with Man introducing the arbitrary discontinuity of species.

Yet today we hold fast to the idea of species as a kind of coadapted gene pool. Rough as it may be, we have erected a scientific classification very different from the individualizing naming by many other peoples, such as the American Indians, who differentiate among, say, all deer, each one, or the totem-worshipping peoples, who may include bears and foxes as one on the same pole. Ours is a species-oriented scientific culture.

Is there a danger that we may become fixated on species? The biologist William Drury, for example, has remarked that "there is a tremendous preoccupation with rare species in the conservation movement. . . . From an ecological point of view, however, a rare species probably isn't very important . . . unless humans think it is very important."[6]

Human beings, however, increasingly think it is important. Thus we have the famous case of the snail darter, an endangered species that held up the construction of a major dam. The argument was that the genetic reservoir, represented by the tiny fish, was more important than the gigantic water reservoir. The controversy reflects the sense that, as a result of their mechanical civilization, humans are not only destroying their natural surround—the other animals—but also depleting the genetic diversity available to evolution. The even more basic, sobering argument behind biodiversity is that certain species are keystones to ecosystems.

The depth of this fear is indicated by a quotation attributed to E. O. Wilson to the effect that loss of genetic diversity will be worse than "energy depletion, economic collapse, limited nuclear war or conquest by a totalitarian government. As terrible as those catastrophes would be for us, they could be repaired within a few generations. The one process ongoing in the 1980s that will take millions of years to correct is the loss of genetic and species diversity by the destruction of natural habitats. This is the folly our descendants are least likely to forgive us."[7]

The extinction of species, however, as I have suggested, is not a new story. As C. D. Darlington reminds us, "In Africa 100,000 years ago men with Acheulian flint weapons exterminated many genera of great mammals which they killed for food. In North America a worse catastrophe befell when man first appeared in the continent with even better weapons 15,000 years ago. And in Madagascar a small repetition was enacted when men arrived 1,800 years ago in that great island. Thus there came about a series of those irreversible disasters which, unnoticed by the inventors, have since paleolithic times followed in succession each new invention with its ensuing access of human prosperity."[8]

Today, Man as inventor does notice. That awareness is more or less new. And what is also new, or at least potentially so, is the increased scale of his destruction as a result of his increased development of machines and mechanical life. How we view this depends to a large extent on our time scale. Sub specie aeternitatis, the Permian or Cretaceous extinction seems to matter little; a couple of hundred million years later, the earth becomes replenished. In our lives, however, we exist now, and the vanishing of even one species may leave an aching gap.

The snail darter itself is, in fact, trivial; its symbolic value, however, is great. Still, the greater danger, perhaps beyond even specific species extinction, is that humans and their machines may be changing the environment in massive and possibly irreversible ways. On the earth it is the destruction of the tropical forests; in the atmosphere it is the ozone. Change in habitat, far more than mutation, which only survives in terms of the surrounding conditions, is the fundamental cause of the coming into and the going out of existence of species, a coming and going that we call evolution. The danger is that the balance may be shifting to the "going out," with a new Permian Age waiting in the wings. (It is depressing to think that generations of humans—starting, quite possibly, with our children—might, through our own folly, be doomed to the poverty of a Permian Age.)

That is only one part of the story. The other side, as mentioned earlier, is that humans have also acquired what appears to be unprecedented power to preserve species.

The preservation of species can take many novel forms. For example, artificial insemination of cows is by now an accepted breeding procedure; such a procedure can be extended to interspecies embryo transfer. Two such transfers have already successfully occurred: the birth of a baby gaur (a wild ox native to India) to a Holstein dairy cow, and a mouflon (a wild Sardinian sheep) to a domestic American sheep. Such projects often fail, but scientists are confident that, in spite of the numerous obstacles, many such transfers can take place successfully, thus preserving endangered species.

Zoos have gotten into this act by insisting on conservation as perhaps their most important role. Thus, for example, it is claimed that "zoos must prepare to become last havens for creatures like the wild horse that would be destined otherwise for genetic oblivion."[9] Unlike embryo transfers, what I shall call the "zoo as ark" concept intends to breed like with like, in a normal manner, in order to preserve endangered species. Inbreeding, of course, immediately looms as a danger. The other difficulty is that if we define an animal partly in terms of its behavior in an environment, it is clear that even in the newly designed "open zoos" we are not preserving the same animal as in the wilds.[10]

There is yet another, though more mechanical and metaphorical, way of "preserving" endangered species: photography. Instead of ornithologists shooting and then preserving a rare species, they are able to "capture" it on film. Painters, of course, have done this on canvas or in engravings, but generally from dead specimens. The camera, especially the movie camera, captures the bird on the wing, or the tiger moving in the forest. The final result, however, is not a living animal; and thus photography leaves our relation to other creatures many steps below that even of the zoo (except, perhaps, in terms of "humanitarianism").

If the problem of preventing extinction of species evokes concern, even greater anxiety may arise around the issue of creating, artificially, new species. The biogenetic revolution, in the form primarily of gene splicing, arouses ancient fears such as we have encountered with automata and Frankenstein myths. This shadow hangs over much of the current work in biogenetics and fills the pages of periodicals such as the *National Enquirer* and the frames of films such as *The Fly*. It appears both in our dreams and in actuality in the form of monsters and monstrosities.[11]

*Monster* is a term used to characterize that which is contrary to nature. In some eras, monsters have been regularly interpreted as a sign from God of our sins. *Monster* differs from *monstrosity*, which is of natural origin. In fact, of course, the line between the two terms is constantly being blurred (and I shall sometimes use them interchangeably). So, too, in the past was the line between imaginary species of monsters and observed animals; thus, Gessner's *Historia Animalium* portrayed monsters alongside more common species. Though Linnaeus, in his *Systema Naturae*, sought to expose fraudulent monsters, other eminent scientists of his time still gave them credence.[12]

The role of gestation in the creation of monstrosities was seen as seminal. Aristotle, for example, attributed deformities to a failure of the male principle.[13] Ambroise Paré attributed them to the mother's overly active imagination affecting her unborn infant. Only gradually, however, did the deformity as a divine sign, the moral overlay, generally give way to the deformity as a subject of comparative anatomy.

With the increasing power of the latter, monstrosities were no longer viewed by scientists as a break with nature. Thus, the freaks exhibited in sideshows, such as the "Young Man of Thirty, Covered with Scales" who was exhibited in London in the early nineteenth century, might now be seen as part of a continuum of sorts in nature. (Incidentally, the scaly Young Man is alleged to have had a great-grandfather who was "found savage in the woods of North America," another kind of continuity.) And even the famous Elephant Man could fall within the order of nature, rather than its disorder.[14]

Indeed, to the eye of some modern genetic scientists, monstrosities take on a positive value, or, as one geneticist labeled them, become "hopeful monsters." This is the view of Richard Goldschmidt, who argues, as Stephen Jay Gould paraphrases him, that "new species arise abruptly by discontinuous variation, or macromutation." Goldschmidt admits that "the vast majority of macromutations could only be viewed as disastrous—these he called 'monsters.' But, Goldschmidt continued, every once in a while a macromutation might, by sheer good fortune, adapt an organism to a new mode of life, a 'hopeful monster' in his terminology."[15] Another scholar is more low-key in her description. "Ultimately every species has to cope with changes in the environment that are unpredictable. And it is only because it continues to produce sports by means of its mutation mechanism—including flies that are blind or unable to fly—that all the possibilities are explored. These sports, which are normally selected out, but which continue to be born from generation to generation, are to some extent the life insurance of the species."[16]

The monstrosities born to humans find little comfort in being a form of life insurance (in fact, they rarely so serve any longer for humankind), and genetic engineering to prevent such monstrous births seems a "humane" act. But tinkering with other animals, possibly producing "monsters," arouses fear and repulsion in many humans. And because there is a spectrum, especially in the imagination, connecting humans and animals, monstrous births in one species seem to threaten to spill over and, obscuring the humaneness of genetic intervention, evoke horror at the possibilities of creating yet new and worse Frankenstein monsters.

In fact, humanity's direct intervention in evolutionary selection is not new. Domestic breeding, as I have already stressed, caught Darwin's eye before natural selection. "Breeders," he said, "habitually speak of an animal's organization as something plastic, which they can model almost as they please." The "great power of this principle of selection," he went on, "is the magician's wand, by means of which he may summon into life whatever form and mold he pleases."[17]

Of course, Darwin's view of human modeling power by means of domestic selection was hyperbolic. New techniques would be needed, that is, biogenetic ones, to summon into life "whatever" new form is desired; and even then there appear to be definite limits to this magic art. Still, we see what Darwin had in mind. His "pure" breeds and hybrids are anticipations of Man's probing into nature, scientifically, to create improved or new beings, plant and animal.

Two major twists mark the path from Darwin's selection to present-day DNA. The first was taken by his contemporary Gregor Mendel. In his 1866 paper, buried in the *Proceedings of the Natural History Society of Brunn*, Mendel set forth his discovery that different characteristics—the color and height of peas, for example—are inherited separately, so that as one commentator puts it "the genetic material must encode morphological instructions in independent units, entities that we now call genes."[18]

The next twist was supplied by T. H. Morgan, working with the fruit fly, *Drosophila*. Using a microscope on the fast-breeding fly, Morgan was able to see how sex determination worked and first observed a spontaneous mutation, a fly with white eyes. The way was open, if I am permitted a giant step (bypassing, for example, H. J. Muller), to the discovery of the structure of DNA and an understanding of how genetic information is encoded.

At this point, humans possess three ways of constructing new organisms: by encouraging mutations (for example, through radiation exposure), by genetic engineering, and by embryonic reconstructions such as grafts and transplants. What have humans done with their knowledge and what can they do with it? As remarked earlier, the field is developing so quickly that anything said here will undoubtedly be outdated by tomorrow's newspaper item.

One current story, for example, is of the creation of a creature with the face and horns of a goat and the body of a sheep, called a geep. This has been achieved by taking cells from a seven-day-old goat embryo and inserting them into a seven-day-old sheep embryo, then implanting the joint embryo into a ewe's womb. The reproductive physiologist who has waved his wand here calls his creation a chimera, after the Greek mythological being. Whereas the chimeras were monstrous, however, he believes his geep to be a useful creature, advancing our ability to preserve endangered species by implantation of fertilized eggs in ordinary surrogate mothers, as discussed earlier.[19] Geeps themselves, however, are an evolutionary dead end, for they cannot breed true as a species.

Another story concerns the intrusion by humans into wildlife itself. By inserting a gene that controls growth in a rainbow trout into a young carp, scientists have gotten it to grow 20 percent faster than its natural relatives. Such changes in the metabolism of fishes in the wilds can also be harnessed to the purposes of aquaculture, or fish farming. In both ways, humans seem "mechanically" to be extending their domination further into the animal kingdom.[20]

Superovulation, ova and embryo implants, and possibly cloning are all different approaches to reproducing superior animals. The first three methods involve sexual reproduction, and therefore surprises and uncertainties. Cloning, in contrast, is asexual and should result in a perfect replication of an individual.

A clear indication that such developments are seen as bringing closer the animal to the mechanical is the issuance of patents. The subhead of one *New York Times* story is "New life forms would be treated like mechanical inventions," and the same paper's heading for an editorial is entitled "Life, Industrialized." In these stories, religious leaders are quoted as saying that "the gift of life from God, in all its forms and species, should not be regarded solely as if it were a chemical product subject to alteration and patentable for economic benefit," and Jeremy Rifkin, an opponent of genetic engineering, laments that "living things are to be considered no differently than chemical products or automobiles or tennis balls."[21]

For better or for worse, in spite of such warnings, the forces of economic "benefit" along with the mechanizing impulse seem to be pressing forward.[22] Sometimes, not surprisingly, the results are disappointing. For example, the insertion of a human growth hormone into pig embryos to make pigs grow faster has resulted in animals that are cross-eyed and arthritic—in fact, "monsters." Unlike Frankenstein, however, present-day scientists seem able to abort their monstrous creations and try again for better specimens.

Ethical questions, of course, will persist, for as one theologian argued, genetic sciences raise moral questions about "what it means to be human."[23] Yet, part of being human seems to consist of pushing on in the direction of controlling nature in various ways (although the question of degree is often subject not to some mystical determinism but to conscious choice, which marks certain interventions as taboo or undesirable). Controlling nature means obeying its laws and imitating its own ways.

Thus humans operating "mechanically" seem also to be operating "naturally." It is only the initiating event that is "unnatural," in the sense that it is human-created. Once initiated, the creation is then generally subject in its development once more to the forces of the environment.[24]

Our biogenetic concerns are situated in both a mythical and a scientific landscape of the past. Thus, thoughts about domination over other species as well as about our contribution to the extinction of species surround the possibility of new creation. In our myths, we converse with other animals while in reality we seek to decipher animals' languages by science. We experience increasingly not only a greater awareness of animal intelligence but a heightened ethical problem of animal rights. In this matrix we must think about and learn to deal with our modern biogenetic challenge.

The key word is *gene*. It has taken on for us almost the importance that the word *Nature* had for our predecessors. The latter term, though it encompasses the genetic, far more suggests the environment, the conditions, in which the genes can develop. The term *gene*, on the other hand, suggests something self-contained and therefore concisely manipulatable. If we can alter the gene, it is implied, then we have altered the world.

Such an extreme interpretation of the genetic must be played off against the other extreme claim: *any* character may be given to any individual by the shaping force of the environment. Applying this view to humans, a nonbiologist, the nineteenth-century reformer Robert Owen, for example, could announce that character, individual and general, is completely the result of external conditions and therefore completely malleable. (Incidentally, Owen also spoke of workers as "living machines.")[25]

There is little question that the effect of genetic inheritance has often been underestimated in the past, frequently as a consequence of scientific ignorance. When it has been given importance, the result has often been misguided, as in the case of nineteenth-century eugenics. Here, the science was narrow and was motivated almost as much by ideology as by the desire to seek the truth.

In our day, eugenics has been supplanted by sociobiology, as the latest effort to give due weight to genetic determinism. Is this the proper scientific and philosophical background against which the efforts at biogenetic change should be evaluated? The subject is a hornet's nest (more properly, perhaps one ought to say "ant's nest," for ants are the specialty of Edward O. Wilson, sociobiology's most prominent proponent), and angels as well as human animals are liable to get badly stung when entering it. Yet, a stab at understanding what is involved is essential for our purposes.

One definition of sociobiology, given by Wilson, is that it is "the study of all aspects of social behavior up to and including the evolution of social behavior in man." Basically, it appears to be a population theory whose ultimate goal is "to predict, from a knowledge of the parameters of population biology, the evolutionary consequences of social behavior." There are two prime movers of social evolution, according to Wilson. The first category consists "of the historical constraints that control the rate of social evolution, including the basic genetic structure of the species, the properties of their immediate ancestors, and their history of adaptation. The second category is composed of the environmental factors in the recent evolutionary history of the species, those physical and biotic agents that determine their particular ecological 'niche.' "[26]

Hence, we have sociobiology, embracing both the genes and the environment and emphasizing behavior. Another attempt at definition may make clearer some of what is involved. As Melvin Konner summarizes it, sociobiology "is the application of natural selection theory to the explanation of reproduction, especially the behavioral aspects of reproduction. Put another way, it is an attempt to see how far one can get in the analysis of the social behavior of animals armed mainly with the assumption that the purpose of such behavior is the maximization of reproductive success." In more popular language, we are confronted with the "selfish gene."[27]

In his book *Sociobiology*, Wilson makes allusion to Samuel Butler's famous aphorism that the chicken is only the egg's way of making another egg, and adds that this has been modernized: "The organism is only DNA's way of making more DNA." As he says of genes, "The individual organism is only their vehicle, part of an elaborate desire to preserve and spread them with the least possible biochemical perturbation."[28] One cannot help feeling here, to paraphrase another statement, that the chicken has been lost sight of for the egg.

Eschewing, however, all the arguments about Wilson's overextension of his theories, his ideological offshoots, and his perhaps overly narrow focus, one must admire both the erudition behind his theories and their emphasis on genetics. He reminds us forcefully that humans as well as the other animals (and plants) come into the world with a set of genetic "givens" that cannot be ignored, whatever the subsequent unfolding and development of those givens in relation to environmental conditions.

Wilson reaffirms for us the basic weakness in strict theories of cultural determinism, with their utopian possibilities. A number of other authors work out in specific detail the relation of genetic factors to the environment and the consequences thereof. Thus Melvin Konner, a biological anthropologist, both builds on and criticizes Wilson while offering us a detailed picture of what he calls behavioral biology; Irenaus Eibl-Eibesfeldt, an ethnologist, updates Darwin's *Expression of the Emotions in Man and Animals*, focusing on love and hate as basic behavior patterns; and Mary Midgley, a philosopher, offers a lucid and informed discussion of the implications both of the new biology and of sociobiology for Man's knowledge of himself.[29] Many other such works could be cited.

The gene is clearly here to stay (as well it should). Or, rather, to be modified and manipulated, if the biogeneticists are to have their way.

How far and to what purposes are, of course, leading questions. The lines of battle are not always clear, and thoughtful opposition to unbounded technological "advance" is possible and desirable. At one end of the spectrum, however, "Luddites" about biogenetics exist now, as they did in regard to machines during the Industrial Revolution. Such new intellectual Luddites (for they are quite different from the early workmen), for either ethical or environmental reasons, or both, oppose further biogenetic work. Their environmental position often puts them in opposition to ordinary workers, who frequently place immediate economic needs above environmental ones and see regulations as limiting their job opportunities. In any case, there are those intellectual Luddites who wish to stop all further biogenetic experimentation and certainly application, thereby taking up the antivivisection cause in the name of species yet unborn.

On the other side are those who envision the new biogenetics as carrying humans to something approximating a new state of perfection, or at least power. Thus even so restrained and sober a thinker as Melvin Konner resorts to hyperbolic terms when he writes, "No one in today's behavioral sciences doubts that biology is making, and is destined to continue to make, a massive, profound impact on those sciences. The understanding of behavior that results from this impact will be as changed from what we have had before as physics was after Einstein, Planck, and Lorentz."[30]

There is a long history of scientific aspiration behind Konner's eulogy. In the 1840s, for example, it took the shape of a program, which we have first encountered in our section on Freud, advanced by a group of eminent biophysicists, whose number included Carl Ludwig, Hermann von Helmholtz, Ernst von Brücke, and Emil du Bois-Reymond. Summarizing a meeting of these four in 1847, Ludwig announced that "we four imagined that we should constitute physiology on a chemico-physical foundation, and give it equal rank with Physics." Earlier, Brücke had stated, thereby echoing La Mettrie, that "the more one advances in the knowledge of physiology the more one will have reasons for ceasing to believe that the phenomena of life are essentially different from physical phenomena."[31]

Such materialist reductionism turned out to represent more a dream (or a nightmare?) than a realizable program. In fact, progress at the time took place mostly in the techniques of histology and vivisection. As Paul Cranefield remarks, "Never at any time did any member of the 1847 group succeed in reducing a vital phenomenon to physics and chemistry."

The paradox, however, is that the same goal of reducing humans to mechanical animals was achieved, at least in theory, by means other than the physico-chemical. As we have seen, Pavlov, for example, who was a student of Ludwig's, achieved his successes by means of vivisection and then via his findings claimed both animals and humans to be mere physical-chemical processes, with a touch of psychology. (Freud, too, as noted earlier, started out as a disciple of Brücke and wrote his "Project for a Scientific Psychology" with the aim of explaining humans as purely physical-chemical beings; only after this effort short-circuited did he turn to a psychoanalytic psychology.)

The attempt, as we can see, to reduce humans to physics, chemistry, and now biology has a long history. Such reduction has certainly been a heuristic goal, leading scientists to fundamental and important discoveries. It has also, strangely enough, served as a moral aim promising to free humans from their imperfect and even corrupted state.

Its latest version, in this regard, I am suggesting, is biogenetics, or at least biogenetics as put forth by some of its practitioners. Quoting Wilson is again instructive. "Scientists and humanists," he tells us, "should consider together the suggestion that the time has come for ethics to be removed temporarily from the hands of the philosophers and biologicized." As he goes on, "The transition from purely phenomenological to fundamental theory in sociobiology must await a full, neuronal explanation of the human brain. Only when the *machinery* [italics mine] can be torn down on paper at the level of the cell and put together again will the properties of emotion and ethical judgment come clear. . . . Cognition will be translated into circuitry."[32]

Is this not the modernized voice of T. H. Huxley, wishing to become a machine as the purchase price for achieving perfect morality? The desire to make humans perfect runs deep. It can take a secular form in science, I have been arguing, in the ambition to free humans from their animality, by way of making them machines (both in theory and then in fact). And it can seek to do this by biogenetic as well as by more overtly mechanical means.

A first step in this direction is genetically to alter the other animals. H. G. Wells (who, incidentally, spent a year studying biology with T. H. Huxley), in his utopian fantasy, *Men Like Gods*, anticipated some of what I have described above as going on today. As his title indicates, Wells attributed to humans a divine prerogative and "called upon them to 'bring to trial' every other earthly organism from the rhinoceros to the tubercle bacillus, and alter it to his satisfaction or get rid of it."[33] More recently, the brilliant and versatile scientist Freeman J. Dyson has suggested the genetic engineering of creatures that can exist and be self-supporting in space. Thus, he projects, for example, an "astrochicken," weighing one kilogram that, we are told, "will not be built but grown by the use of genetic engineering, and . . . will depend on artificial intelligence and solar-electric propulsion for its operation." Other creatures such as a "Martian potato" and a "space butterfly" are on his drawing pad.[34]

The next step, clearly, is to tinker with humans. Thus a respected molecular biologist, William Day, predicting the future evolution of humanity, tells us that "he [man] will splinter into types of humans with different mental faculties that will lead to diversification and separate species. From among these types, a new species, Omega man, will emerge, either alone, in union with others, or with mechanical amplification to transcend to new dimensions of time and space beyond our comprehension—as much beyond our imagination as our world was to the emerging eucaryotes." The means by which Omega man will arise, Day implies, is through genetic engineering.[35]

A few more examples will suffice. Thus Joshua Lederberg, a brilliant Nobel prize–winning biologist and sometime head of Rockefeller University, wrote in 1978 (and would probably not write so today), "Now what stops us making supermen? The main thing that stops us is that we don't know the biochemistry of the object that we are trying to produce." The implication is that we will come to know the biochemistry and that we will go on to produce supermen. And Francis Crick, another Nobel laureate, also writes of the long view that "provided mankind neither blows itself up nor completely fouls up the environment, and is not overrun by rabid anti-science fanatics, we can expect to see major efforts to improve the nature of man himself within the next ten thousand years."[36]

We are clearly not far from the eighteenth-century philosophe Condorcet, only instead of his social art conveying us into the realm of the new Man, it is sociobiology, or rather biogenetics. Perfection, even if newly conceived, still beckons us.

How seriously should we take these predictions? What grounding, if any, do they have in our present day? A start has certainly been made, as I have tried to show, on the Wellsian program of genetically altering other species. Now what about humans?

Artificial insemination is now a standard, available medical technique. But biogeneticists go further and, in an effort to eliminate abnormalities or malignancies, seek to extend their techniques from the other animals to humans. The emblem on a brochure issued by the Jackson Laboratory, one of the preeminent research laboratories in the United States, reads "Mouse. Gene. Man." Learning first on mice how transplanted tissue can be accepted or rejected, the research has laid the foundation for successful organ transportation in humans (winning the Nobel prize in 1980 for Dr. George D. Snell). Knowledge of DNA and the resultant gene splicing promises to prevent human birth defects.

Such intervention can be seen as merely corrective "surgery" of a sort, only carried out before birth rather than after. What we are seeing is the substitution of technology for biology, so to speak, at earlier and earlier stages before normal birth term. From cesarians to delivery and incubation of a six-month fetus to surrogate motherhood to in vitro births is simply a spectrum, carrying us back earlier and earlier to the creation of the oocyte, or incipient egg. "Corrective" action is theoretically possible at any of these stages, on humans as well as the other animals.

Such intervention, as our earlier discussion has shown, can be seen as "monstrous" as well as being viewed as the prevention of the monstrous. Biogenetics appears to place us between the hope, for some, of producing a superhuman, and the fear, by many, of conceiving monsters. I share the view of most reputable scientists that neither is likely. Is there another possibility, however, whether hopeful or monstrous, in the technology of cloning, as applied to humans?

Claims have been made for the application of cloning to the production of amphibians and even suggested for tissue from a wooly mammoth found frozen in Siberia (technology for the latter hope is still far away). Why not to humans? The first thing to note is that cloning of humans as a scientific achievement is neither present now, nor likely for a long time, *if ever*. The technical problems, according to experts, are staggering.

Even if achievable, the ethical problems might prevent its realization. Would society itself wish to clone future Einsteins? Would it allow a single individual, say of great wealth, to perpetuate herself or himself in this manner? Even if cloning were technically possible, would an Einstein result from an Einstein, or is nurture as important as nature in forming such a being? After all, genetic programming prepares an infant to respond to society, but it does not imprint the exact shape of his response, nor predicts what his particular socialization will be like, nor, in fact, tells us what his society will be like.

Such questions abound. But experiments concerning identical twins may help provide answers. Some of the evidence suggests an extraordinary role for the genetic inheritance, with twins brought up separately still exhibiting astonishingly similar behavior. The psychological problem of being a twin is also striking; and one has to speculate on what would result from having not just one alike but, say, eight or eighty in the world.[37] The subject is, indeed, mind boggling (and, one might add, increasingly open to scientific criticism of the original research) and revives in biogenetic form the psychological fear of the "double" that so haunted nineteenth-century fiction.

Rather than pursuing here, however, the chancy but troubling subject of cloning, I would like to conclude our consideration of biogenetics with a few general assertions. Let me start with a sweeping statement: genetic alteration of human beings, except in the cases of correction of birth defects alluded to earlier, is not a likely event. I see neither supermen nor monstrosities emerging from gene splicing.

What I do see is a continuing extension of "prosthetic Man," to use a term found in Freud (and to be discussed further in my concluding chapters). As I have argued earlier, humans have evolved by extending their "reach," that is, achieving the vision of the eagle by means of the telescope, the power of the horse or elephant by the invention of the steam or internal combustion engine, and so forth. Most of this prosthetic extension has been and will be in terms of machines. What I see in the biogenetic developments is the "animal" side of this same development.

For example, the mechanical provides humans with artificial hips, or pacemakers for the heart. The biogenetic (or, in this case, perhaps the biochemical) involves the attempt to implant animal hearts (rather than "plug in" mechanical devices) in ailing humans: the transplanted chimpanzee heart in the 1977 operation by Dr. Christian Barnard, or the baboon heart in Baby Fae. More promising are such efforts as the fabrication from cultured cells of a thyroid gland equivalent by MIT scientists.[38] Efforts such as these promise to make the human a being increasingly made up of both mechanical and animal replacement parts.

The larger context, I believe, in which our understanding of the implications of biogenetics for the human sense of identity must be sought is in the historical antecedents to this search, in regard to both animals and machines. These antecedents tell us of the constant attempt by humans to shape and control nature: such has been the human evolutionary direction at least up until now. As C. S. Lewis reminds us, "*Nature* is all that is not man-made; the natural state of anything is its state when not modified by man."[39]

Biogenetics represents the most extensive intentional modification by humans of the animal (and plant) world. Humans have moved from hunting, domestication, and domestic breeding to genetic manipulation and new creation. They have increasingly "mechanized" the biological. The potential economic and medical consequences of these extensions are clearly breathtaking. And, in a sense, so are the philosophical and psychological consequences of this intrusion into nature, turning it to a certain extent into a Man-made state.

Yet, I think it would be wrong to exaggerate the importance of this development for Man's sense of himself or his place within the world. Some argue that being able to breed by biogenetic means for a particular quality—intelligence, musical ability, and so forth—will make Man into a race of animals more akin to ants than to existing humans. Aside from particular issues—such as what kind of "intelligence" is intended, how, politically, this will come about, and so forth—I find the idea more a matter of fantasy (Huxley's *Brave New World*) than of science, social or natural.[40] As fantasy, of course, it figures as a serious part of our inquiry.

The human world is still a world dominated by natural selection, of which humans are only a part, and will remain so unless human beings ever are able totally to create an artificial environment (a species-long dream, perhaps to be realized in the future on some distant planet?). Thus, Man's genetically modified or created new species may survive and flourish under artificial protection, but these species still must also exist in a broader surround of natural selection. (Or will humans make a zoo of the whole earth?)

This is not to say that a range of very important changes is not to be expected. In comparison with machines, however, such as the computer, these changes will be more quantitative than qualitative for the simple reason that society will exert a conservative force. Thus while the partial elimination of unwanted genetic characteristics can be expected to be welcomed and encouraged, the creation of new characteristics is likely to be blocked.

Machines, in contrast, are not immediately seen as being so personal; they do not strike so close to our immediate selves (though, as we shall see in the next chapter, we do identify with them). Moreover, we see ourselves as *creators* of the machine; we are hardly likely to wish to exchange that commanding position in order to be the *subject* of "animal" breeding, with ourselves as the animal.

In sum, then, though the biogenetic is important, I believe that in regard to our study it takes second place behind the development of the machine.[41] Or rather, to put the matter in more positive terms, the biogenetic takes its place in symbiosis alongside the "mechanical," with developments interweaving the two becoming more and more important and discernible. The "mechanical," of course, has itself been changing as a result of the computer-brain revolution, which forms the subject of chapter 9.

## **Chapter** Nine

We come now to the modern computer. In earlier describing its origins in the work of Charles Babbage, the emphasis was on situating it in the context of the Industrial Revolution, of which it formed a part. Babbage's "Engine" was "mechanical" in essence, even though transcending the mechanical in principle. By the twentieth century, we speak of the Information Revolution as succeeding the Industrial Revolution, or overlaying it, and thus providing a different context for our handling of the very computer that has brought about the new revolution. In this new context, the mind, not the machine, is the dominant metaphor.

In considering the modern computer, we come to the furthest extension of the fourth discontinuity and its potential ending, as well as reaching the last phase, for the present, of our consideration of Man's effort to define his own nature in relation to animals, on one side, and machines, on the other. In this chapter I shall start off with some cautionary remarks. Then I shall try to provide an overview of the emergence of computers and to raise questions about its significance. Next, I shall look briefly at the arguments as to the nature of AI (artificial intelligence) and mind. Last, I shall say something about the linking of computers to robots, or our automata of chapter 3. I shall reserve for the final chapters an assessment of the implications of all that we have been saying up to now.

In attempting to carry out these tasks, I must express more than the usual humility that should be suffusing this book. Not only is the subject of computers both more technically demanding and more intellectually complicated, for me, than most of our earlier topics, but, like biogenetics, it is also changing literally almost day to day. We are very nearly forced to pass from history to futurology.

I must also, therefore, stress again the importance of distinguishing fantasy from reality, a distinction that applies throughout this book. Part of what I am looking at is how humans regard, or feel about, the computer, as earlier they regarded other machines and other animals.[1] This is one reality, so to speak. It may be quite different from actual reality; that is, for example, a fear of the computer coming to exercise dominion over humanity may have no "real" grounding in the "facts." The same comments can be made about aspiration and realization: the first may reflect utopian hopes and the second potential achievements.

One other preliminary comment is necessary. Different individuals react differently to machines, and especially now to the computer. For example, Sherry Turkle, in *The Second Self,* has studied the way different children experience the computer, some seeing it as alive, others as dead, some feeling threatened by it, others supported and enhanced by it. What for some is welcome precision, for others is intolerable constriction. What is more, taking a developmental perspective, Turkle subtly explores the way reactions may change over time. As she summarizes her work, "My discoveries about the individuality of computer relationships as a function of personality and cognitive style, and as a function of distinct moments in the life cycle, exclude simplistic notions about a 'modal response' to the computer."[2]

Turkle's work is based on research about individuals. Such individual reactions, of course, form part of the cultural reaction. Yet, culture can take on a shape and a life of its own, in the sense that certain dominant themes come to be expressed in classical form, by leading thinkers and artists, and establish the terms of discourse. I will be concentrating on this aspect of the topic.

To complicate our problem, part of that culture consists of psychological patterns, which, in a complex culture, can change over time. Whereas, for example, the nineteenth century was marked by the classical neuroses of hysteria and obsession, the twentieth century is characterized by narcissistic disorders, the "empty self." And inasmuch as attitudes to machines may be seen as projections of personal and cultural anxieties (on the individual level, Turkle talks of coming to see oneself as a computer in order to provide protection from feeling, and so forth), different periods will manifest different dominant reactions.

This is a path we will not pursue further here, though Turkle's work beguiles us in this direction. Instead, we will return to our focus on the overall cultural reaction in regard to what I have been calling the fourth discontinuity.

The line begins, I am arguing, with Man's assertion of mastery over the animals, epitomized by his power to name them, and made actual by his command of tools with which to kill and subdue them. Such mastery over other animals intimately involves Man himself, for in conquering by the use of reason, which replaces instinct, the beasts around him, he was also exhibiting, by using that same reason, the conquest of his own animal passions within. Bodily impulses were seen as "animal" ones, to be subdued.[3]

This theme is one of the most powerful in human thought, and especially so in the West. It finds classic expression, of course, in the Greeks, who first raised philosophy, and thus reason, to an early pinnacle. The relation of reason to the mechanical is crucial to our subject, and a short digression is, therefore, in order here.

In *The Republic*, Plato advocates the rejection of passions and appetites and extols the philosopher who "stands apart from human needs and limitations" and whose viewpoint is "detached and extra-human." As Bernard Knox summarizes the position, "Plato's hero . . . through the exercise of reason, rejects the passions and appetites completely, and lives a life spent in contemplation of eternal unchanging truths, free from internal value conflicts and immune to luck."[4]

In her marvelous book *The Fragility of Goodness*, Martha Nussbaum argues that Plato's appeal to the absolute was in contrast to the dramatists, who argued for contingency and conflicting passions, values, and obligations. *Antigone*, for example, offers a "famous celebration of the *technai*, the arts and sciences which have brought man, step by step, from helplessness to mastery of his environment." *Technē* "is the instrument by which man can make himself immune to *tuchē* [luck]. In the event this proves to be a delusion."[5]

Nussbaum's own conclusion is that "there are certain risks that we cannot close off without a loss in human value, suspended as we are between beast and god, with a kind of beauty available to neither."[6] This message, she claims, is also to be found in Aristotle, who accepted humanity's animal nature but also saw the human as the sort of animal that is rational. Thus, whereas Plato rejected contingency and chance, embracing unchanging reason, Aristotle and the Greek dramatists recognized the power of both partial rationality and *tuchē* (luck) and accepted the necessarily ambiguous human condition.

The irony is that Plato's absolute has come back in modern times to haunt humans in the shape of *technai,* the material embodiment of his ideal aspiration to rise above all the passions. In the beginning of mechanization, this was not the case. Automata were first built not to dominate nature but to copy it. They were to imitate nature, not to go beyond it. Such a view of technology, it can be argued, predominated up until the Renaissance. Increasingly, from that time on, technology and science took on their own authority. We have already noted how the visual representations by men like Taccola, da Vinci, and Paré "exposed" the mechanical nature of artifacts—animal, human, and tool—and thus gave humans control over their inner workings. What before were mysteries now became mere mechanical contrivances, created by humans.

Such creation also promised to give humans power over themselves, their passions, as well as over things. The price, as we have seen, for example, with La Mettrie, or T. H. Huxley, or Pavlov was that Man the creator also became Man the artifact. At the time of the Industrial Revolution, Carlyle most dramatically realized what was happening, or could happen. There is a nice touch in Carlyle's being, as we have noted, T. H. Huxley's favorite author, his personal mentor, and yet that Huxley at one point read him to a conclusion that the earlier prophet would have rejected: Man, in becoming mechanical, becomes perfect, freed from moral error.[7]

Huxley, the materialist, joined hands across the centuries with Plato, the idealist. Reason had become embodied in the machine. In the nineteenth century, the face of the machine was still that of the clock, but in our time, it has become the computer. What the computer represents, however, is not only the embodiment of human reason but also the creation of a reason that may be equal to or even able to go beyond human reason. In the world of fantasy at least, if not (yet?) in that of actuality, humans may be seen not only as machines—computers—but also as coming under the computer's domination. Such a fear, as we have seen, is not new—we need think only of Frankenstein's monster. What is new is that the computer-machine expresses not only our animal passions but also our human reason, in potentially "monstrous," that is, mutational, form.

I want to pause for a moment before going on with this line of thought. As the reader must have seen, I am intrigued with T. H. Huxley's willingness to become a machine in order to become morally perfect. An extraordinary notion, it epitomizes perfectly one part of the human-machine relationship. Let us explore some of its implications a bit further.

In his classic article "Computing Machinery and Intelligence," A. M. Turing discusses abstract machines and comments that "these abstract machines are mathematical fictions rather than physical objects. By definition they are incapable of errors of functioning. In this sense we can truly say that 'machines can never make mistakes.'"[8] In principle, then, in becoming a machine of this sort, Huxley could have his wish realized.

Or could he? In fact, as Turing himself recognizes, Gödel's laws (that any logical system cannot itself be proved logically) limits even the machine's perfectibility. In short, the "perfect" machine is itself imperfect.[9] Error is built into the universe. So much for Huxley's renunciation of his humanity, for it turns out also to be a renunciation of the cosmos.

There is another dilemma. What is the machine that Huxley wishes to become like? In the modern discussions of AI, one line is to say that machines can be made to think like humans, that is, that there is no real difference between humans and machines—in this case, the computer—because they are exactly alike thinking machines. If this were, in fact, the case, then, since humans err, machines must do so likewise. In which case, we have the paradox that Huxley's desired perfection cannot be reached even on earth by our becoming a machine.

The alternative, of course, is that the machines are or can become more rational, more perfect, than we are, without being totally perfect (because of Gödel's theorem). Thus while Huxley's desire cannot be perfectly realized, it could nevertheless be approached asymptotically. If humans are "human, all too human," as Nietzsche said, then computers are also "computer, all too computer," and we must settle for that limitation. So much for perfection!

Humans, being human, however, do not wish to settle for such a limited condition. They aspire to be angels, if not God, which is as close to perfection as we are able to imagine. Where Plato, however, sought to realize this aspiration in the shape of the philosopher, more recent thinkers have aspired to do so in the form of the machine, now computer.

Since Darwin, such hopes have increasingly been clothed in evolutionary garb. Evolution, not salvation, is to bring Man to perfection. Darwin himself was careful to disassociate his findings from the arrow of perfectibility (though he occasionally faltered). Immediate followers, such as Ernst Haeckel, were more likely to fall into hyperbole, as when

Haeckel declared, "We are proud of having so immensely outstripped our lower animal ancestors, and derive from it the consoling assurance that in future also, mankind, as a whole, will follow the glorious career of progressive development, and attain a still higher degree of mental perfection."[10]

Darwin had claimed that he used the term *natural selection* to stand as a counterpart to Man's "power of selection" manifested in the breeding of domestic animals.[11] Conceptually, it is easy to extend the notion of artificial breeding to machines, as well as to nature, and this is what Samuel Butler did. Thus, the machine—for example, an automobile or an airplane—can be "selected" for its speed, just as domestic breeding selects in the case of a racehorse. This is the true "artificial" breeding practiced by humans; and in this sense they are being true to their own "nature." When such machines, however, take on the quality of general purpose machines, as computers promise or threaten to do, linking up the separate extensions of human or other animals' powers, they appear to have the potential of actually becoming "superhuman."

This potential tends to connect with aspirations of perfection; and the aspirations frequently match with the propensity for prediction, which, in turn, often verges on wishful prophecy. This line of development can start with a sober estimate of fact, as when one author notes that "we are here [in the early twentieth century] at the limit of the mechanical world: we are precisely at that dividing line beyond which electronics and cybernetics would eventually lift the idea of 'tool' to a level so different that the continuity seems lost."[12] And it can go on to the hyperbolic statements of Robert Jastrow, who envisions a day when our brains will be replaced by the silicon-based intelligence of computers, when we will be in a state, if not of perfection, then at least of immortal life, and thus of an eternity of time in which to achieve perfection.[13]

Edward Feigenbaum, a practicing computer scientist, and Pamela McCorduck express similar ideas in more restrained fashion: "The essence of the computer revolution is that the burden of producing the future knowledge of the world will be transferred from human heads to machine artifacts."[14] Many other such comments could be cited. Let me settle for one more by perhaps the most brilliant thinker now working in the AI field, Marvin Minsky.[15] As he remarks, "The amount of intelligence we humans have is arbitrary. It's just the amount we have at this point in evolution. There are people who think that evolution has stopped and that there can never be anything smarter than us."[16] Going further, Minsky is also reported to believe that "real computing machines are now almost self-replicating. One uses a computer to program the design of a computer and this design is given to a computer that supervises the actual physical construction of the new computer."

The world of Samuel Butler seems to have arrived—and then some! We must remember that we are in the presence of different "generations" of computers, changing reproductively at high speed. It took the human eons to develop a limbic system in the brain; we inherit it immediately at birth now. The cerebral cortex is a relatively new part of the brain, allowing for what we recognize as culture today. That culture has allowed us to develop machines and now computer machines. As Turing (who discusses Babbage in his classic article and cites Butler in his bibliography, thus marking his own lineage for us) says, "The survival of the fittest is a slow method for measuring advantages. The experimenter, by the exercise of intelligence, should be able to speed it up."[17]

And speed it up we have. By the exercise of intelligence, or what I am calling artificial breeding, humans have produced at least five generations of computers that can be described as follows: starting with the electro-mechanical relay of 1944 (as zero generation), we have a next generation of vacuum tubes in 1946, transistors in 1959, integrated circuits in 1964, medium- and large-scale integration in 1969, and very large-scale integration in 1978.[18] And now new ones.

If the past is prologue to the future, we can see why some observers are given to hyperbolic predictions. The computer is here not only to stay, barring some Butler-like renunciation, but also to develop and "evolve." Whereas in the past, we came "face-to-face" with our animal nature in relation to the other animals, now we are "faced" with machines.

The environment in which this encounter is to take place is one created increasingly in an artificial way, equal to the creation of the computer itself. I have said earlier that Man's evolutionary drive, for better or worse, until now has seemed to be in the direction of creating his own surround, whether it be city or factory, and thus moving further and further away from his animal nature.

Yevgeny Zamyatin, the Russian author of the dystopia *We*, which was published in English in 1924, catches this human aspiration perceptively when he has his hero, D-503, declare that " 'Man ceased to be a wild animal only when he had built the Green Wall, when we had isolated our perfect machine world from the irrational, hideous world of trees, birds, animals.' "[19]

In chapter 8, we discussed the problem of extinction of species. Now, even if only in fantasy, we see that humans can envision the destruction of species as clearing the ecological space so that only humans and their machines are left. In the nineteenth century, one writer, William Delisle Hay, in *Three Hundred Years Hence,* imagined a future age in which all wild and domesticated animals throughout the planet are destroyed: "We needed the land and we needed its productions; we could not afford to retain animals; the earth had no longer need for them. Man found substitutes for the food and clothing he had formerly derived from the brutes."[20] In the twentieth century, Frank Herbert in *The Green Brain* writes less drastically of the elimination merely of all insects (in this case, with dire consequences). To eradicate the animal in himself, Man is willing, at least in imagination, to eradicate them in the world at large.

And perhaps in actuality. Already, as I noted earlier, there are more motor vehicles—over 300 million—in the world than there are humans either in the United States or in the former Soviet Union. Such machines do not do away, at least as yet, with their creators, for human beings have been proliferating like the proverbial flies. These motors, however, do take the space of many other animals. And motor vehicles are only one species of machine.

As Carlyle might say, such are the signs of the times. They point to a world inhabited solely by humans and machines, with the computer as the intermediary link, or "interface." That world itself is one more or less created mechanically by humans, in their own increasingly mechanical image. It is an artificial world; and it is certainly an imaginary one at this time. Are there elements of reality to it? An extension of our discussion of computers to their hookup with space exploration may offer us some hints.

The human desire to fly above the earth, and eventually to leave it, has a long history and is symbolized by the myth of Daedalus.[21] It became real in the summer and autumn of 1783, in France, with the advent of balloon flight. Louis-Sébastien Mercier, author of one of the first modern science fiction works, *L'An 2400* (1770), witnessed the subsequent historic ascension by Pilâtre de Rozier and the Marquis d'Arlandes in a Montgolfier balloon and described the balloon itself as "superb in the sunlight, whirling aloft like a planet or the chariot of some weather-god." Then he added, "It was a moment which never can be repeated, the most astounding achievement the science of physics has yet given to the world."[22]

Mercier had glimpsed the future reach to the planets of the heirs of intrepid balloonists. Although their precise moment, of course, could never be repeated, comparable ones were to appear. First came the movement in imagination. The balloon flights took place a few years before Thomas Malthus's dire prediction in his *Essay on Population* (1798) that Man would outrun his food supply—"man is necessarily confined in room," Malthus intoned. The Industrial Revolution, as we know, deferred the Malthusian specter. Yet, in principle, it still hovers over the earth. One way of defeating it for all time seems to be by escaping the embrace of the earthly room entirely and populating outer space. In 1862, Jules Verne, publishing his *Five Weeks in a Balloon*, took up where Louis-Sébastien Mercier had left off. This was followed by *From the Earth to the Moon* in 1865, and Man, at least in his mind, broke loose from the earth's pull and floated out into space.

Back on earth, more mundane work was needed to make the fictions realizable. The Russian scientist Konstantin Tsiolkovsky pioneered in envisioning the principles of rocketry, both in his 1883 diary, *Free Space*, and his 1903 paper, "Exploration of Cosmic Space with Reactive Devices," where the multistage rocket is projected. The way was now open to the work stretching from the American Robert Goddard to the German Werner von Braun. The aspiration embodied in their work was expressed by Tsiolkovsky when he exclaimed, "If we can even now glimpse the infinite potentialities of man, then who can tell what we might expect in some thousands of years, with deeper understanding and knowledge. There is thus no end to the life, education and improvement of mankind. Man will progress forever. And if this be so, he must surely achieve immortality."[23] Here, clearly, the technological hyperbolic is alive and well, solving not only the Malthusian problem but in addition the question of salvation and eternal life.

I want only to touch on two other related lines of thought before coming back to our own main line of concern. The first involves the idea that we need not actually go, physically, in a spaceship, say, to the Moon or Mars, but could simply be teleported there. Norbert Wiener, the late eminent cyberneticist, argues that it is conceptually possible: "Since all traits of 'life' seem to involve the body's structure on a molecular level, might it be possible to scan a human, molecule by molecule, and by the use of a pulsed code, and a suitable supply of chemicals, construct an exact duplicate? By breaking down the body in this manner, we could then send the information to a machine on Mars that would then reassemble the person from elements on Mars."[24] In teleporting, then, cloning takes on a mechanical garb rather than a biogenetic one, as discussed earlier.

The last idea we need to consider is the reverse of our colonization of space. It is the invasion of earth by creatures from outer space. From

H. G. Wells's *The War Between the Worlds* to the movie *The Body Snatchers*, to mention only two examples, our own projections and projects come back to haunt us.[25] Here, the fabulous creations of our minds, hurled out into space along with ourselves (if we are not teleported), boomerang and come falling back to earth.

For our purposes I want to make a number of points about space travel in general. The first is that both Verne-like fictions and Tsiolkovsky-like formulae are given actual flight only by the guidance of the computer. The computer takes us into outer space, just as much as the missile; or, rather, the computer and the spacecraft are as one. Second, the computerized spacecraft is a machine, an artificial creation, which also provides a totally man-made environment. Third, even on arrival at the Moon or Mars or wherever, humans will still have to live in an artificial environment, which they bring along with them or construct on the site. Fourth, as far as we know there are not and will not be any other animals inhabiting these planetary bodies (unless we bring them with us, in constructs like Biosphere II).[26] Thus, in sum, space colonization promises to create exactly the denuded earth, emptied of other species, and totally mechanical, with humans inseparable from the computer, which we have earlier seen described in fiction and prophesy.

Gerald O'Neill, an imaginative proponent of space colonization, has tried to draw up actual plans to make possible the realization of his hopes. In 1974 he published a short paper on the feasibility of constructing artificial habitats in space, where "communities could be as comfortable as the most desirable parts of the Earth, with natural sunshine, controlled weather, normal air, apparent gravity and complete freedom from pollution."[27] A moment's reflection on the list suggests that only the sunshine and air are actually to be found under normal conditions on present-day earth; the space colony would have a man-made, improved environment. Thus, the colony may be more beneficent than our present human condition, but it will certainly be a more artificial creation. And behind the sunshine still lurks the fantasy-cum-future realization of a completely Man-machine-computer world.

In this book there is no way to avoid mentioning the genre of science fiction, both in books and in films. Arguably, some of the best (as well as some of the worst) and certainly most important literature of our time is to be found in this genre.[28] In this type of literature and film, the current obsession, for no less a word is warranted, with the human-machine question is constantly in view.

I shall restrict myself to two examples of the genre for purposes of illustration. The first is the film *Blade Runner*, which takes its origin from the novel by Philip K. Dick, *Do Androids Dream of Electric Sheep?*[29] The film is undoubtedly more familiar than the book, but I will refer to both. Their plots represent a twenty-first-century, high-tech update of Capek's *R.U.R.*, with the new robots taking the form of Nexus 6 Replicants, or androids (incidentally, only gifted with a four-year life span), but evoking the same threat of the machine and the question as to what marks the difference between humans and androids. In the movie, the Blade Runner (I cannot find out the source or meaning of this title) is acted by Harrison Ford, of *Star Wars* and Indiana Jones fame (with all the resonances thereto).

The time is around 2019. Set in a perpetually foggy, rainy Los Angeles, inhabited (if that word can be used) by a mongroid populace, the movie conveys far more powerfully than the book the sense of urban decay and class differences of the new century. The replicants are androids working off-planet mines who have escaped and found their way to earth.

I shall not discuss the plot, such as it is, but simply touch on a few of the leading themes (without particularly distinguishing between the film and the novel). One is the distinction between humans and androids. The Voigt-Kampff Empathy Test—shades of the Turing Test! (see further this chapter)—tests for empathy in terms of a vague religious sense called Mercerism; other differences are that androids do not "blush" in reaction to morally shocking stimuli (reminding us of Darwin's views) and that they do not have the "normal" human revulsion to such foods as boiled dog.

In fact, the book and film can be read as undermining the differences between human and android. The sexual barrier turns out to be permeable, with humans having "android mistresses": "So much for the distinction between authentic living humans and humanoid constructs," the hero muses.[30] What is worse, the hero sometimes feels empathy for the androids, and the latter seem suspiciously close to developing traces of that feeling themselves. What is more, the hero comes to realize that, in his cold-blooded killing of the replicants, for that is his job, he has come close to being inhuman, if not in fact crossing the line.

Dick's work evokes many of the great themes of the fourth discontinuity, but neither the book nor the film is distinguished aesthetically. The movie does play off effectively, however, with its dark, dank version of the future, against the shimmering, antiseptic movie *Star Wars*. Let me state forthwith that I think *Star Wars* is a great film, one of the classic expressions of a wonderful mythical theme, in its way a twentieth-century counterpart to the epic accounts of Homer. (I must add that, as a continuing epic—it is to consist of nine parts in all—I found *The Empire Strikes Back* and *The Return of the Jedi* disappointing; alas, like pornography, sci-fi can become pompous, repetitious, and boring.)

In *Star Wars* we encounter space colonization with its realistic accompaniment of war. Even in the immensity of space, ordinary human nature is omnipresent: Han Solo, as his name implies, is the American cowboy ranging the stars; Princess Leia, his sexless love; Luke Skywalker, the unknowing incestuous hero; and the Jedi and Darth Vader the forces of good and evil. The result is not a realization of the perfection and immortality promised us in the film's technological hyperbole (though the heroes, Solo, Leia, and Skywalker, seem immune to death, perhaps because they begin by being more or less lifeless figures, that is, mythically timeless) but is another encounter with the petty human limitations we have always known, exhibited against a cosmic backdrop.

In other words, we are presented not with utopia, but with a "realistic" picture of Man in outer space (and the renaming of the Strategic Defense Initiative as Star Wars is an apt representation of this fact). So, too, animals are not eliminated from that world but are brilliantly transmogrified. We are shown a kind of hybridization, or mongrelization, of humans, animals, and machines. Who can forget the barroom scene, where half-human animals are playing musical instruments? And Chewbacca, the gorillalike "wookiee" who walks, though he does not talk, like a man. Then there are the mixtures of humans and machine: the humanlike robots, R2D2 and C-3PO (and, as a mixture of animal and machine, one might mention the mechanical, dinosaurlike towers, the so-called snow walkers, in *The Empire Strikes Back*; and, for the sexual threat, the scene with the huge froglike Jabba the Hut and bikini-clad Princess Leia in his hand—shades of *King Kong!*).

And especially Darth Vader. That croaking, computerlike voice strikes a deathly mechanical note. Joseph Campbell, the well-known student of mythology, captures the matter when he says, "*Star Wars* deals with the essential problem of modern existence. Is the machine going to control humanity, or is the machine going to serve humanity? Darth [and I myself can't help adding, what a wonderful, almost Joycean, play on the words *Death* and *Darkness*] Vader [and here we have the echo of *invader*] is a man taken over by a new machine, he becomes a machine."[31] The "new machine"—in fact, Darth Vader is still a man, although many of his parts are mechanized—is a computer-minded robot, and Darth Vader the symbol of its dark side. We have already noted a sunshiny technological hyperbolic (mistakenly, some may see *Star Wars* as fitting into this category); now we must acknowledge a somber apocalyptic voice as Man discourses both on earth and in space with his "mechanical" *Doppelgänger,* the computerized robot.

It is time to return to earth. We are faced here with developing forms of the computer and the robot. Leaving aside for the moment the latter, we must ask: what is the nature of this computer that we have created? Is it a form of mind, or a clever matter of programming? Can the machine be made to think like people, or have people always thought like machines? We are in the presence of a new epistemology, and the questions abound, touching on the deepest part of our human nature: our sense of self.

I sit at my computer, whose identifying number I hereby acknowledge—serial number OERGJ—for its assistance. It has no name (though I could arbitrarily assign it one): like Yahweh, when asked to give His name, it seems to respond by saying, "I am that I am." The fact is that its namelessness is troubling; or rather, we are troubled both by its namelessness and by its being a number (and giving one line of computers the name Apple does not solve the problem, only pays it a compliment). Computers, like typewriters and automobiles—other machines—have serial numbers stamped on them. That is their "name." The number is impersonal; it says that there is no real person behind it. When we wish to dehumanize a person, for example, in prison, we take away his or her name and hand out a number, usually stenciled on the back of the uniform. Or worse, as at Auschwitz, on the wrist. In making someone a number we remove his or her quality and leave him or her only as a quantity. Thus, in *We,* Yevgeny Zamyatin's antiutopian novel, the inhabitants all bear numbers, to indicate their basic interchangeability.

Let me offer another illustration. The building in which I work at MIT has a number, E51 (for East Campus, Building 51), but no name. This is not atypical at MIT, and it bothers many people. Why? Why is it better for the building to be graced with the name of a benefactor than to be called Building X? Obviously, benefactors enjoy immortalizing themselves by placing their names on the bricks and glass, but the general public can hardly share in such egoistic satisfaction.

Looked at from one angle, in terms of identification, direction, and layout of a campus, numbered buildings (just as numbered streets) make sense. Such numbering also avoids the invidious glorification of a particular person; why should it be seen as "his" or "her" building? The answer appears to be that we prefer the inequality of names to the impersonality of numbers. When we can, we domesticate our autos, buildings, and other mechanical products by naming them. Even the B-52 bomber over Hiroshima was given a name, the *Enola Gay*.

When we name something we make it human. Or at least we think we bring it under human control, make it our "familiar." This is what we have done with the other animals. Such "domestication," however, seems to be resisted by machines: though there are animal trainers, there are no machine trainers (unless one thinks of programmers or testers in this way). Machines, by refusing to bow down before our nomenclature, seem to defy and threaten us. They become Frankenstein's nameless creation, potential monsters.

Thus in discussing the nature of the computer we must be aware that for many people there is a kind of nameless dread surrounding the topic. For others, there is a kind of fabulous magic. I can attest personally to the latter, having successfully (or so it was alleged) completed a one-week course at MIT in the "Structure and Interpretation of Computer Programs," where, "having demonstrated an ability to conjure spirits either by name or by value," I was declared a Member in good standing of the GRAND RECURSIVE ORDER OF THE LAMBDA CALCULUS, with the rank of SCHEME Hacker, 1st class, attested to by a document signed by two Grand Wizards and their Sorcerers' Apprentice (the three teachers from the electrical engineering and computer science departments).

This was all in good fun. Yet it points to an important feature of computers. Basically, what is involved in computer design is an abstraction to simplicity in order to build more complicated entities. With a name (not a personal name for the computer, but a "mailing" name, so to speak), we can manipulate things. A new language is necessary; for example, when LISP was invented in 1957 by John McCarthy, it was different from FORTRAN in that it was able to evolve. By use of such languages, the world can be decomposed into objects, which then send messages to one another. As my teachers pointed out, what is involved is comparable to sorcery and to a witch's formulae: it must be said right (as any user knows, a period or letter out of place and the command goes unobeyed). It is an "occult" business.

But so, essentially, is human thinking. In order, for example, to answer the question as to whether computers are "conscious," we have to know what consciousness is in human beings. And we are not sure. Work in brain science and artificial intelligence is raising old questions in new guises. Philosophers and psychologists join biogeneticists and computer engineers in discussing a host of such issues. Books abound on the subjects. This present book will not be one of them. Instead, hovering at the periphery of the philosophical issues, I will be hinting at the ways they relate to our general theme of humans (animals) and machines.

One of the first questions is how, in fact, to define the question. In his classic article, Alan Turing puts aside the question "Can machines think?" as wrongly phrased and sets himself to substitute in its place what he calls the "imitation game." This is the famous Turing Test. Basically, it says that if a computer behind a curtain gives answers to questions set by a human who then cannot tell whether the respondent is human or machine, then the machine has passed the test and can be said to "think." The real question then is whether a digital computer can be designed that can correctly play the "imitation game" (to help the machine pass, it can even be programmed to make humanlike errors). It would then qualify as a "thinking machine."

The philosopher John Searle, for example, disagrees. He opposes to the Turing Test the "Chinese room." Behind the curtain, so to speak (actually in a room), he imagines an homunculus who can hold up appropriate letters in response to a Chinese person outside the room telling a story in Chinese. According to the Turing Test, the native Chinese speaker might be convinced by what he saw that the homunculus (a machine would do equally well) was actually understanding and conversing with him. But, as Seale points out, we would know that the machine, in fact, was merely reproducing letters whose *meaning* it did not *understand*.

If Searle is right, then the computer merely manipulates formal symbols but attaches no meaning to them. He concludes that the Turing Test is an example of "simple-minded behaviorism" and that we should take the computer for what it is, a useful machine, without insisting that it also possesses the property of thought.[32]

At this point, however, it seems important to make a distinction between what is called information processing and emergent AI. The first is a matter of pure logic, that is, the use of Boolean algebra, which manipulates symbols instead of numerals, and is embodied in a machine that follows the rules programmed into it. Such, certainly, were the early computers. When their schema is extrapolated to the human brain, as it has been by some, and the latter described as simply an information processing entity, the question must then be raised: who has written the program for the human brain?

In emergent AI, this problem can be bypassed. Instead of rules as such, a network of independent elements is set up inside the computer, and the interaction of these elements produces intelligence. The machine, then, is not so much taught as allowed to learn. As Sherry Turkle comments about such a computer, "Its sustaining images are not drawn from the logical but from the biological."[33]

A further extension of the biological is to be found in the work of the Nobel prize winner Gerald M. Edelman. His theory, called Neural Darwinism, takes the "view that the brain is a selective system more akin in its workings to evolution itself than to computation." According to him, brains accomplish such tasks as perception, learning, and memory through selection on the basis of experience. The details are enormously complicated, but Edelman's conclusion is simple and straightforward: "We are not clockwork machines, and we certainly are not possessed of brains that are like digital computers."[34]

To both test and explain his theories, however, Edelman has resorted to what he himself calls repeatedly "a new kind of automaton," whose latest version he has called Darwin III. His work, he claims, may lead to a whole new generation of machines that, being able to react to novelty, that is, to learn, may be more like animals than like computers.[35]

Such statements touch on fundamental issues. Information processing computers can be programmed to assemble a machine, for example, because a machine is designed to be put together. But, as Marvin Minsky remarks, "Nobody's ever made a machine that could build a bird's nest. The debris lying around on the floor of a forest isn't designed to be made into nests." As he concludes, the complexity of real life is beyond the computer.[36]

Will it, however, always be beyond the ability of some future Darwin III? Much of the problem may lie in the question of the computer's ability to generalize. This was the barrier, we remember, that Descartes felt the machine could never pass (*his* version of a Turing Test?). In fact, this ability to recognize classes of things under different conditions, for example, letters of the alphabet even when they are in different fonts, sizes, or handwritings, is now claimed for Edelman's most recent automaton. On his scheme, could not a computer be created that could "learn," through "selective experience," even how to build a bird's nest? (One wonders, incidentally, how adept humans are at building birds' nests?)

It would be a bold person who, in the light of the developments that have already occurred with computers, would rule out categorically such a future development. Are we then to expect to be presented with a computer that thinks no differently from a human being? Obviously, the work now going on plunges us into the workings of the brain, inspired by new insights as to computer processes, and vice versa. The brain, as we know, is a chemical system as well as an electrical one. Can this dual system be duplicated in the computer? Can there be functional equivalents, even if not the actual systems? These are preliminary questions before we can go back to assessing the question of whether brains and computers think alike.

Even if the answer to the chemical-electrical question were to be "yes," we would have to explore more deeply the questions "What is thinking?" and "Is thinking all that we have in mind when we talk about mental processes?" As the British philosopher Gilbert Ryle pointed out, the equating of brains with minds is a "category mistake." The brain may be a physical-chemical, physiological-electrical, and even biological mechanism; the mind is an entity possessed of consciousness, intentions, and meanings. Will machines, even emergent AIs and neural Darwinian automata, possess such qualities? And what about emotions?

These are the terms in which current philosophical reaction to the computer often clothes itself. The arguments swirl about us.[37] There is little that I can add to them here (though I shall take a stab at some of the implications in my concluding chapters). Fortunately, our primary task at the moment is to study how human beings are reacting to the computer "machine" and not to answer the grand questions themselves.

One last general issue, however, needs consideration. It concerns the question of simulation, which takes a number of forms. The first emerges from the Turing Test: is the machine merely simulating a human reaction—saying, for example, that it is thirsty—without actually duplicating it, that is, *being* thirsty? This version of simulation clearly echoes some of the questions raised earlier and adds relatively little that is new.

The second version of the machine's ability to simulate, however, is, in my view, of much greater importance. For example, using high-speed digital computers, astrophysicists can build a model of a supernova, on the basis of known physical laws, and set it running. Though we could never get inside an exploding star, we can simulate what would happen in such an explosion. It is a new version of our "exploded" three-dimensional drawings of the Renaissance period (see chapter 2). Or, to put it more broadly, in this case the exploded drawing can be said to be combined with a "thought-experiment" that we can now make "alive" through a dynamic simulation.[38]

Such "actual" developments are merely specific illustrations of the way the computer allows us to generate artificial worlds, in which we can simulate the behavior of economic, political, or other systems, or what you will. Pure mathematics already offers us one such possibility; the computer allows us to take giant steps forward. In constructing such worlds, which can come to include personal relations (as in sci-fi), we come dangerously close to creating the totally human-made environments that, as we have noted in an earlier context, appear to be one of humanity's deepest aspirations. In such artificial worlds, we transcend completely our animal nature, or so we think. It is easy to lose oneself in such computer-constructed worlds; anyone watching a child playing Pac-Man knows what is meant here. In such worlds, the lines between fantasy and reality fuse and become confused. Simulation appears to become new creation, by a new creator, the computer.

The computer as a thinking machine able to learn and to create artificial worlds acts in symbiosis with Man. As a chess player, it enters into direct rivalry with him. For many absorbed in AI questions, this contest is the true test, taking the place of the Turing "imitation game." Critics say that a machine will never be able to rival the subtlety of thought, the generalizing abilities, found in the great human masters; proponents claim that it is just a matter of time. In the eyes of the latter, moreover, work on the chess computer is analogous to the breeding experiments on *Drosophila* by Thomas Hunt Morgan, which, as we noted earlier (chapter 8), prepared the way for later genetic engineering.[39]

In fact, the first chess machine goes back to at least 1770, when Baron Wolfgang von Kempelen constructed a wooden automaton, claiming it could play a skillful game of chess. Known as the Turk from the turban on its head, it did indeed play skillfully, beating Benjamin Franklin among others. The only problem was that like others of its kind, it was operated from inside by a human player, skillfully if difficultly hidden. We are in the early stages of the magic of the machine.

Edgar Allan Poe wrote a piece called "Maezel's Chess Player," debunking the Turk. The Turk, he pointed out, made occasional mistakes; a true chess machine would not err. In a short story by Ambroise Bierce, "Monxon's Master," the threat embodied in the chess automaton is carried to its agonistic conclusion when the machine kills its human opponent, its "master" (the Persian for checkmate means literally "the king is dead"). Here, in imagination, the future victory of the chess machine over a live chess master is depicted.

Will it become reality? I remember hearing some years ago my colleague Norbert Wiener vindicating the possibility in principle but pooh-poohing it as reality. For, as Wiener contended, it would require a machine the size of Rockefeller Plaza to have the wherewithal to play skilled chess. The extraordinary pace of miniaturization that followed shortly thereafter, and the enormous gains in computer design that have taken place since, rapidly made Wiener's practical limitations obsolete. We now have chess machines, such as CRAY BLITZ and HITECH (notice the new names to go along with the numbers), that can beat all but the world masters.

The human mind is fixed in its number of neurons and possible synapses. In principle, the computer is not; more and more circuits can be built into it and, with parallel processing, made to handle more general thought, and faster. In principle, a world champion chess master in the form of a computer will emerge. Lest we humans take undue fright, it should also be pointed out that a slight change in the rules of the game, midway through the contest, would leave the machine helpless, while its human opponent could adapt. Who knows, though, whether a further future will bring a machine that could survive even in the face of changed rules?

The computer chess player, as it now stands (or rather sits), may be able to think and to play an unbeatable game, but it cannot literally move. Thus, however threatening the existing chess machine may be to some, it is not as if it were mobile, that is, in some sense "alive." When such motionless "minds," however, are linked with robotic machines, then both the threat and the promise to humans appear to be enhanced. In our earlier discussion of automata (chapter 3), both real and mythical, we examined some of the classic reactions. With the advent of powerful computers, robots can take and are taking on new forms of life. If the computer allowed an astronaut on the Moon to take "a giant step for mankind," it is also allowing robots to take enormous strides forward. How will humans react?

Actual robots today, as I noted earlier, can now take over a range of tasks from humans. A robot can work on an assembly line, doing simple and repetitive chores with fewer errors than human operators. It can do spot welding, spray painting, and a whole array of similar tasks without breaks for coffee, the bathroom, or what have you. On economic grounds alone, it is often worth substituting robots for what Marx called the "slave labor" of humans. In fact, the number of robots coming "on line" in Japan, the United States, and other advanced industrial nations is growing by leaps and bounds.[40]

Robotic devices, as suggested earlier, can also be used in situations too dangerous or impossible for humans: they can enter hazardous radiation areas, detonate terrorists' bombs, or dive beyond human depths in the sea. They may also aid physically handicapped people, serving as prosthetic devices, and, eventually, as mechanical "nurses." In everyday life, they can take the place of watchmen, serve as drink caddies, and perhaps eventually clean the house. Their possible service to humans is still being explored on the drawing boards, but the future seems very promising.

There already exist a variety of robots. "Teleoperators" are robots controlled from a distance, as in deep ocean diving. The human operator, through closed-circuit television, "sees" with the eyes of the robot and uses it as an extension of his or her hands. Such teleoperated robots are also used in nuclear "hot labs" and in outer space.

Other robots have self-contained programs and operate in that sense "automatically." What makes them different from merely automated machinery is that they can be reprogrammed, that is, retooled, so to speak, for a changed production line. Research on better eye-hand coordination has provided increased flexibility for such robots, and improved feedback mechanisms in general have extended their range greatly.

One issue, of course, is whether robots should be made in humanlike shape or not? The fact is that robots need to fulfill certain functions, and the human form may not be the best one in which to do them. Nature made legs; humans have made the wheel (which is not to be found in nature). But what counts is the motion involved (one recalls here the Wheeler man in *Ozma of Oz*). Thus, Edward Fredkin, an MIT professor, has been designing a robot that "will be shaped like a long-stemmed upside-down *T* and have a single moveable joint located near the middle of the stem. This joint will be the only moveable part of the robot. The crossbar of the *T* acts as a foot and prevents the robot from tipping over. The robot should be able to balance on its single leg, hop or jump forward or backward, and do somersaults." It will not, however, look like a human, although, as Fredkin, a sober-minded man, remarks, "We envision future two-legged versions of this robot with the strength of a bulldozer, the grace of a ballerina, and the agility of a cat."[41]

Graceful as it might be, such a robot would still be perceived as hard, cold, and metallic. Do we need to keep them that way, so that they may be perceived as being clearly different from humans? Or would we prefer them to be soft, quiet, warm beings, with whom we could be on truly user-friendly terms? Robot enthusiasts claim that the problem itself has been technologically outdated. Thus the author of the *Robot*

*Catalogue* tells us that the "historically deep-rooted vision of robots as a threat to mankind, and their creation as a violation of nature, has been fundamentally altered by the rapid developments in the robotics field. The refined capabilities of today's industrial robots, as well as the emerging new personal robots, have thrust us into an age where myth is superseded by the daily science."[42] As an example, he then mentions the Japanese, where workers greet their robots with a friendly "good morning." As one Japanese psychologist remarked, "We give them [the robots] names. We want to stroke them. We respond to them not as machines but as close-to-human beings."

How close can they get without becoming scary? The industrial robots are merely information processing machines. As we have seen, emergent AI and Neural Darwinism promise us learning machines, capable of generalized thinking. When these are "implanted" in robots capable of great strength and agility, might we then not have a new "creature"? Moreover, such robots, in unmanned factories, will actually be able to make other robots.[43] What will then be the "nature" of that machine, and its relation to us?

I am prepared here to go out on a limb. While I do not believe in technological determinism—science and technology are human creations, a major theme of this book, and thus potentially subject to human control—I believe that a combination of economics, human aspiration, and technology (not to mention politics) is pushing, or pulling, us in certain directions. One push is to develop computers with greater and greater intellection. I see every reason to believe that, as the telescope and microscope far surpass human eyesight, so the computer will far exceed specific human powers of computation and ratiocination. They already have. I am not so sure how far computers can be made to go in the direction of generalizing ability; but I see no reason to draw an arbitrary boundary.

Robots are clearly a present reality, not a fantasy, and improvements are proceeding apace. The possibilities for computerized robots, given time enough, are almost as limitless as the technological hyperbolists would have it. Does this mean that computerized robots will become humanlike, or that humans will become obsolete? Will the robots come to exercise dominion over us, or, however humanlike, will they still remain under our control? These are the questions, of meaning and significance, not of technical achievement, to be considered in our final chapters. Having acquired some knowledge of what is called the computer-brain revolution, to place alongside the biogenetic revolution, we can now turn to that task.

## **Chapter** Ten

We have come a long way—from the beginnings of evolution to the latest computers. It is time now to reflect on the evolutionary journey; indeed, humans have been doing this practically from the beginning—asking who they are and how they relate to animals and, especially more recently, to machines. Thus our work is a reflection on reflections.

I have tried to follow this human questioning through: a close look at some important modern framings and framers of the problem—the seventeenth-century debate over the animal-machine issue in its Cartesian and anti-Cartesian forms, culminating in La Mettrie; a treatment of automata, as the forerunner of the robot; a chapter on the Industrial Revolution, as bringing Man into a truly mechanical civilization; a look at various modern prototypic figures, first Linnaeus and Darwin, then Freud and Pavlov, and then Charles Babbage, T. H. Huxley, and Samuel Butler; an overview of the biogenetic revolution of our time; and a similar survey of the comparable revolution in computers and brain science.

My emphasis has been on intellectual history, on how humans have reflected on the actual changes in science and technology rather than on the changes themselves, though I have tried not to neglect the material world entirely—quite the contrary, as chapter 4, on the Industrial Revolution, demonstrates. It must also be said again that my approach has been neither systematic nor truly ecumenical; I have not tried to narrate the entire story of human reflections on our subject but rather have chosen what I consider to be the most revealing instances in the context of what is basically a Western-oriented discourse. In short, my intent has been philosophical, though my perspective has been historical.

Now, in two concluding chapters, I shall try to come to grips with some of the fundamental questions: in the first concluding chapter, I shall discuss what appear to be the unique characteristics of human beings; and, in the second, to inquire into what lies behind the apparent human drive to mechanize the world, taking seriously the possibility that machines represent an evolutionary step.

What is Man's nature, or, to put it more dramatically, what is unique about him? This, as Huxley put it, is the question of questions and reverberates down the passages of human existence. It is worth invoking at this time the psalmist's version as he sang, "What is man, that thou art mindful of him?" and gave as his answer, "For thou has set him above the animals, and made him a little lower than the angels." This is the Hebrew response.

The other great stream of Western thought rises among the Greeks. We can take the wonderfully evocative definition of Man offered by the chorus in *Antigone* as representative. It is a long passage, poetically listing Man's conquest of the birds and the beasts, his use of language, and how "clever beyond hope is the inventive craft he possesses," especially as it leads to building cities. In the summary given by Martha Nussbaum, "The men of the Chorus reflect that the human being is, in fact, a *deinon* thing: a wonderful and strange being not at home in, or in harmony with, the world of nature; a natural being who tears up nature to make itself a home, who then modifies its own nature to make itself cities."[1] (The Greek word *deinon* is a difficult word to translate; as Nussbaum tells us, "It can be used of the dazzling brilliance of the human intellect, of the monstrousness of an evil, of the terrible power of fate.")

As these passages suggest, both the Hebrews and the Greeks agonized, in the sense of wrestling constantly, with the question "What is Man?" There are other ways of phrasing this question, but they are all forms of the same self-reflective question: What is unique, if anything, about the human species? There are also other traditions—the Chinese, the Indian, the Islamic, and so forth—in which these same questions are raised, and answers given. When I speak of humans, then, I am drawing here, as already remarked on a number of times, only on the reflections of Western humanity. Because the West, as I have argued, has been at the forefront recently of scientific and technological achievement, an achievement that has now been appropriated and added to by other non-Western cultures, I am in hopes that my effort at an answer to these large questions will have more than parochial import.

The first and most fundamental thing that must be said of humans is that they are evolutionary beings. Thus, they are changing beings, and characteristics that might help define them at one stage of their evolution might not be accurate at another. On the other hand, it is clear that, over long stretches of time, certain aspects of their biological nature run deep and largely constant.

The other fundamental statement that must be made about humans as evolutionary beings is that what they are is a particular combination and degree of traits, many of which individually will be shared with other animals (and later, machines). The point about evolution is that change in any one part or trait requires change or adaptation in others: as we noted in an earlier chapter, descent from the trees seems to have meant an upright posture, an upright posture to have freed the front paws, now hands, for tool use, a larger brain to have meant a larger female pelvis, and so on, in intercausal fashion.[2]

One other point is simply that almost every assertion I shall be making is a matter of intense scholarly debate and could be the subject of many paragraphs or chapters in themselves. With this caution, I shall start with what is obvious: that the human is that animal among the primate mammals whose closest relatives today are the chimps and gibbons, and whose earlier antecedents go back millions of years. In the beginning there appears to have been *Australopithecus afarensis*, emerging in Africa (though perhaps elsewhere at the same time, such as China), coming down from the trees and walking. *Homo habilis* was begot by *Australopithecus*, and, in turn, begat *Homo erectus*.

More recently, if we go back only 100,000 to 250,000 years, we find the Neanderthals as cousins on a collateral branch of the human tree; the Cro-Magnons, who emerge some 30,000 years ago, are modern humans, whose anatomy and brain size are already ours. Man's animal origins were first seriously discussed in the West in 1699, by Edward Tyson, the eminent English anatomist, who dissected a chimpanzee sent from Africa to London, thereby discovering its close resemblance to humans. Not until 1856, however, only fifteen years before Darwin wrote his *Descent of Man*, were the fossils of Neanderthal discovered.

Thus arose the problem of the so-called missing link. The search for a "missing link" was finally successful around 1891–1892, when Eugène Dubois, a Dutch physician, discovered and then reconstructed the skull cap and the femur of a creature whom he called *Pithecanthropus erectus*, or the "ape-man who walked upright." More popularly called Java man, and later redesignated scientifically as *Homo erectus*, as referred to above, this creature is now a well-documented ancestor of humankind, with remains discovered in three continents.[3]

The brain of *Homo erectus* was roughly two-thirds the size of that of the modern human, and this statement alerts us to the fact that brain size and weight are key determinants of what is a human. Important characteristics of our human are someone who walks upright, with a brain of some 1,200 cubic centimeters, and a body weight of about 180 pounds on average (though, in fact, the variations are enormous among individuals). Measured by the relationship between brain weight and body weight—for humans are certainly not the largest in absolute brain size, as a glance at whales and elephants will show—humans may be considered the brainiest creatures on earth. The other thing to note about the human brain is that it has three separate evolutionary layers: reptile, limbic, and cortex, and it is the coordination of all three layers that defines human mentality.

What I have tried to suggest by the shorthand above is that an answer to the question "What is unique about Man?" must start by seeking the answer in human evolutionary biology. In the language of Georges Canguilhem, "It is Darwin's merit to have substituted for the idea according to which Man is an approach to or a 'failure' of the human, the idea according to which Man is an evolved animal, that is to say perfected."[4] Without taking "perfected" too seriously, we must stress the changed viewpoint about Man's relations to the other animals that results from Darwin's work.

It should then be pointed out that humans are similar to almost all other animals in that they are characterized, as David Landes puts it, by "circadian ('about a day') and circannual biological rhythms. They are stamped in our flesh and blood; they persist even when we are cut off from time cues; they mark us as earthlings."[5] (And immediately we can see that with the advent of clocks and "Man-made time," Man's "nature" is subject to change—in the form of tension if nothing else.) Our account would then have to go on to say that the human creature needs amino acids, requires a constant range of body temperature, and so forth. In short, we need to presume a medical, as well as biological, textbook as a basis on which to continue our reflections about what is human nature.

So presuming, I will now proceed in the same free-wheeling way, but more in terms of particular subjects than overall, long-term evolutionary development. I take up next the fact that humans have bodies, animal bodies, and not, for example, as computers do, frames or mainframes. These bodies are liable to all the "ills that flesh is heir to." Humans, for example, fear to have broken parts. We catch the flavor of this characteristic when we counterpose it to machines, as in a recent sci-fi novel where machines are coming to dominate humans. As the machine says, "I—indeed, all mechs—am used to being broken into parts, repaired, and reassembled. That is the natural way."[6]

It is not altogether clear what is "natural" for humans. What *is* clear is that humans have a developed consciousness that enters into their awareness of their own bodies. Many feel repelled by their bodies and their bodily functions. It is natural for most animals to defecate in the open, to be attracted by the smell of feces and urine, to use them to mark their territories, and so forth. When did humans diverge from this path? All we know is that over time, they came to surround their bodies with "manners," such that, for example, defecation in public became distasteful.[7] Again, we see change at work, related to other changes, such as the movement toward "civilization."

The human body is not something Man takes without reflection or as a given. Man ornaments it, mutilates it, and disguises it. The body is "created," even if by destructive means such as circumcision. It is as if humans try to do away with their "human" bodies, making themselves new, artificial creatures. Eyebrows are plucked, faces shaved, hair is cut and coiffed, holes are pierced in ears and noses, lips are painted, the body is tattooed—the list seems endless. The desire behind the actions appears ambivalent, partly motivated by the wish to be more attractive while partly springing from a revulsion against the body. It is as if the animal, sick of itself, were trying to shed its skin and become "unnatural."[8]

The quest for attractiveness reminds us that the human body also is a sexual body, distinguished in part by its procreative function. Moreover, its evolutionary nature has been strongly shaped by sexual as well as natural selection. I have already alluded to human year-round sexual activity (in chapter 6). What must be added is that sex in humans has also become psychological: they particularly if not uniquely can have the term *perverse* applied to their sexual practices, whether these practices be of a sadistic, an "unnatural"—that is, bestial—or a displaced nature. In Freud's analysis, indeed, as we have seen, sex has the widest possible function, not only naturally creating new beings but also in making them into fully human beings, which is to say "unnatural" psychological animals.

I wish here not to hover over the Freudian implications of sex but rather to focus on sex's social meanings. The first is that sex acts as a kind of magnet, holding humans together in a family. The long gestation period, the extended dependency of the newborn, the year-round nature of sexual attraction, all seem to play a part in keeping parents and offspring together. What I want to emphasize, however, is that the family then takes on psychological and social attributes beyond (at least in degree) those of other animals when it establishes kinship lines, lineage groups, and rules as to mating, such as the incest taboo.

Man, therefore, not only produces offspring but in the process also sets up society, of which the family is the first example; and humans do this mainly by establishing rules. As Melvin Konner sums it up, "Kinship generates most of the rules of the social system in . . . cultures, including rules of marriage, group membership, exchange, inheritance, authority, and descent."[9] Humans, in short, have a social as well as a biological genealogy.

Such social genealogy, in turn, is a means by which humans seek to control their own breeding. It is the social form of domestic breeding, or what Darwin called artificial selection in regard to the other animals, but now with humans as its object as well as its subject. The genetic consequences are explored in C. D. Darlington's *The Evolution of Man and Society*, with due attention to the incest taboo but also to the other means, including adoption, by which control over birth lineage is achieved.[10]

Other animals also have means of regulating births and controlling population numbers, through such methods as fetal absorption and infanticide. Man alone seems to control reproduction by custom, as well as by a wide range of devices in addition to infanticide, such as abortion and various contraceptive measures. The artificial nature of the latter, made increasingly mechanical in modern times, marks Man off from other creatures. Such conscious control, along with the more customary social structuring of who may mate with whom—the sense of kinship and of social hierarchy—means that generations are active agents in the process of generation itself.

Human society, as has been said, is first made up of families, and these give themselves lineages, that is, named and identifiable ancestors. Other animals do not have such an "inheritance" (unless given to them by humans).[11] Families, marked by lineage and kinship ties, come to compose a society (which later expands its basis, for example, by forming tribes, provinces, nations, and so on). Unlike, for example, insect societies, such societies are held together by human ties (by definition), and, as I am trying to suggest, these can be constructed in new and different ways. Thus, the construction of a society is by choice, even if that choice is vague and sometimes unintended as well as strongly shaped by tradition and custom. (In passing, it might be noted that ornamentation serves another function not yet mentioned, which is that of marking status and lineage differences; and these, in turn, serve further as a form of breeding control.)

Where there are societies, there are cultures. Cultures embody the values as well as the acquired, material knowledge of the group. Culture as a subject is huge, the focus of innumerable anthropological and other studies, and I will remark here on only a few aspects. The obvious one is that human evolution has become cultural far more than physical. The human "physical being" (though not "body," for, as I have been trying to suggest, that is a distinctly social or cultural entity) has persisted more or less the same over the last 30,000 years or so, but with an enormous difference in its settings: one need only compare (without passing any moral judgment) Bushman society and culture with twentieth-century Western society and culture! In fact, the question of what is unique about humans is itself a cultural question, changing its shape in Promethean fashion as humans have evolved over the centuries since the ·advent of Cro-Magnon Man.

Cultures have many components. One major component of all cultures seems to be some form of religion. Religion may be defined as a system of faith and worship that gives order and meaning to the universe. It generally gives, in terms of myth, some explanation, or rather story, as to the origin of all things, as well as providing rituals to reenact the original becoming. Religion also structures society by enforcing particular restraints and taboos and sets up role models by its account of heroes. As far as we know, no other creature has religion, that is, a system of beliefs and ritualistic worship that gives "meaning" to existence. (It should be noted, however, that many premonotheistic religions set up gods that were half animal as well as half human, thus marking a continuum: in Egypt, Horus, Thoth; in India, Hanuman and Ganesh; and so forth.)

At the core of religion is often the subject of death. As best we can tell, humans alone appear *fully conscious* of the death that awaits them and establish ways, generally religious, of dealing with it.[12] Deliberate burial of the dead occurred for the first time that we know of among the Neanderthals.[13] Most cultures subsequently have devised elaborate ceremonies to mark the passing from life. Many insist that life goes on after apparent "death" and imagine an afterlife and an eternal existence.

Again, I need hardly go into details; what I wish to stress, instead, is that death for humans seems critical because of our consciousness that each of us is an individual, that is, an unrepeatable combination of body and mind (or is this merely a Western concept?), which at some point is then gone forever (except as saved by religious belief—for example, reincarnation—and practice). William Godwin and others in Western culture have more or less postulated the end of death, but in their secular version of a religious solution we recognize a utopian state. Such an eternal condition would mean a changed human being, not the one we know now. As of now, we can say that *consciousness* of death, *as a future state,* is a fundamental part of the human condition that distinguishes it from the other animals, as well as machines (can the latter be made "conscious" of their "deaths"?).[14]

If religion and consciousness of death are pivotal features of cultures, so, too, are music and art (often linked to religion, as in dirges and funereal representations). Humans are, of course, not unique in their exercise of music; one need only think of songbirds and some of the whales. It is, therefore, a question of degree. So, too, other animals dance; but it is the complexity of the dance and the stories and values of humans embodied in these performances that makes the difference.

As for art, other animals "build" and shape objects. Man alone can be said to have architecture (where buildings are first imaged in the mind and on paper and then constructed), to make sculptures representing or symbolizing the human body and those of other animals, and to draw and paint (one thinks immediately of Cro-Magnon cave drawings) both bodies and natural objects and scenes, whose results are then preserved on a surface, such as a wall or a parchment. Again, if we are to understand the unique qualities of humans, the emphasis must be on the degree of difference from the "artistic" productions of other animals.

We have hardly exhausted the components of culture, in treating of religion, death observances, music, and art. These particular examples are meant both to illustrate some of what constitutes a culture and to serve as leading examples of humanity's distinguishing traits. I want now to turn in a slightly different direction and deal with what, in the past, has often been alleged to be the most unique feature of humans, sharply distinguishing them from the other animals (and until recently, machines). It is reason.

Not all cultures insist on the primacy, or even importance, of reason. Insistence on it is itself a cultural belief. Because it is so central to the Western conception of the human, however, it deserves rather special, even if again brief, consideration.

The emphasis on reason springs from Greek thought (its absence in the Bible is striking; there the emphasis is on morality, which is known through revelation—God's literal voice—rather than reason). Its classical origin is, of course, Plato. Again Martha Nussbaum sums up the argument, ending with a quotation from the *Phaedrus:* "However much human beings resemble lower forms of life, we are unlike . . . in one crucial respect. We have reason. We are able to deliberate and choose, to make a plan in which ends are ranked, to decide actively what is to have value and how much. . . . If it is true that a lot about us is messy, needy, uncontrolled . . . it is also true that there is something about us that is pure and purely active, something that we could think of as 'divine, immortal, intelligible, unitary, indissoluble, ever self-consistent and invariable' [Plato]."[15]

The Platonic belief in rational self-sufficiency eventually entered into the Christian belief system so that it too (or central versions of it) insisted that Man's distinguishing quality was reason. Reason allowed him thereby to participate in the Godhead.

In chapter 2, I devoted a good deal of attention to Descartes. Here I shall merely highlight the way he became, in the seventeenth century, the epitome of this way of thinking, replacing religion by science as the mode of establishing what is unique—reason—about humans. In Descartes's words in the *Discourse,* he knew himself as a thinker ("I think, therefore I am"), that is, as "a substance whose entire essence or nature is only to think." Later in the *Meditations,* he declared that he was in fact "a thinking thing," nothing more nor less.

By his rules, laid down in the *Discourse,* Descartes insisted that anyone could be sure of never making a mistake, finally "arriving at the knowledge of everything." Having declared earlier that "God is pure intelligence," Descartes, a believing Catholic but unknowing libertine, clearly was convinced that he had shown Man not only his true nature but also how that nature was at one with God, as long as it followed Descartes's rational rules. Since God was perfect, it followed that Man, too, was perfect; or at least perfectible, Q.E.D.

This was how humans differed from the other animals. Reason, according to Plato, Descartes, and their followers, was the means by which humans repudiated their own animality, rising out of the animal kingdom into the realm of pure thought. Only in the twentieth century has such hubris lost much of its conviction in Western thought.

Is there anything to be salvaged from the idea? A modest proposal might be the following. Humans do, indeed, have a kind of special reason, though reason itself is not unique to them. The reason that most sets off humans from the other animals is first and foremost a cultural artifact. Humans are special in the sense of being able to see "connections" among phenomena (though other animals also possess this ability, it is the length of the chain of connections that is at issue here), which they are then able to arrange systematically and to pass on as culture, that is, by some form of abstract language, by conscious education, and by logical argument. Humans have reason, then, in the sense of being persuadable, educable, by rational discourse.

One needs to stress that reason is embodied both in the species, by means of inherited ideas and institutions, as well as in the individual; the individual, left to his or her own devices, or born into a "primitive" society, might still believe, for example, that the earth is flat. Surely, mere observation would seem so to suggest. It is, in fact, only the cumulative "reason," as elaborated by the species, that corrects and orders the "observation," making it into a truer observation. Perhaps, therefore, we can sum the matter up by saying that humans are not only the brainiest animal around but also the most "rational" by virtue of their culture.

In the hands, or mind, of Descartes, reason was more or less severed from emotions—and this, as noted, in spite of Descartes experiencing his revelation as to the unique power of reason in a dream. I cannot follow him in this piece of surgery. In any event, one must ask whether emotions are unique to humans. As stated, the answer to the question must be "no," for the evidence is abundant that other animals also exhibit behavior characterized by emotion. As Konrad Lorenz, for example, declares, "In the Greylag Goose and in man, highly complex norms of behavior, such as falling in love, strife for ranking order, jealousy, grieving, etc., are not only similar but down to the most absurd details the same."[16]

Thus, the question must be rephrased to ask, what kind of emotions are particularly human? For example, the emotion associated with pain appears to be one shared with other animals. Only humans, however, seem to delight in inflicting pain on other members of their own species. Cats may play with mice, but there is no evidence that they deliberately delight in causing pain to other cats. Torture, in fact, seems a uniquely human attribute. Human pleasure from inflicting pain on other humans, it appears, is a grisly claim to uniqueness and one that cannot be dismissed as part of our "bestial" nature. Rather, it seems to stem from our peculiar psychological "makeup."

Some humans even seem to be without "human" emotions; we call them psychopaths. Presumably, they do not even derive pleasure from torture but practice it without any emotion. We tend to think of such members of the species as "inhuman," abnormal, underlining the fact that a normal person does have emotions.[17] One such emotion is guilt over misdeeds, and the psychopath is without a sense of guilt.

What of intentions and motives? Are these uniquely human or at least importantly different from the other animals in terms of degree? Certainly humans have conscious intentions, which assume a certain level of thought about the future. Further, as Mary Midgely points out, human society requires that each individual have motives and that he or she can grasp that others also have them.[18] Friendship, ambition, a willingness to barter—these must be understood in the other as well as in oneself—and this, because of our reason, our social arrangements, and our other attributes, appears uniquely possible for human beings. We are, as stated earlier, a "psychological" creature.

Once more, it is obvious that a whole chapter or book is needed for the subject. Deprived of humanity's claim to uniqueness because of reason by the challenge of the "thinking" machine, that is, the computer, some philosophers now place the emphasis on emotions, which they deny as a possibility to the new artificial intelligences. My own position is that it is the *relation* between emotions, which are hardly unique to us in comparison with the other animals, with our particular reason, again hardly unique to us, that is a distinguishing mark. (I am leaving open the possibility that "emotions" could be "built" into computers.) All of our thinking is tinged with emotions, intentions, and motives, and our emotions, intentions, and motives with thinking. A philosopher may separate them; human life does not.[19] We are thus returned to the totality of our evolutionary nature.

Having stumbled through, or into and about, this difficult subject, that is, feelings, I want to turn to another old chestnut in the discussion: language. It, too, has been alleged to be unique to humans. Recent work with apes and observations of bee dances, for example, have exploded this notion in its simple form. What seems to be worth further consideration is how human language allows for symbolic manipulation rather than mere communication, and the *extent* to which it allows it.[20] Though even the uniqueness of symbolic manipulation has been challenged, the question of extent, it seems to me, cannot be.[21]

In what is a complex and specialized subject, I wish to make only two points, of special relevance to our concerns. The first relates to feelings, which we have just discussed. In the case of humans, the use of symbolic signals gives access not only "to information but to the emotions."[22] Letters on a page from a loved one can serve both functions. The other point, even more important, is made by Konrad Lorenz: "Among animals, symbols are not transmitted by tradition from generation to generation, and it is here, if one wishes, that one may draw the border line between 'the animal' and man."

To extend and expand on this point, it must be emphasized that human language is a *historical* matter (again, of course, we are dealing with degree; the language of some birds, for example, is also "historical" in one sense of that word), that is, that the meaning of words is historical and, indeed, changing. The symbols humans use are fraught with meaning, and that meaning is historical. (It is also ambiguous, trailing its disorderly and confused history with it; thus, the word *cleave* in English means both to separate, as done by a butcher's knife, and to cling to, as embraced by lovers.) As Joseph Weizenbaum puts the point in its most sweeping terms, "Language involves the histories of those using it, hence the history of society, indeed, of all humanity generally."[23] Clearly, computers have their work cut out for them!

The mention of the word *history* raises the question whether this is a defining term of humans and their uniqueness. The Spanish philosopher Ortega y Gasset, for example, says simply that "Man is his history." History, of course, has two meanings: the totality of all that has happened to humans in the past, and the structured attempt to understand the meaning and patterns of selected parts of that past, and to put them down in writing. The first can be said almost to be a synonym for evolution, in its human phase. The second is a comparatively recent awareness, emerging prominently with the Greeks and their attempt to discriminate between history, that is, inquiry (the literal meaning of the word) and myth.

Both myth and history are attempts to know and understand the past, and in this sense both depend on memory of a special sort and a transmittal over generations, by cultural means, of the particular memories. In this regard, humans do seem to be unique. History as such, of course, is a more scientific attempt than myth and has evolved out of a specific cultural development, in order to give sense to and derive knowledge from the past. It marks a dramatic separation from nature, construed as eternal, recurrent time, and the demarcation of human, or novel, unique, "constructed" time. (Once history exists in this sense, then it can be turned back on nature, and nature itself historicized, as with Lyell and Darwin.)

In writing this book, dealing with (Western) humanity's reflections on its relations to animals and machines, and speculating on the subject myself, I am, of course, "doing" history, as well as being a historical animal. I am also conscious of what I am doing. Consciousness, or self-awareness, may also be a unique attribute of humanity. Of course, we cannot know for sure of the inner attributes of the other animals (and, in the future, of machines). It is the thesis, however, of Julian Jaynes that human beings alone have evolved into consciousness, rooted as it is physiologically in the cortex, but developing psychologically in historical time. Jaynes claims (see further note 14, this chapter) this development as occurring somewhere around three thousand years ago, and gives as an example the Greek experience. His thesis is a controversial one but does point accurately, I believe, at human consciousness as being tied to history and culture in a fashion not now known in other animals.

From consciousness, one is naturally led to the unconscious. Until Hartmann and Freud at the end of the nineteenth century, psychiatrists and psychologists resolutely denied its existence (and some still do). Again, we are at the entrance to thorny woods, for psychoanalysis, the domain of the unconscious, as well as conscious, is obviously still a controversial subject. I confess that I find the evidence for the existence of unconscious mental processes in humans to be overwhelming (though one can argue usefully as to how it reveals itself and works). Some of what needs to be said, I have tried to say in chapter 6. Acceptance of parts of Freud's work would mean taking seriously such notions (while rejecting others) as primary process thinking (where, for example, the usual Aristotelian syllogisms no longer apply), dream interpretation, and so forth. It means assigning a specific mental life— marked by unconscious mental processes such as repression, displacement, projection, reaction formation, and so forth—to the human animal, which it does not share with other animals, though it takes its root from humankind's animal evolution.[24] It gives Freudian form to the human as a psychological animal.

What of morality? Is that unique to humans? Darwin, in *The Descent of Man*, stresses the continuity of humans and the other animals, including thought and feeling, and then declares that it is "the moral sense of conscience" that is "by far the most important" distinction.[25] In its most elaborate, formal development, this moral sense generally manifests itself for most of humanity as religion. Other animals, such as dogs and cats, do seem to exhibit feelings of what we can call shame or guilt. Do these approach what we mean by morality (though not religion)? It would seem, as with all the characteristics that we have enumerated, that once again it is a question of degree.

Morality necessarily means choice. One must choose between two actions, one more "moral" than the other. Antigone wants to obey the rules of the city but also wants to obey family rules and bury her brother. Whichever she does, she will also "want" to do the other. Other animals may also find themselves in what appears to be a similar dilemma—one thinks of Buridan's ass—but do they freight the choice with moral overtones? (And what about a computer, which, it would appear, chooses one path or another but doesn't "want" either or both?) And do other animals (such as the elephant) exercise moral choice in a time continuum akin to that lived in by humans? In this special sense, then, morality may indeed be unique to humans. It appears to spring out of consciousness, as discussed above, and can lead to greater self-knowledge and growth as a result of committing an error; one yearns and learns to do better. Huxley, in seeking to eliminate the possibility of a wrong moral choice, can be said also to eliminate much of what is involved in being human.

One could go on and on, seeking to enumerate possibly unique traits in humanity. For example, one would want to discuss humor and laughter: are these to be found in other animals? Then there are dreams: are they unique to humans, emerging out of the unconscious, or are only their contents unique? What of memory: is human memory unique in certain features (for example, in relation to dreams)? Man has been defined as *Homo ludens*, the playful animal: how is this trait different in humans than, for example, in playful otters? The list seems almost inexhaustible (unlike this writer's and the reader's patience in touching on them).

I want, therefore, to mention only two other traits, one of which will then form the subject of my concluding chapter, and to come to an initial conclusion of sorts here as to what is unique about "human" nature. The first of these traits revolves around what has come to be called the "built environment." Humans attempt to substitute their own created "surround" for that of nature. Oddly enough, when, for example, beavers build dams we think of them as part of "nature." Bower birds build elaborate nests, and we also think them natural. However, when humans build homes and dams, we consider them part of a "built environment" and unnatural. Obviously, part of what is involved is a semantic issue, and a matter of degree.

Humans, more or less like other animals, build because the world is a dangerous place and caves and cities help us survive (at least against the other animals and the climate). A totally built environment would presumably be a totally safe environment (again, excepting the threat of other humans). This attempt completely to eliminate nature in favor of human-made structures appears uniquely to characterize the human animal (in fact, being the paradoxical animals they are, humans in advanced civilizations also seek to preserve nature, in the form of parks, zoos, and so forth—but these, too, are their "constructs").[26] From the all-enclosed capsule that provides a life-support system in space to the cities on earth that snatch a space from nature, humans seek to control their environment by building it, rather than accepting it as given. The extent of their desire—and their success—places humans at the end of a spectrum in this regard.

Closely related to the idea of the built environment is Man's creation of machines. In its most primitive form, a tool, the machine, has been held to be the defining feature of Man by, for example, Benjamin Franklin, who, as we have noted, referred to his fellow men as tool-making animals (a usage followed by Karl Marx). Recent work, especially on tool making and use by chimpanzees, has undermined the unqualified claim by humans as such.[27]

Machines, however, as the more extended and complicated form of tools, seem to represent a quantum jump, placing humans well beyond the other animals. Indeed, I would emphasize as strongly as possible that a leading definition of humanity would be: a human is that animal who breaks out of the animal kingdom by creating machines.

In this context, it is useful for a moment to think of the words *Creator* and *creatures*. In Western thought, we speak of a Creator, or God, and we designate the animals whom he creates, "creatures" (in German, for example, the comparable terms are *Schöpfung* and *Geschöpfe*). As the Bible tells us, "And God said, Let the waters bring forth abundantly the moving creatures that hath life."

In making machines, humans have become themselves Creators who endow their creations with movement. Automata, as we have seen, express this form of creation dramatically. An automobile, a locomotor, an airplane, these also move under human inspiration. Until the Renaissance, it appears, as I noted earlier, that Western Man built automata and other machines not so much to dominate nature, but to copy it; not to rival God, but to imitate him. Increasingly, however, in the West, humans came to smudge the image of God as the Creator and to substitute their own, first turning God into a Newtonian machine and then merging him with nature as an evolutionary process. In doing so, humans united within themselves extraordinary powers of destruction—we have already noted their ability to exterminate—and of creation. Whether in taking on creative powers humans are also able, in the form of their machines, to bring into being a new evolutionary step remains our next question. If Man succeeds in taking this step, he would certainly be doing something admittedly unique.

I shall try now to sum up the findings of this present chapter in regard to the question What is a human? In seeking an answer, I have tried from the beginning to be both succinct and synthesizing. We have ranged therefore through a number of attributes, darting brief glances at them, asking in what ways they are unique to humans. The absolutely essential perspective is the evolutionary one: humans are animals that have evolved in a particular way unique to them—as the oyster's evolution is unique to the oyster, and the bat's to the bat. Human traits, almost all of which are shared in one degree or another with other animals—thus emphasizing the continuity of life (even allowing for punctuated equilibrium)—are unique only in the particular configuration and extent in which they are found. It seems a truism, but an important one, frequently overlooked: to repeat, humans are unique only in the totality of their humanity.

One attribute of humans, however, is their drive to seek simplicity and order. Thus, a human asks, Amidst all the attributes, what is my essence? Is it Reason? Is it Emotion? A moral sense? A creative power, expressed in a built environment and machines? Surely, amidst all the attributes, some are more essential than others? The answer, given human nature, is that humans' conceptual powers incline them to single out of their totality some traits that are more important, more striking, though not necessarily more necessary, than others. For I have already tried to establish that it is the conjunction, the interrelating causality, of human attributes that makes for a human.

Still, though all attributes are equal, some are more equal than others. A human is that "creature" (to use the earlier religious terminology) that has evolved to become an upright animal, characterized by neoteny, that is, an extended childhood, and a large brain relative to weight; who possesses highly developed rational and emotive powers; manipulates symbols; has a high degree of consciousness and self-awareness (as well as an unconscious), part of which involves a sense of extended time, and thus death (defied by constructing a humble coffin or a grandiose pyramid); manifests an acute sense of morality, often embodied in religion; has emotions, especially about sex, but also about other humans; enters into social relations with other humans, involving kinship lines, family organizations, and such, up to the conscious entity we have come to call society; has history, both personal and social, that is, a remembered, structured past, transmitted over many generations; constitutes himself or herself and society in terms of "culture," which allows for accumulation and inheritance in a novel, nongenetic form; and, as part of that culture, has come not only to regulate "artificially" his or her own breeding but to create mechanical creatures, potentially a new "being" in the process of evolution, using the term broadly.

The above, in short (!), is what defines a human and the human condition (in fact, other characteristics could easily be added). It is the combination and its changing nature that form a human's essence, or uniqueness; thus, it is a matter of totality rather than of a single attribute. What I have given is a description of a tenuous, imperfect existence, fraught with ambiguity and ambivalence, and filled with change and possible development. One such development is creation beyond themselves, as humans make machines. Having tracked Western humanity in its removal of the "Thou" (who putatively had created humans) from the question What is a human? and having instead tried to answer that question in evolutionary terms, I want now to turn in that same spirit to the new development of humankind, which some think may be in the process of taking on independent "life": the machine.

## **Chapter** Eleven

I have argued that part of the uniqueness of humans is their drive to create machines. In creating machines, humans appear to take on God-like, or at least Promethean, qualities; but, as humans in more modern times have moved to replace the concept of God, or gods, with nature, they have gone even further and appear to be that being, or becoming that being, that has taken on the truly unique role of conscious evolutionary agent.

What has possessed humans to move in this direction? What does it mean to say that humans are a (or the) conscious evolutionary agent? What are the possible results of such a step? What is the future of machines? What are the implications for the human condition and Man's conception of self? I shall address these questions in this final chapter.

When humans first appear, they are already holding tools. Whatever the evolutionary steps leading to this development, our fossil remains are of human and tool together. Freed from pawing the ground, the released human hand can now hold a stone axe, that is, shaped stone, which obviously gives an adaptive edge. The first reason for tools, then, is that they are part of the process of natural selection, giving humans an advantage in their evolutionary struggle.

We cannot, of course, recapture the mind of early humans, but we can be reasonably certain that they had little consciousness about their tool use: it helped them survive, and that was enough. Tools could be directly used in the hunt (of either other animals or other humans), and could then be used to make better weapons. They could be used to construct artificial shelters, make pots, weave textiles, shape canoes, and so on in the process of humans building an "artificial" environment, with "artificial" extensions of their own bodies' powers.

Somewhere along the way, tools began to turn into machines. With the coming of cities and civilizations, we can speak of mechanical artifices, whether water devices, grinding mills, or, indeed, automata. A full history of technology would give us the details. For our purposes, however, to answer the question "What drives humans to mechanical construction?" I want instead to move from natural selection as the key to Man's many-millennia history to modern times and to place beside natural selection the economic impetus.

As I have already argued, the real entrance to mechanical civilization occurs with the Industrial Revolution, though it was preceded by centuries of invention. In fact, such an extended mechanical civilization first flourishes in a particular form of society, the capitalist. Fernand Braudel, for example, takes the period 1400–1800 as the time in which Western capitalism reshapes material life and prepares the way for a new, industrial civilization.

Both in the run-up and then certainly in the fully developed industrial society, there is an economic advantage to be gained by the use of machines. It is the new form of survival advantage. Human workers can be expensive in ways that a machine need not be; a machine, once capitalized, can work tirelessly and uncomplainingly, and when superannuated can be scrapped rather than put on a pension. The tractor, unlike the horse, does not eat when not in use.

As for the extent of utilization, this appears limited only by the extent of the market. As J. H. Plumb tells us, the effort at "improving nature" rests on an "ever-expanding consumption based on industrial production."[1] Thus, the drive to mechanize is explosively fueled by an incitement to consume. This is itself a late historical development, intimately related to the Industrial Revolution. In sum, a major material factor in the impulse to mechanization is the presence of certain social conditions that are initially capitalist and consumerist in nature (with at least the consumerist aspect certainly needing qualification today, in view of the environmental effects).

Besides the forces of economic and natural selection, are there others, perhaps less materialistic and psychologically more fundamental, at work in the increasing move to machines? Certainly, one seems to be sheer wonder. Humans are curious beings, in both senses of the word.

They are filled with wonder at how things work. They tinker, take things apart and put them together again, and invent. They do technology and science because of an inquiring brain. Herein, surely, is the least materialistic force in back of the human creation of tools and machines.

A vaguer, rather different "spiritual" force emanates from the way a human feels about his or her body. As I argued earlier, the human body is a cultural as well as a physical entity. Who has not felt at times the "foulness" of the body and the desire to shake it off? Has not felt revulsion at the "base" necessity of bowel movements, or perhaps even of sex? Humans, as much of this book has shown, have desperately tried to separate themselves from their "bestial" nature and to become pure spirit, or as close to it as they could come. In its worst state, the beast in humans becomes the monster, a sign of moral depravity rather than of genetic difference. In its best state, the animal in humans leads to an approximation of the angelic.

In the West, a battleground for this struggle has been Christianity. Though filled with ambivalences, the Christian religion places a strong emphasis on escaping from the body, and especially abjuring sex. Asceticism is not unique to Christianity; but Christian theology and clerical practice have been much shaped by its chastening message. By denying the body, the claim is made, we become free. For many Christians, as Elaine Pagels explains, "the 'good news' of Christianity meant autonomy: that a Christian could actually defy destiny by mastering bodily impulses. Forces conjured by such names as Aphrodite and Eros . . . must now yield themselves, like beasts before a lion tamer, to the rational will . . . ascetic Christians were no longer at the mercy of uncontrollable forces—neither the powers of destiny, or fate . . . nor the passions that arose from within."[2]

Now, it is hardly the case that ascetic Christians spent much time inventing machines—quite the contrary. What I am suggesting here is simply that the human desire to escape the flesh, which took one form in asceticism, might take another form in the creation of machines. Thus, the wish to rise above the bestial body manifested itself not only in angels but in mechanical creatures. Certainly, once machines existed, humans clearly attached to them feelings of escape from the flesh.

Angels were a marker on the Christian way to human perfection. Machines took on the same quality for more secularly minded humans. They did so in two ways. One way, embodied in the idea of progress, was to lead humans into a mechanical paradise in which they were perfectible because they had entered into a perfectible society, with all bodily tasks performed by machines, thus leaving the human as a purely spiritual creature, with all social problems solved. The other is that, the machine being perfect, in the sense that it could not err, for humans to become more mechanical meant that they, too, were fast approaching perfection. That this interpretation involves fantasy does not detract in any way from its power.

To take an example from the world of music, let us pause to consider the piano. It is "mechanical" in that a note cannot be struck wrong (we are reminded of the mechanical nightingale of Andersen). Nevertheless, even the piano can be played differently and subjectively by individual pianists. Indeed, they cannot help doing so; even if the note is exact, the touch and tone will vary. (An irony, of course, is that even the subjective playing of a Horowitz is reproduced note for note in a recording.) With a "player piano," however, even this human touch is eliminated, and we get a completely mechanical, exactly repeatable performance. Jacquard "cards" replace human hands. It is worth noting that *Player Piano* is the title of Kurt Vonnegut's replay of Samuel Butler's story of a human uprising against the machines that have threatened to take over life.

Why rebel against the "player piano," which for our purposes can symbolize the machine in general? After all, the machine promises perfection, and, if it threatens to take over life, in return it promises to do away with death. As Harold Searles puts it, "Our frustration at the knowledge we are merely mortal is vastly intensified by the knowledge that we have created a technology which, seemingly omnipotent and immortal itself, has not extended our own alloted life span much beyond the biblical three score years and ten. So we identify unconsciously with this technology which, being inanimate, cannot die."[3] If for some, such as Carlyle, the machine symbolizes, as we have seen, death, for others it promises eternal life.

In the previous chapter, I tried to offer a synthetic picture of human nature, to indicate the elements that make for the unique being we call the human. Now I want to argue that it is exactly the most characteristic traits of the human condition—for example, fear of death, loathing of the body, desire to be moral and free of error—that, along with the desire for evolutionary mastery of the natural world, comprise the fundamental forces that increasingly impel humans toward the creation of machines. In the course of evolution, it is a part of human nature that has grown more and more powerful. Or, to put it another way, humans are riven creatures, whose most "human" qualities also drive them toward "inhumanity."

Out of humanity comes machines. In the words of Freud, they have made Man into a "Prosthetic god."[4] More narrowly speaking, tools are an extension of humans, while machines may be said to impose their own rhythms and rules on them; but this is a semantic difference whose boundaries are easily crossed. A spear extends the human hand, as does a hammer; so does a textile machine.

In our time, Norbert Wiener suggests the broader definition of the "engineering of prostheses" when he writes of how "the dolphin propels itself through the water by its flukes, and avoids obstacles by listening for the reflections of sounds which it itself emits." Then he continues, "What is the propeller of a ship but an artificial pair of flukes, or the depth-sounding apparatus but a vicarious sound-detecting and sound-emitting apparatus like that of the dolphin? The wings and jet engines of an airplane replace the wings of the eagle, and the radar its eyes, while the nervous system that combines them is eked out by the automatic pilot and other such navigation devices."[5]

Thus, the idea of machines as an extension of humans is a commonplace. The next step involves a more invasive form of prostheses—the actual implantation of mechanical parts within the human body. An artificial hip, a pacemaker, a mechanical heart, these are major physical intrusions of the mechanical into the human body. They are "plugged" in, so to speak. The naked animal is replaced by a machine-human.[6]

How far will this process go? In the realm of fantasy, it has gone very far indeed. Human-machine hybrids are the new form of the ancient centaurs and mermaids. In 1975, a comic strip in Japan that has quickly spread to the West introduced a man-robot called Goldorak. Goldorak is actually an extension of a man, Actarus, a scientist from another planet. His body parts are given names borrowed "both from human anatomy and from machine images: retrolaser, clavicogyre, carnefulgur, and fulgurpoing."[7] In the movie genre, there is not only *RoboCop* but *RoboCop II* (and by now perhaps *III*; for competition there is also a series of Terminator films).

Robert Jastrow, a serious space scientist mentioned earlier, lyricizes about how "at last the human brain, ensconced in a computer, has been liberated from the weaknesses of mortal flesh. Connected to cameras, instruments and engine controls, the brain sees, feels, and responds to stimuli. It is in control of its own destiny. The machine is its body; it is the machine's mind. The union of mind and machine has created a new form of existence, as well designed for life in the future as man is designed for life on the African savanna." Then in the language of technological hyperbole, which comes pretty close to pure fantasy, Jastrow offers a concluding hymn to this new form of intelligent life: "Housed in indestructible lattices of silicon, and no longer constrained in the span of its years by the life and death cycle of a biological organism, such a kind of life could live forever."[8]

The furthest extension of such fantasies comes when the symbiosis turns into complete possession, and the machine takes over the body wholly, a fantasy touched upon briefly earlier. For example, the film *Invasion of the Body Snatchers* (1956 and 1978) arrives at this point when it has mysterious pods from outer space generate exact physical replicas of the human beings whom they touch and "after the cloning process is completed, replace the original human with a newly-minted creature which, unlike the prototype, is devoid of all emotions, indeed all personality—is, in short, a pure automaton."[9]

Of course, at this point we have crossed the line from prosthesis to complete substitution. Retreating to the simpler form of prosthesis, we must regain our sense of what is possible and what is pure fantasy. A sense of humor—a particular human attribute?—is helpful; Herman Melville in *Moby-Dick* supplies it. In the scene where the carpenter is making Ahab a new wooden leg—a prosthetic device—we have the following dialogue: Hailing the carpenter as "manmaker," Ahab muses that "that old Greek, Prometheus, who made men, they say, should have been a blacksmith, and animated them with fire." Then he continues in manic mood: "Hold; while Prometheus is about it, I'll order a complete man after a desirable pattern. Imprimis, fifty feet high in his socks; then, chest modelled after the Thames Tunnel; then, legs with roots to 'em, to stay in one place; then, arms three feet through the wrist; no heart at all, brass forehead, and about a quarter of an acre of fine brains."[10]

We are not intended to take too seriously the ravings of Ahab; in fact, they are a parody of the technological hyperbolic *avant la lettre* and violate all the rules of allometry, defined as the possible relation of size to shape (with volume growing more rapidly than surface). Still, the subject itself is a serious one, the prosthetic wooden leg being the precursor of more mechanical replacements of human parts. Only a foolish person could with certainty say when humans will or must call a halt to their prosthetic intentions, both as extension and intension of their human physique.

The old saying "If you can't beat them, join them" is a slightly macabre way of putting the prosthetic possibility. Can humans, in fact, "beat" the machine? Legends such as that of John Henry, the American hero who killed himself trying to compete with the machine, pose the question somberly and pessimistically. The fear that machines can outdo humans, and that they will, in fact, replace or displace them, looms large in the collective imagination (existing ambivalently, cheek by jowl, or lever by gear, with the belief that machines may also bring humans power and immortality).

The early nineteenth century in the West is filled with forebodings about Man losing his dominant place and even being destroyed. Fictions abound, such as Mary Shelley's book *The Last Man* (1826), which tells of the destruction of the human race, in this case by plague, until only one person remains. Others, to name just a few more examples, are Bulwer-Lytton's *The Coming Race* and H. G. Wells's *The Time Machine*, where the human is replaced by a superior species. Earlier, we have Diderot's wonderful "D'Alembert's Dream," where one of the dialogists, Dr. Bordeu, asks, "Who knows whether our species is not simply a hatchery for another generation of beings who will supplant our species after the lapse of countless centuries, during which successful modifications will occur?"[11]

With Diderot, we encounter an incipient version of evolutionary theory that permits him to envision a superior species coming into being and going beyond Man (even though Diderot has d'Alembert espouse belief in the Great Chain of Being). Diderot's version of evolution is Lamarckian—he believes in spontaneous generation and that "our organs produce our wants, and the other way around too—wants produce organs." So inspired, he can have Dr. Bordeu (who, incidentally, is probably modeled on La Mettrie) imagine that "the original shape of a creature changes and develops in response to necessity and habitual use. People nowadays walk so little and work so little, and they think so much, that I wouldn't be surprised if man should wind up by becoming all head."[12]

We are still far from machines as such supplanting humans (in spite of Diderot's materialistic position). The seeds of such an idea are there, however, in the shadowy intuition of evolution. When that theory becomes more scientific and pervasive, as it does with Darwin, and is coupled to the reality of the Industrial Revolution and its mechanical developments, we are on the edge of the new conception.

Darwin himself was vague as to possible developments. In the last paragraph of *The Descent of Man* he does say that the theory of evolution offers Man "hope for a still higher destiny in the distant future."[13] It appears that by higher destiny Darwin meant a superior human, with more advanced morality and perhaps reasoning powers.

Darwin's remarks can, however, be read in a different light. Darwinian evolution could also mean a higher animal species and not just a higher grade of human. This was the reading taken by Tennyson, who was exercised that, as one scholar puts it, "mankind might turn out to be, like the wooly mammoth, merely a false start, or a species to be superseded in some as yet ungraspable 'progress.' " As Tennyson wrote to John Tyndall, "I should consider that a liberty had been taken with me if I were simply made a means of ushering in something higher than myself."[14]

What if the "something higher" were a machine instead of a more advanced animal? In Darwin's time, as we have seen, only someone such as Samuel Butler went beyond him, envisioning, even if satirically, evolution's higher destiny in the shape of machines rather than humans. Today, Butler's speculations can be put in new, more concrete form, revolving around the computer revolution.

The computer revolution dramatically extends our discussion of Carlyle's "head and heart" effect.[15] As we recall, Carlyle had recognized that a new society, the industrial, was forming around him. His was a Mechanical Age. Its effect was to make Men mechanical in head and heart as well as hand. By the extension of their sensory apparatuses, especially of the hand by the new textile machinery, Men were becoming "hard" in their hearts and "calculating" in their heads. The new Man was a calculating Man, even at that time.

Today, Carlyle's concern with "calculating" takes on a new extension: that is, the mind itself and its reach are extended. Where nineteenth-century mills afforded greater mechanical power, twentieth-century versions of Babbage's arithmetic mills are giving humans vastly extended mental power. They are also raising the question whether the human mind is programmed; whether humans are, in fact, simply thinking machines.

The question, I am now suggesting, goes well beyond even this and raises the further, and furthest, question: is a new species—"machiaspecies," as it has been called—arising, perhaps to replace humans? It is, in fact, the Butlerian version of evolution that we must now take seriously. One can distinguish phases in that evolution: prosthetic extensions; prosthetic joining of human and machine, culminating in human-cum-computer; and the coming into being, at the hands of humans, of a new type of species, the thinking machine.[16]

A striking feature of the general question that we are posing is that it arouses anxiety among humanists but not where one would expect it most, among religious fundamentalists. There is no Scopes trial to

223

challenge the new theories that posit a being beyond Man. In fact, fundamentalists everywhere are as eager to use the new machines as anyone else. Do they believe the new computer-brain theories are not important, in fact, are mere fantasies and of no consequence? Or is it simply that the instrumental use of the computers makes them into tools, which, though they are extremely useful in spreading religious doctrines, are without other spiritual consequences?

Many humanists, on the other hand, are much disturbed over the possibly malignant consequences of a computerized world. Carlylean in approach, they are concerned over a dehumanization of humans, in which they are reduced to computerized beings. In their worst fantasies, or thoughts, they perceive Frankenstein's monster in new computer robotic form, but this time multiplying and exercising dominion over a world in which humans are no longer the dominant force.

What reality lies behind such thoughts and fantasies? It is time we confronted this question head on.

To answer this question, we must first ask, as we did with humans themselves, What is the computer machine that humans have made? What is its nature? As it now stands, the computer is an information processing system, dependent on a program inserted by a human and with a memory that allows for total recoverability (when functioning correctly). Within its program, it never errs (allowing for the same caveat). It operates at great speed and even now does calculations well beyond the reach of any human.

Implanted, so to speak, in a robot, the computer acquires a "body" that allows it to move. This can mean movement of parts, such as a "hand," or locomotion of the entire machine. So endowed, the computer robot (let us henceforth call it the *combot*) can execute tedious tasks, of mind and motion, previously the lot of human slaves (wage or otherwise). As I noted in some detail in chapter 9, it can do such things as enter areas and execute tasks too dangerous for humans. It may also be able to enter into "service," that is, take over routine household tasks, or perhaps even low-level nursing duties.

The combot can do all of these things, and more, right now. Can it go beyond rote instructions and devise new solutions to problems and tasks? With the introduction of parallel processing and other innovations, the answer seems to be "yes." The fact is that we are on the edge of these developments and do not know their limit.

Can the combot also reproduce itself? Again, the answer appears to be "yes." As early as 1964, in *God and Golem, Inc.*, Norbert Wiener wrote that it is "natural to assume that machines cannot make other machines in their own image; that this is something associated with a sharp dichotomy of systems into living and nonliving; and that it is moreover associated with the other dichotomy between creator and creature." He then gave his opinion that "machines are very well able to make other machines in their own image." Indeed, Wiener goes so far as to believe that they can do so with variations, with the machine itself acting as an "archetype, even as to its own departures from its own archetypal pattern."[17] More recent developments support this general prognosis.

We are, in short, on the verge of a new field: machine genetics. One of the most imaginative and informed students of artificial intelligence, Joseph Weizenbaum, who has pioneered in recognizing the dangers of the technological hyperbole, does grant that the modern computer "can form a model of itself which could, in some sense, be considered a kind of self-consciousness. When I say therefore that I am willing to regard such a robot as an 'organism,' I declare my willingness to consider it a kind of animal."[18]

There seem to be no bounds, in principle, to the expansion of intelligence in such machines. They seem prepared to take off from the limits reached by the human brain. I have already noted that the human is the "brainiest" animal around, as a result of human evolutionary development. Increased brain size, as Stephen Jay Gould points out, "added enough neural connections to convert an inflexible and rather rigidly programmed device into a labile organ, endowed with sufficient logic and memory to substitute non-programmed learning for direct specification as the ground for social behavior." "Flexibility," he concludes, "may well be the most important determinant of human consciousness; the direct programming of behavior has probably become inadaptive."[19]

Reaching the limits of actual usage of neural connections (for there is greater potential than ever utilized) in the brain, humans have stored their increasing knowledge in the form of culture. One part of culture has been the development of machines, and now combots. Combots can, in principle, be endowed with more "neural connections" than humans—we simply do not know the limit to this development—and, as I have been arguing, can be made to enjoy *flexibility* and *creativity*, in the sense of producing both new solutions and new versions of themselves (itselves?).

Some very brilliant scientists, such as Herbert Simon and Alan Newell, seem to be saying that the combot can imitate anything humans can do, and more. Thinkers such as Simon and Newell appear to base their faith in this accomplishment on the reduction of humans to a programmed animal-machine—and we have seen the tradition in Descartes and Pavlov and others on which they can build—whose mentality can be mimicked by an "artificial intelligence." At this point fantasy can take hold, as in the Chinese automaton of two thousand years ago or in Asimov's humanlike robots, with combots in human "drag" indistinguishable from humans (although, in fact, more powerful). In the claims of Simon and Newell, pioneers in the new world of computers, we may ask whether fantasy is fusing with hard-headed, calculable reality?

Let us seek to render unto combots what is theirs. The future stretches before them, and us, and we must peer into it, even though through a monitor darkly. Even now, we speak of "generations" of computers (and combots to come). We have conceded that combots can be made to devise new solutions to problems and can thus think "generally." They can be made to replicate themselves and even to do so with variations, thus, in principle, entering on a continuing development of themselves. In this process, we may even see "monstrous" combots, in the sense of machine "genetics" going haywire and producing "abnormal" creatures (that is, contrary to the intentions of their original human progenitors).

I am prepared to concede, further, that computers will someday—and I have in mind decades and even centuries—be endowed with "emotions," and thus potentially with "motives." As combots, they have motion and thus will be able to act on their intentions. Beyond this, I cannot even speculate (one must turn at this point to science-fiction writers). All one can say is that reality has been catching up with fantasy time after time, and that given enough time, the evolution of combots simply cannot be predicted. The limiting factor may actually be humans, if in a Butlerian mood they decide to pull the plug à la Hal in the movie *2001*—and do it in time.

I will allow myself, however, one additional speculation. It involves extraterrestrial life. In his book *Wonderful Life*, Stephen Jay Gould argues for the sheer chance and contigency of evolution. The emergence of humans, as they are, was a most unlikely event. Indeed, according to Gould, if the *Pikaia*, the world's first known chordate (that is, with a notochord or stiffened rod along the back that evolved into our spinal column), had not survived—a matter of chance—"we are wiped out of future history—all of us, from shark to robin to orangutan."[20] If this is the story on earth, what, then, are the possibilities of some form of life evolving in outer space?

In reviewing Gould's book, the distinguished biologist Richard Lewontin said that "if life exists elsewhere in the universe it will not look anything like life on earth, for its evolution will have been another of the many potential realizations of history."[21] If such life does exist, a highly uncertain and contingent assumption, would it also create machines? And if so, what would those machines look like? Presumably, they would no more resemble our machines than extraterrestrial life our human beings. Or would certain universal principles of physics dictate the construction of their machines, too? These are "spacey" thoughts. More mundanely, we know only the machines, and now the combots, that we have created on earth.

Having tried to give the combots their present due, I want now to argue that, whatever their nature, and possible future evolutionary nature, they are not and will not be humans. This follows directly from what was said in the previous chapter about the uniqueness of humans. It is not a matter of one or two or even many qualities—such as rationality or emotions—but of the unique, experiential, and evolving combination of these qualities that constitutes human nature.

Let us imagine a typical academic conference, with its predictable exchanges. The participants, of course, are humans. Now, let me suggest a thought experiment: a conference in which the moderator, for example, recognizes the "computer in the back row"—for the conferees are all combots. For this to approach the human situation, we must further imagine the following: that the "debate" has mass-effects, for example, contagion-effects; that there be imitation; and that personalities, ideologies, and interests, for example, intrude into the "rational" exchange of thoughts.

In fact, the situation is unimaginable, so to speak; it is a fantasy. As Freud knew, and novelists before him, humans are more irrational than rational; thus Freudian "talk" is not just language. It involves free association, empathy, transference, sexual memories, and a host of other such attachments. Such "talk" is not just reserved for the therapeutic hour; it spills out and around our conferences as well. The effort to build all of this into combots seems to border on the bad dreams of mad scientists (incidentally, if machines do not sleep it is difficult to see how they would dream).

It is a constrained imagination that insists that combots could exchange ideas only by imitating human beings in conferences. There may well be utterly different ways of combots creatively communicating with one another; and these should not be ruled out. All that I am saying is that combots will be combots, and humans, humans. To turn one into another, or vice versa, seems a sterile exercise. Combots can have little or no equivalent to human "historical" experience, personal or as a species, no socialization in a nuclear family, no political, social, and economic interaction in a society, and so on.

Even if, to grant an argument, one could achieve all of the above, building my qualifications into combots, why would one want to do it? Making machines, that is, combots, like humans simply runs against one of our own major reasons for making such machines: our desire for perfection. If the machine is perfect, it is not human. And if it is not perfect, then, in this mode of thinking, we do not want it. Imperfect, it will also err, and in the erring evolve in a different direction from existing humans. Being more "brainy" than humans, the combots become, in effect, a different species. In sum, Man's age-old fantasy of merging with his creation, the machine, is itself a part of his uniqueness—and the fantasy is not about to be realized.

We are now at the end; though it is an end that posits a new "evolutionary" development: the combot of unknown dimensions. In the past, humans have struggled intensely with the question of their being: animal or angelic, human or machine? They have posed the problem for themselves in zoos and circuses, automata and robots, exploded drawings and simulated models. In more scientific form, they have named the animals, established classifications, dissected bodies, speculated about animal-machines, dug up fossils, conceived evolutionary theories, opened pouches into dogs and behaviorally manipulated them and then themselves, and, in a different direction, descended into the innermost reaches of their own psyche. They have also entered upon an Industrial Revolution, creating a civilization of machines, and now more recently, moved toward a biogenetic and a computer-brain revolution as well.

What meaning does all this have? I have spoken of the human as a prosthetic god; and he or she will continue to be that. Humans will, indeed, also become more mechanical, both in body and in mind. In body, they are increasingly hooked up to mechanical parts—the macabre end point manifesting itself in life-support systems from which they need a "right to die" in order to free themselves from such unwanted, purely mechanical "life." In mind, Carlylean mechanization is now supplemented by metaphors of programming and artificial intelligence; and since humans think and feel in terms of metaphors, they approximate more closely in this regard to the mechanical-cum-computer. All in all, then, something like a new species will eventually emerge—*Homo comboticus*—that will compete with and very likely replace (or convert) most of the human types that have existed before about 1970; that is, precomputer Man.

Having said this, I want to argue further that even this evolved human form, *Homo comboticus, as I have defined him with an emphasis on the metaphorical life,* will still be human, subject to the constraints of the human condition. He will still be an uncertain and erring creature, forced to make choices whose results are unknown and often unintentional. In his historical world (that is, a real existence in physical and social time and not in a laboratory or mere built environment) he will be subject to all the irrationalities, enthusiasms, and swirling economic and social movements that have characterized his past. Death will still remain the individual's fate, with all its attendant fears.

Choice is part of the human condition. Humans may opt to try to become more and more mechanical, emphasizing the *comboticus* side of their beings. Or they may try to diminish and eliminate that tendency, doing away with further mechanical development. Or they may decide to rejoice in their present, precarious human condition. (Or some of all three possibilities.) If they emphasize the last option, they must face the paradox that part of being human is to seek to escape one's humanity by the creation of machines, which then reshape their creator. (In this sense, the last choice embraces all three options.) In short, it will take enormous courage to rejoice in being "human," when being "human" means being in a continuing state of change. Change and choice, it seems, go together.

What of the Butlerian option that machines will develop into a new species? I think that option is also open and realizable. Humans have consciously created a new "creature"—the first such mechanical creation that we know of on the earth. It emerges as part of Man's own evolutionary nature. How far this new creature will be allowed to "evolve" in its turn is an open question, initially to be decided by humans themselves.

In order to think more precisely and firmly about this question, we must finally, *and now in the context of all that has been said before,* address the definitional problem frontally: what does it really mean to talk of the machine's "evolutionary" nature?

Our starting point must be the use of the term *evolution* in biology itself. As Robert Richards says, the term "is pregnant with its history."[22] It originally referred in the seventeenth century to Swammerdam's theory of the preformation of the adult within the embryo. Evolution, therefore, meant the unrolling or unfolding of what was already in the embryo. A synonym might be *development:* the oak tree develops from the acorn.

Gradually, in the eighteenth century, the thesis emerged that the embryo recapitulated the forms of lower species; and this notion, in turn, became attached to that of species alteration. Supporters of this view "came to believe that the embryo traversed the forms that species went through in their gradual evolutionary transformation."

Thus, the words *evolution, development, transformation,* and *transmutation* tended to be used almost indiscriminately for change in both the embryo and the species. Darwin, as we have noted, did not use the term *evolution* itself in the *Origin of Species* (only once speaking there of "evolved"); yet, after Darwin, the term came to mean what Darwin was talking about in his theory of natural selection in regard to species.

On one side, the early usage became caught up in the debate, waxing vigorously in the nineteenth and twentieth centuries, over the issue of ontogony recapitulating phylogeny.[23]

On another side, which was mainly a detour, it filtered out in a discussion over the existence of archetypes, or in Goethe's language, an *Urbild,* in which, for example, all parts of a plant are modifications of a single structure, the leaf. In this view, "All parts of a plant are 'transformations' of the leaf in the same sense that a circle is a 'transformed' ellipse."[24] (I cannot help thinking of Hegel's use of this idea and his famous example of the dialectical development in which the bud disappears when the blossom breaks through, and the blossom when the fruit appears, all as "moments of an organic unity" necessarily unfolding from the beginning.)[25]

This "idealist" view is no longer taken seriously, and certainly not in regard to evolutionary theory. Still, it reminds us how amorphous are the words *evolution* and *development.* What further complicates our usage is the loose fashion in which the term *evolution* is used: we talk of thoughts evolving, of a tennis player's game evolving, and so forth.

Words mean what I say they mean, announced Humpty-Dumpty, and he is approximately right. Words themselves "evolve," as my initial quotation from Richards suggest. Nevertheless, we should be as precise as we can in these matters; and our use of the term in regard to machines is no exception.

What suggestions can we get from comparable uses, that is, those more serious than tennis players? On one side, we have statements by accomplished scholars that "modern science has evolved and continues to evolve."[26] Here, then, in regard to the very science that gave birth to Darwin's evolutionary theory we have the assertion that ideas, too, can usefully be seen as "evolving."

The key word turns out to be *selection*. This is the argument that David Hull pursues at great length in his chapter "Science as a Selection Process."[27] As he acknowledges, Thomas Kuhn had already indicated the outlines of a supporting argument. In Kuhn's words, "The analogy that relates the evolution of organisms to the evolution of scientific ideas can easily be pushed too far. But with respect to the issues of this closing section it is very nearly perfect. The process described . . . is the selection by conflict within the scientific community of the fittest way to practice future science."[28]

Similar terminology has been used in regard to technology. Thus, Thomas Basalla argues in his book *The Evolution of Technology* that new inventions undergo replication, selection, and extinction, just like species. Joel Mokyr, in *The Lever of Riches*, also claims that the evolution of technology is to be compared to the evolution of biological species, with successful new forms being measured by cost-effectiveness, a form of competitive selection.[29] In an earlier note, I alluded to Richard Nelson's "Evolutionary Modeling and Understanding Technological Change."

Such usages of the term *evolution* by distinguished scholars in science and technology give some coloration to my use of the word in regard to machines, and especially the combot. Nevertheless, caution is advisable. The shift from the biological discussion of evolution by means of an ecologically contextualized process of natural selection to the more general discussion of the evolution of cultures, their science and technology, must remain problematic.

Thus in the case of the fourth discontinuity, I wish to emphasize that my use of the term *evolutionary* in regard to combots is at this stage metaphorical. The process of *selection*, how it works and how it might work, is not yet spelled out sufficiently. Domestic breeding is not really *evolutionary*, in the Darwinian sense, and, so far, that is the leading analogy to the selection process in regard to machines.

One of my main points in this book, however, is to indicate the openness of future *development* (and I am using the word in the non-idealist, undetermined sense). The combot, I would argue, may be "pregnant" with a possible new or extended sense of the term *evolution*. Meanwhile, I speak guardedly of the *evolution* of this "new creature," stressing the extended metaphorical meaning. I should add that 100, 500, 1,000, or 10,000 years are, in the eye of time, a mere wink; and that it is in terms of such extended time (assuming humans do not destroy themselves in the meanwhile) that I am speaking of possible *evolution*.

However the combot develops, I do not believe that it will replace humans. Like other species, it will become one that coexists alongside them, in symbiotic relation. It may, in fact, have certain competitive advantages in a changed environment. Combots will not need oxygen; they can flourish even in polluted surroundings. With solar-powered batteries, they would be able to derive their "food," that is, fuel, directly from the sun; in this sense, they will be more like plants than animals. Thus, if numbers are indicators of success, they would have the advantage of being able to exist in far greater numbers than any plant- or animal-eating creature that is higher on the food chain. And so forth.

As for humans, they are a species interbreeding with themselves. They cannot, except in fantasy, produce human-machine hybrids, unless in the form of what I have called symbiosis, or mechanical conjoining—*Homo comboticus*. On the other hand, whatever the development of, say, the combot, it can be stated categorically that though perhaps able to create other, varied combots, machines will not create humans.

Humans, then, *are* unique *so far* in the sense of *consciously* creating other, different "beings"—biogenetically, and especially mechanically—at the same time as these same creative powers play a most powerful role, in the form of culture, in creating their own evolving human nature.

Earlier, I cited Darwin and his claim, building on the existence of physical laws that are continuous throughout the entire universe, that there was grandeur in the view that "from so simple a beginning endless forms most beautiful and most wonderful have been, and are being evolved." Human pride may have been humbled by the recognition, as a result of evolutionary theory, that there was no longer any discontinuity, any sharp break, between ourselves and the other animals, and by the deepening awareness of our psychological nature. Yet, further reflection allows humans to share in the grandeur of evolution itself.

I should like to make the same argument for the ending of the fourth discontinuity.[30] Our pride, shaken anew by the deepening awareness after Freud of our psychological nature, may be humbled even further by the recognition that we are on a continuum with the machines we have created, though the continuum is of a different kind from that which connects us with the other animals. The continuity of which I am speaking lies in the recognition that human biological evolution, now best understood in cultural terms, forces upon humankind—us— the consciousness that tools and machines are inseparable from evolving human nature. It also requires us to realize that the development of machines, culminating in the computer, makes inescapable the awareness that the same theories that are useful in explaining the workings of mechanical contrivances are also useful in understanding the human animal—and vice versa, for the understanding of the human brain sheds light on the nature of artificial intelligence.[31] In this view we can now discern another kind of grandeur, surrounded as it is with attendant danger—this time mainly of our own making.

### Chapter One: Introduction

1. *The Standard Edition of the Complete Works of Sigmund Freud*, trans. from the German under the General Editorship of James Strachey (London: Hogarth Press, 1953–1974), vol. 16, 284–285.

2. Ibid., vol. 17, 139–141.

3. When challenged by his friend Karl Abraham, the founder of psychoanalysis admitted pridefully, "You are right in saying that the enumeration of my last paper may give the impression of claiming a place beside Copernicus and Darwin." (Quoted in Ernest Jones, *The Life and Work of Sigmund Freud*, 3 vols. [New York: Basic Books, 1953–1957], vol. 2, 224–226.) There is some reason to believe that Freud may have derived his conviction from Ernst Haeckel, the German exponent of Darwinism, who in his book *Natürliche Schöpfungsgeschichte* (1889) compared Darwin's achievement with that of Copernicus and concluded that together they had helped remove the last traces of anthropomorphism from science. Whatever the origin of Freud's vision of himself as the last in the line of ego shatterers, his assertion has generally been accepted by those like Ernest Jones, who refers to him as the "Darwin of the Mind" (Jones, vol. 3, 304). Jones's view of Freud's relation to Darwin should be compared with that of Frank J. Sulloway, *Freud, Biologist of the Mind* (New York: Basic Books, 1979). For the allusion to Haeckel, see Ernst Cassirer, *The Problem of Knowledge: Philosophy, Science and History Since Hegel*, trans. William H. Woglom and Charles W. Hendel (New Haven: Yale University Press, 1950), 160.

4. For Bruner's views, see his "Freud and the Image of Man," *Partisan Review* 23, no. 3 (Summer 1956), 340–347. I would suggest Galileo in place of both Bruner's sixth-century B.C. Greek physicists and Freud's Copernicus as the breaker of the discontinuity that was thought to exist in the material world. It was Galileo, after all, who first demonstrated that the heavenly bodies are of the same substance as the "imperfect" earth and subject to the same mechanical laws. In his *Dialogue on the Two Principal World Systems* (1632), he not only supported the "world system" of Copernicus against Ptolemy but also established that our "world," that is, the earth, is a natural part of the other "world," that is, the solar system. Hence, the universe at large is one "continuous" system, a view at best only implied in Copernicus. Whatever the correct attribution—Greek physicists, Copernicus, or Galileo—Freud's point is not in principle affected.

5. I should add that I also recognize that there is a "gender and science" debate within the history of science; my hope is that another scholar will approach the fourth discontinuity more fully from that standpoint.

6. Sherwood L. Washburn, "Tools and Human Evolution," *Scientific American* 203, no. 3 (September 1960), 63–75. This is still a classic statement of the position, though new evidence suggests modifications of some of the details.

7. For Darwin's comments on the role of tools, see Charles Darwin, *The Descent of Man* (New York: Modern Library, n.d.), 431–432, 458.

8. Karl Marx, *Capital*, trans. Eden and Cedar Paul, 2 vols. (London: J.M. Dent & Sons, 1951), vol. 1, 172. Compare 341, footnote 3.
9. For a discussion of these matters before the discounting of the dedication theory, see Ralph Colp, Jr., "The Contacts Between Karl Marx and Charles Darwin," *The Journal of the History of Ideas* 35, no. 1 (January–March 1974). Subsequently, Lewis Feuer, Margaret Fay, and Ralph Colp, Jr., have all published articles showing that Darwin's letter supposedly directed to Marx was actually written to Edward Aveling. See, for example, Ralph Colp, Jr., "The Myth of the Darwin-Marx Letter," *History of Political Economy* 14, no. 4 (1982). The overall relations of Marx and Darwin, however, are little affected by this scholarly disagreement.
10. Marx, *Capital*, vol. 1, 392–393, n. 2.
11. In semifacetious fashion, I have argued with some of my more literal-minded friends that what most distinguishes humans from existing machines, and probably will always so distinguish them, is an *effective* Oedipus complex. I will try to spell out this topic more seriously in chapter 10. For an excellent and informed philosophical treatment of the difference between humans and machines (*sans* Oedipus complex), see J. Bronowski, *The Identity of Man* (Garden City, N.Y.: The Natural History Press, 1965).
12. As in so much else, children "know" what their parents have forgotten. As O. Mannoni tells us, in the course of explaining totemism, "Children, instead of treating animals as machines, treat machines as living things, the more highly prized because they are easier to appropriate. Children's appropriation is a virtual identification and they play at being machines (steam-engines, motor cars, aeroplanes) just as 'primitive' people play at being the totem [animal]." (*Prospero and Caliban: The Psychology of Colonization*, trans. Pamela Powesland [New York: Praeger, 1964], p. 82.) Sherry Turkel, in *The Second Self* (New York: Simon & Schuster, 1984), updates Mannoni, studying children's appropriation of the computer.
13. A certain amount of caution is needed on this topic, as Jared Diamond reminds us when he points out that "we often consider the evolution of the human body to have ended by Cro-Magnon times, 35,000 years ago, but genetic anti-malarials have been continuing to evolve in the last few centuries." ("Blood, Genes, and Malaria," *Natural History* [February 1989], 8).
14. The earliest version of what I am setting forth in this book is my article "The Fourth Discontinuity," *Technology and Culture* 8, no. 1 (Winter 1967). That article itself has been anthologized a number of times. It has also apparently spurred on a few other papers as well as inspiring a critique, suggesting that the topic is of interest and worth being pursued further. The papers are Laurence H. Tribe, "Technology Assessment and the Fourth Discontinuity: The Limits of Instrumental Rationality," *Southern California Law Review* 46, no. 3 (June 1973), and Gerald Holton, "Science, Technology, and the Fourth Discontinuity," Keynote address for the conference "Psychology and Society: Information Technology in the 1980s," Houston Symposium III, Department of Psychology, University of Houston. The critique is by Arndt Sorge and Michael Fores, "The Fifth Discontinuity," Discussion Paper Series, International Institute of Management, Wissenschatszentrum Berlin, IIM/dp 79–84, August 1979. Another, perhaps more weighty, indication that the topic is of continuing importance is the conference on "Humans, Animals, Machines: Boundaries and Projections," Stanford University, April 23–25, 1987 (where I presented a draft of the section on Babbage in this book).

15. Francis Bacon, *Advancement of Learning* and *Novum Organum* (New York: Colonial Press, 1900), 46–47. Bacon here seems to anticipate Marx (see note 10, above).
16. I have tried to wrestle with some of the ideas and issues raised by postmodernist modes of thought in other works: "The Flaneur: From Spectator to Representation," in *The Flaneur*, ed. Keith Tester (London: Routledge, forthcoming), and "The Deculturization of Culture" (forthcoming).
17. See, for example, Foucault's comments on the "Man-the-Machine" question in *Discipline & Punish: The Birth of the Prison*, trans. Alan Sheridan (New York: Vintage Books, 1979), 136, and, of course, *The Order of Things: An Archaeology of the Human Sciences* (New York: Vintage Books, 1973). For Foucault's indebtedness to Bachelard and Canguilhem, see the illuminating treatment in Gary Gutting, *Michel Foucault's Archaeology of Scientific Reason* (Cambridge: Cambridge University Press, 1989). A related figure of great worth and interest is Georges Gusdorf; for an excellent account see Donald R. Kelley, "Gusdorfiad," *History of the Human Sciences* 3, no. 1 (February 1990).
18. The kind of evidence that supports this statement can be found, for example, in the penetration of modern science fiction, as well as science and technology, into non-Western societies. Thus, in his work on Chinese science fiction, Rudolf G. Wagner points out that "all writers trace Chinese phantasy fiction back to Lu Xun. The preface to his 1903 translation of Verne's *From the Earth to the Moon* is the *locus classicus* for the official definition of the potential of science fiction" (36). Wagner shows how science fiction was used to popularize science itself and then explores the particular Chinese features of the genre, such as its identification of evil science with imperialist powers, and so forth. ("Lobby Literature: The Archaeology and Present Functions of Science Fiction in China," chapter 1 in *After Mao: Chinese Literature and Society 1978–1981*, ed. Jeffrey C. Kinkley, Harvard Contemporary China Series 1, Cambridge, 1985.) I owe my knowledge of this piece to my friend Karen Gottschang and its being made available to me to the author himself. Research into other non-Western use of science fiction and of attitudes to science and technology is clearly needed.

### Chapter Two: The Animal-Machine

1. See, however, work by such historians of science as Frances Yates, Betty Jo Teeter Dobbs, and G.E.R. Lloyd.
2. "Leonardo da Vinci," IBM Booklet (n.p., n.d.). Compare *Leonardo da Vinci: Engineer and Architect*, ed. Paolo Galluzzi, illustrated (Boston: The Montreal Museum of Fine Arts/Northeastern University Press, 1988).
3. IBM Booklet, "Leonardo da Vinci," Illus. #20.
4. The counterparts in recent times have been the holograph and laser pictures.
5. My main guide here is Samuel Y. Edgerton, Jr., "Man and Machine: The Development of Scientific Illustration," MIT Exhibit, January 3–24, 1979. This is the accompanying text to the exhibit (from which the quotations in the rest of this section are taken). I have also found extremely useful on this matter (as well as on much else relating to the fourth discontinuity), Thomas S. Hall, *Ideas of Life and Matter* (Chicago: University of Chicago Press, 1970), vol. 1, especially pp. 218–229.
6. George Boas, *The Happy Beast*, in *French Thought of the Seventeenth Century* (Baltimore: Johns Hopkins University Press, 1933).

7. *The Autobiography of Michel de Montaigne* (Boston: Houghton Mifflin, 1935), 118. (I wish here to acknowledge the research assistance of my Undergraduate Research Opportunities Program [UROP] students, Yildiz Dalkir, Mike Goodwin, and Anvradha Vedantham, on this and other related topics.)

8. Michel de Montaigne, *Les Essais* (Paris: Livre de poche, 1965), 466.

9. The first quotation I use here is a paraphrase given by Boas, *Happy Beast*, 82. The second is from Lenora Cohen Rosenfield, *From Beast-Machine to Man-Machine* (New York: Oxford University Press, 1941), 19.

10. For an excellent treatment of Aristotle's views, see Martha Nussbaum, *The Fragility of Goodness* (Cambridge: Cambridge University Press, 1986), chapter 9. For Descartes's own allusions, see, for example, his *Discourse on Method*, trans. Laurence J. Lafleur (New York: The Liberal Arts Press, 1950), 29–30. If I were trying to cover the entire subject of this book in a consecutive manner, I would certainly need an extended section on Aristotle.

11. Rosenfield, *From Beast-Machine*, xxiv–xxv. The next quotation is from p. xx. An interesting coupling is made of Descartes's views on the animal-machine and early-nineteenth-century industrialization by Karl Marx. Discussing the role of machines in the creation of surplus value, as they replace human labor, Marx remarks that "Descartes, who defined animals as mere machines, was contemplating them from the outlook of the manufacturing period as contrasted with the outlook of the Middle Ages, when animals were regarded as man's helpers. . . . Descartes, like Francis Bacon, looked forward to an alteration in the form of production, and to the effective control of nature by man, *as a result of a change in the ways of thinking*" (italics mine). (*Capital*, trans. Eden and Cedar Paul, 2 vols. [London: J.M. Dent & Sons, 1951], 413–414.)

12. René Descartes, *Discourse on Method*, trans. Lawrence J. Lafleur (New York: Liberal Arts Press, 1950), 18. The next quotation is from p. 21. Later, however, Descartes seems to contradict himself, as when he writes, "For the mind is so dependent upon the humors and the condition of the organs of the body that if it is possible to find some way to make men wiser and more clever than they have been so far, I believe that it is medicine that will find it" (40). Here the Freudian demon seems to be making its appearance.

13. René Descartes, *Meditations on First Philosophy* (1641), trans. Laurence J. Lafleur (Indianapolis: Bobbs-Merrill, 1960), 13. The next quotation is from *Discourse*, 22.

14. Descartes, *Meditations*, 59.

15. Descartes's dream sequence has puzzled many scholars. Some have dismissed the dreams as inconsequential; others have given various fragmentary or unpersuasive interpretations. Freud himself, aside from a few rather random remarks, declined to give an interpretation, citing that the dreamer was dead and could not free-associate to the dream elements (a fact, however, that had not stopped Freud from seeking to analyze a recurring dream of Leonardo da Vinci's). Finally, a scholar who is versed in both Cartesian studies and Freudian dream interpretation has given what I consider to be a sound reading of the dreams, by situating them in the context of Descartes's personal life and the history of his times. See John Cole, *The Olympian Dreams and the Youthful Rebellion of René Descartes* (Urbana: University of Illinois Press, 1992). The reader should be warned, however, that the book is necessarily heavy going.

16. Descartes, *Discourse*, 35.

17. For details, see Rosenfield, *From Beast-Machine*, 4.

18. Descartes, *Discourse*, 38.
19. Rosenfield, *From Beast-Machine*, 137.
20. Descartes, *Discourse*, 29–30.
21. Ibid., 35–36.
22. Ibid., 36–37.
23. Ibid., 38.
24. In his important book *Diderot and Descartes: A Study of Scientific Naturalism in the Enlightenment* (Princeton, N.J.: Princeton University Press, 1953), Aram Vartanian supports the view that metaphysical dualism was itself the "first great step toward naturalism, paradoxical as this might seem" (10).
25. Quotations are from Rosenfield, *From Beast-Machine*, 8, 70. (All translations, including what follow, are mine.) For Descartes's qualification of his position, see Vartanian, *Diderot and Descartes*, 211.
26. Quoted in Boas, *The Happy Beast*, 141, 142.
27. Quoted in Rosenfield, *From Beast-Machine*, 156.
28. Ibid., 112.
29. See ibid., 143.
30. Julien Offray de La Mettrie, *Man A Machine*, based on a trans. by Gertrude Carmen Bussey (La Salle, Il.: Open Court Press, 1961). Because of its availability, when possible I will use this translation. The scholarly edition to be used is *La Mettrie's L'Homme machine: A Study in the Origins of an Idea*, critical ed. with an introd. monograph and notes by Aram Vartanian (Princeton, N.J.: Princeton University Press, 1960). As Vartanian points out, La Mettrie's espousal of sexual libertinism had a scientific purpose as well: La Mettrie's aim was "to break down the common system of barriers that had been created by the same religious authorities against both intellectual and sexual curiosity" (33).
31. La Mettrie, *Man A Machine*, 135, 88. La Mettrie's inspiration here, as in so many other places, is Boerhaave, who spoke of "une science médicales certaines, non plus réduite aux hypothèses." Cf. Vartanian's edition, 77. For a further discussion of what La Mettrie means by *machine*, as well as situating *L'Homme machine* in the corpus of his work, see Ann Thompson, *Materialism and Society in the Mid-Eighteenth Century: La Mettrie's Discours préliminaire* (Geneva: Librairie Droz, 1981), especially 40 ff.
32. La Mettrie, *Man A Machine*, 90, 93. The images of the paralytic and the soldier will recur in T. H. Huxley; see chapter 7 of this book.
33. Ibid., 114–115.
34. Although La Mettrie himself was somewhat inconsistent and his thought complicated, his reputation was that of a simple materialist. See, for example, the statement by Ann Thompson, discussing his *Discours préliminaire:* " 'Psychological' problems are thus those which interest him most, and which he tries to resolve in material terms. It is thus paradoxical that his reputation has been that of a crude mechanist who reduced man to an automaton and who sought to deny his 'spiritual' dimension" (*Materialism and Society*, 56).
35. Ibid., 103, 145. La Mettrie also published a work, *L'Homme plante* (1748), facetiously comparing man to a plant and attempting to show similarities between different parts of his anatomy and the parts of a plant. La Mettrie's ellision of the difference between plant and animal is not so farfetched as it might seem. See, for example, Stephen Jay Gould, *Ever Since Darwin* (New York: W. W. Norton, 1977), chapter 13, "The Pentagon of Life," and such comments as "Enter plants or animals. Our basic conception of life's diversity is based upon this

division. Yet it represents little more than a prejudice spawned by our status as large, terrestrial animals" (113).

36. La Mettrie, *Man A Machine*, 140–141. See chapter 3 of this book for a discussion of the work of Vaucanson and others like him.

37. Ibid., 98. There is another nice satirical touch in La Mettrie's dedication of *L'Homme machine* to the pious Albrecht von Haller.

38. In fact, La Mettrie was more sophisticated—and inconsistent—than I portray him in this sentence. He was aware of the need to vitalize the Cartesian "dead mechanism" approach to biology and thus introduced the notion of irritability into his conception of the living machine. Compare Vartanian's edition, 19 and 89.

39. Writers such as Rousseau—"I see nothing in any animal but an ingenious machine"; Diderot, who in his dialogue "D'Alembert's Dream" spends page after page arguing the validity of such assertions as that "if anyone wants to describe . . . the steps in the production of a man or animal, he will need to make use of nothing but physical agencies"; and Laurence Sterne, who takes up the question mockingly in his *A Sentimental Journey*—carry on the discussion. Among scientists, to name just a few, Cabanis, leader of the early nineteenth-century *Idéologues*, propelled La Mettrie's thesis into the mainstream of modern science, while as late as the 1870s, DuBois-Reymond was orating on La Mettrie's views before the Prussian Academy of Sciences.

### Chapter Three: Automata

1. See Joseph Needham, *Science and Civilization in China* (with the collaboration of Wang Ling), vol. 4, part 2 (Cambridge: Cambridge University Press, 1965), 54. This book is a mine of information on the subject of automata, as well as on its more general subject. Further on automata, compare Alfred Chapuis and Edouard Gélis, *Le Monde des automates* (Paris: A. Chapuis, 1928).

2. Needham, *Science and Civilization in China*, vol. 2, 53. Comparison with statements by La Mettrie spring quickly to mind.

3. Quoted in Julian Jaynes, *The Origin of Consciousness in the Breakdown of the Bicameral Mind* (Boston: Houghton Mifflin, 1976), 336.

4. For one such attempt, though a brief one, see John Cohen, *Human Robots in Myth and Science* (London: George Allen & Unwin, 1966).

5. Needham, *Science and Civilization in China*, 165.

6. Quoted in ibid., 164.

7. Frances A. Yates, "The Hermetic Tradition in Renaissance Science," in *Art, Science, and History in the Renaissance*, ed. Charles S. Singleton (Baltimore: The Johns Hopkins University Press, 1967), 258, 255.

8. Ibid., 257.

9. Quoted in ibid., 259.

10. Radu Florescu, *In Search of Frankenstein* (Boston: New York Graphic Society, 1975), 233. This book is a marvelous work, well printed and illustrated, and, at the time I bought it, a wonderful buy. Compare the article by Michael Uhl, "Living Dolls," *Geo*, July 1985, and its quotation of one observer who delicately noted that Vaucanson's duck duplicated the process of digestion in full view of the spectators, "ending the digestion process as naturally as it began" (86). Thus, long before Pavlov, the idea of a viewable pouch in the stomach was employed, not in a dog, but in an automaton.

11. In the seventeenth century, Sir Kenelm Digby, member of the Royal Society, had already declared that birds were machines, whose motions when feeding their young or building their nests were no different from the striking of a clock or the ringing of an alarm. See Keith Thomas, *Man and the Natural World* (New York: Pantheon Books, 1983), 35.

12. *Folk-lore and Fable: Aesop. Grimm. Andersen*, in *The Harvard Classics*, ed. Charles W. Eliot (New York: P. F. Collier, 1909), 325. The next quotation is from p. 326.

13. Ibid., 328.

14. Ibid., 329.

15. There is some evidence for this origin in Needham, *Science and Civilization in China*, 157.

16. See Florescu, *In Search of Frankenstein*, 223–225, for this and other details.

17. Ibid., 41.

18. Aldini, *On Galvinism* (London, 1803), 194, quoted in Michael Kita, "Mary Shelley's *Frankenstein*: Two Contexts," unpub. ms. I owe to it inspiration for some of the above, and for what follows on *Natürphilosophie*.

19. See Floresco, *In Search of Frankenstein*, 65 ff., for his tracking down of the possible influences on Mary, who supposedly visited a Castle Frankenstein in the Rhine country, inhabited in the eighteenth century by a Konrad Dippel, an alchemist accused of strange experiments.

20. Mary Shelley, *Frankenstein* (New York: Dell, 1975), 46.

21. In fact, Mary Shelley herself, in a subsequent novel, *The Last Man* (1826), makes the connection when she writes about Man as an "automaton of flesh . . . with joints and strings in order" (quoted in William A. Walling, *Mary Shelley* [New York: Twayne Publishers, 1972], 93).

22. Shelley, *Frankenstein*, Dell, 7. The next quotation is from p. 12.

23. Ibid., 51.

24. William Godwin, *Enquiry Concerning Political Justice, and Its Influence on Morals and Happiness*, 3d ed. in 2 vols. (London, 1798), vol. 2, 528.

25. Baum's own identity is not as simple as it might at first appear. Some writers on Baum see him as a social critic and a populist; see, for example, Henry M. Littlefield, "The Wizard of Oz: Parable on Populism," *American Quarterly* 16, no. 1 (Spring 1964). For an overall treatment, see Raylyn Moore, *Wonderful Wizard Marvelous Land* (Bowling Green, Ohio: Bowling Green University Popular Press, 1974), who suggests that "for the first time in the history of the fairy tale, Baum produces monsters which are mechanical, in whole or in part" (143). For a number of critical essays on Baum, see *The Wizard of Oz by L. Frank Baum*, ed. Michael Patrick Hearn (New York: Schocken Books, 1983); also Martin Gardiner, "The Royal Historian of Oz," in his *Order and Surprise* (Buffalo, N.Y.: Prometheus Books, 1983).

26. The edition I have used is L. Frank Baum, *Ozma of Oz* (Chicago: Reilly & Lee, 1907).

27. In the *New York Times*, February 11, 1982, there is a claim that *robot* was a term coined by Karel's brother, Josef.

28. Karel Capek, *R.U.R.*, trans. Paul Selver (Garden City, N.Y.: Doubleday, 1923), 10–11.

29. In fact, neither Frankenstein nor God could have created a twelve-foot human, for it violates a known law concerning size and shape, wherein volume grows more rapidly than surface (for details, see Stephen Jay Gould, "Size and Shape,"

in *Ever Since Darwin* [New York: W. W. Norton], 1977). Domin himself has a glimpse of this fact when he adds, "For no reason at all their limbs used to keep snapping off" (16).

30. Quoted in Florescu, *In Search of Frankenstein*, 14.
31. Isaac Asimov, *I, Robot* (New York: Fawcett Crest, 1970), 16. (The title might be intended to suggest either an ironic or an egoistic identification with the author, who is frequently cited as I. Asimov.) Asimov's more recent book *The Robots of Dawn* (New York: Ballantine Books, 1983) is, unfortunately, not quite up to the standard of its predecessor, being rather repetitious and crude in its attempts at salaciousness. *I, Robot* itself, however, is a classic.
32. Ibid., 28.
33. Ibid., 53.
34. Ibid., 63. The next quotation is from p. 129.
35. Ibid., 159–160.
36. Ibid., 187.
37. Ibid., 192.
38. Sigmund Freud, "The Uncanny," in *Standard Edition*, vol. 17.
39. *New York Times Magazine*, January 10, 1982, 62.

### Chapter Four: The Industrial Revolution

1. It may be useful, however, even on this continuum to distinguish between a scientific instrument, such as a microscope or water barometer, and a machine that does work—for example, a spinning machine or pumping device. It may also be useful to remind ourselves that the meaning of the word *machine* changes over time. For example, in the seventeenth century it would conjure up the idea of some form of physical contact, the moving of an object, as by a lever or gear. By the twentieth century, it could be a computer; as a calculating "machine" it would no longer be seen as doing physical work. It is interesting also to reflect on the origins of the word *engine*. It comes from the Latin *ingenium*, meaning natural ability, genius. This is further connected to the Latin and Greek words for *engender*, thus carrying the sense of giving birth to something new (see *Webster's New Collegiate Dictionary*).
2. Among the many excellent books on the Industrial Revolution are Phyllis Deane, *The First Industrial Revolution* (Cambridge: Cambridge University Press, 1965), David S. Landes, *The Unbound Prometheus* (Cambridge: Cambridge University Press, 1969), Peter Mathias, *The Transformation of England: Essays in the Economic and Social History of England in the Eighteenth Century* (London: Methuen, 1979), E. J. Hobsbawm, *Industry and Empire* (New York: Pantheon Books, 1968), and T. S. Ashton, *The Industrial Revolution: 1760–1830* (London: Oxford University Press, 1948), which, though outdated, is still a useful short account.
3. To carry the metaphor a bit further, we can say that the production of mass clothing was subsequently matched by the production of mass culture, that is, Carlyle's other "clothing."
4. This and all the following quotations from Ure are from the excerpts from his book, *The Philosophy of Manufactures* (London: Charles Knight, 1835), in *The Development of Western Technology Since 1500*, ed. Thomas Parke Hughes (New York: Macmillan, 1964).
5. The factory as palace was a frequent trope at the time. Disraeli and many others

employed it enthusiastically. One gets a different picture reading writers such as Carlyle, Engels, and Dickens.

6. See Deane, *First Industrial Revolution*. For an analysis in depth of the interlocking nature of one part of the Industrial Revolution, in this case the railroad in nineteenth-century America, which includes the administrative, social, political, and intellectual, as well as the technological and economic aspects, see *The Railroad and the Space Program: An Exploration in Historical Analogy*, ed. Bruce Mazlish (Cambridge: MIT Press, 1965).

7. Landes, *Unbound Prometheus*, 97. The next quotation is from p. 98.

8. Lewis Mumford, *Technics and Civilization* (New York: Harcourt, Brace, 1934), 157.

9. Since the weighing of live animals was not possible until around 1814, according to my colleague Harriet Ritvo, this claim must be taken with a certain reservation.

10. Sigfried Giedion, *Mechanization Takes Command* (New York: W. W. Norton, 1969), 209–246.

11. Linnaeus offered a delightful variant on this view of marking time. He advocated that "a *Floral Clock* should be assembled for each different climate, governed by the awakening of the different plants, so that every man might know the correct time of day, even if he has no watch or the sun is hidden" (quoted in François Delaporte, *Nature's Second Kingdom: Explorations of Vegetality in the Eighteenth Century*, trans. Arthur Goldhammer [Cambridge: MIT Press, 1982], 183).

12. Sidney Pollard, *The Genesis of Modern Management: A Study of the Industrial Revolution in Great Britain* (Cambridge: Harvard University Press, 1965), is a superb and pioneering work dealing with a largely neglected aspect of the early Industrial Revolution. For the more modern period, of course, one must conjure with the name of Frederick Jackson Taylor and his "scientific management."

13. Compare E. P. Thompson, "Time, Work-Discipline, and Industrial Capitalism," *Past and Present* 38 (December 1967). For an excellent account and analysis of the development of the new managerial system in nineteenth-century America, see Alfred D. Chandler, *The Visible Hand: The Managerial Revolution in American Business* (Cambridge: Harvard University Press, 1977).

14. Karl Marx, "Economic and Philosophical Manuscripts of 1844," in *The Marx-Engels Reader*, 2nd ed., ed. Robert C. Tucker (New York: W. W. Norton, 1978), 76–77.

15. Neil McKendrick, "Josiah Wedgwood and Factory Discipline," quoted in *The Rise of Capitalism*, ed. David Landes (New York: Macmillan, 1966), 68. The quotation from Bentham that follows is in Gertrude Himmelfarb, *Victorian Minds* (New York: Alfred A. Knopf, 1968), 38.

16. Quoted in *The Rise of Capitalism*, ed. David S. Landes (New York: Macmillan, 1966), 67.

17. Giedion, *Mechanization Takes Command*, 47.

18. J. Bronowski, *William Blake and the Age of Revolution* (New York: Harper & Row, 1965), 5.

19. Derek Bok and John Dunlop, *Labor and the American Community* (New York: Simon & Schuster, 1970), 268, quoting Benjamin Aaron.

20. The quotation from Byron is given in Thomas Pynchon, *The New York Times Book Review*, October 28, 1984, 40. In another sense, of course, Byron can be said to have been right: the Lutherans were also "backward" looking, appealing to an earlier purity in Christianity.

21. Eric J. Hobsbawm and George Rudé, *Captain Swing* (New York: Pantheon Books, 1968), 17.

22. Worthington C. Ford, ed., *A Cycle of Adams Letters, 1861–1865* (Boston: Houghton Mifflin, 1920), vol. 1, 135. See *The Education of Henry Adams* (Boston: Houghton Mifflin, 1961), 342 and 380, for the passages on the dynamos.

23. Ironically, as Sigfried Giedion remarks, "The greater the degree of mechanization, the further does contact with death become banished from life" (*Mechanization Takes Command*, 242). Meat, for example, is no longer killed before our eyes or even hung as a carcass in a butcher's shop, but simply presented in a plastic wrapping.

24. Quoted in M. H. Abrams, *Natural Supernaturalism* (New York: W. W. Norton, 1971), 211. The next quotation is from Abrams, *The Mirror and the Lamp* (New York: Oxford University Press, 1953), 65.

25. See my article "Carlyle's 'Depressive' Vision of Industrialism," in the collection of essays on biography, ed. Frederick Karl (forthcoming).

26. Thomas Carlyle, "Signs of the Times," in *Carlyle: Selected Works*, ed. Julian Symons (Cambridge: Harvard University Press, 1970), 22 and 30.

27. For an extended discussion of the theme of the cash nexus and its importance, see Bruce Mazlish, *A New Science: The Breakdown of Connections and the Birth of Sociology* (New York: Oxford University Press, 1989; pbk. State College: Pennsylvania State University Press, 1993).

28. Compare note 22, however.

29. See, for example, Giedion, *Mechanization Takes Command*, 347–359.

30. Nikolaus Pevsner, *High Victorian Design* (London: Architectural Press, 1951), 73.

31. It is useful to recall the origins of the word *technology*. It was coined apparently by Johann Beckmann, who initiated lectures at Göttingen University "on agriculture, mineralogy, market research, and financial administration under the generic title of 'technology,'" and published a textbook on the subject in 1777 (W. H. G. Armytage, *The Rise of the Technocrats: A Social History* [London: Routledge and Kegan Paul, 1965], 37). The botanical roots of technology are still echoed, for example, in our linguistic usage: *plant*, for *factory* (the connection being through the plantation as a productive system). A moment's reflection suggests further the way Erasmus Darwin, Charles's grandfather, was involved in the two worlds of biology and machines.

32. See Christopher Hobhouse, *1851 and the Crystal Palace* (London: John Murray, 1950), 27.

33. *Great Exhibition of . . . 1851: Official Descriptive and Illustrated Catalogue* (London: Spicer, 1851), vol. 1, 3–4.

34. Patrick Beaver, *The Crystal Palace, 1851–1936: A Portrait of Victorian Enterprise* (London: Hugh Evelyn, 1970), 37.

35. See the fascinating treatment of Dostoevsky and Chernyshevsky in Marshall Berman, *All That Is Solid Melts into Air: The Experience of Modernity* (New York: Simon & Schuster, 1982), 235–248.

36. George W. Stocking, Jr., *Victorian Anthropology* (New York: The Free Press, 1987), 5.

37. I should add that a fuller consideration of the social effects involved—not the focus of this present work—would pay further attention to the fact that the workers frequently felt, with much justification (though the issues are complicated), that mechanization was to be opposed because it eliminated their jobs,

took away their control over the means of production, increased job-related accidents, and mainly benefited their employers. Why, they might have asked, would the embracing of the machine as one of us improve our conditions? My answer is that there is no certainty that it would. Elimination of the fourth discontinuity, I am arguing, would mark a major shift in the climate of opinion, which then in turn would allow for our decisions in regard to the machine and its uses to be made more consciously and humanely. As will be clear from chapter 10, the necessity of human choice would still be with us.

38. E. L. Doctorow, *Ragtime* (New York: Random House, 1974), 112. Another American, earlier, had also been struck, during a visit to a plant in Cincinnati, by the speed with which hogs were butchered. Frederick Law Olmsted recounted how "we took out our watches and counted thirty-five seconds, from the moment when one hog touched the table until the next occupied its place" (quoted in Verlyn Klinkenborg, "Books," *The New Yorker*, July 29, 1991, 79). The shadow of Frederick Winslow Taylor, as well as Henry Ford, already seems to hang over Olmsted's observation.

39. Thomas P. Hughes, *American Genesis: A Century of Invention and Technological Enthusiasm* (New York: Viking, 1989), a pioneering book. We can further envision the development of highly organized technological systems not only as a replacement for Ure's factory system, but also as an extension of our conceptualization of the "linkages" of the early Industrial Revolution.

40. For a more serious look at the effect of computers on workers, see Shoshana Zuboff, *In the Age of the Smart Machine: The Future of Work and Power* (New York: Basic Books, 1988).

### Chapter Five: Linnaeus and Darwin

1. One very early specific link between the biological and the mechanical is that an upright posture—a biological change—is requisite for tool development.

2. Some writers, however, have written in exactly this way. See, for example, Richard Nelson and Sidney G. Winter, *An Evolutionary Theory of Economic Change* (Cambridge: Harvard University Press/Belknap, 1982). They look, for example, at "competing" engines—diesel, gas, steam—and can be said to supply a working model for how Samuel Butler's fancied tool and machine development might take place (see section on Butler, chapter 7 in this book). For a sobering discussion of the dangers of a loose use of the term *evolution*, see Mary Midgely, "Evolution as a Religion: A Comparison of Prophecies," *Zygon* 22, no. 2 (June 1987), and "Fancies about Human Immortality," *The Month*, November 1990. As I remarked earlier, however, I reserve my own fuller discussion of this issue toward the end of this book.

3. Compare Andrew Dickson White, *The History of the Warfare of Science with Theology in Christendom* (New York: Macmillan, 1965). Like many in the Enlightenment who were anticlerical, Linnaeus nevertheless retained a strong religious sense. As one scholar puts it, "At some moments it may appear as though, with his sober intellect and his clear eyes he belonged entirely to the Age of Enlightenment; at other times he reverts to simple superstition and bizarre fancies" (*Linnaeus: The Man and His Work*, ed. Tore Frangsayr, with contributions by others [Berkeley: University of California Press, 1983], 37).

4. The first quotation is from Linnaeus, *Egenhandiga anteckningar*, 1823, quoted in the unpublished doctoral thesis of Lisbet Koerner, *Nature and Nation in*

*Linnean Travel* (Harvard University). Koerner is fluent in Swedish (I have no ability in the language) and draws on a wide range of sources; her thesis is an invaluable addition to the literature, advancing especially the notion that Linnaeus's work must be seen in a mercantilist, economic context. The second quotation is from Heinz Goerke, *Linnaeus*, trans. from German by Denver Lindley (New York: Charles Scribner's Sons, 1973; orig. 1966). This is an excellent biography, emphasizing Linnaeus's work as a physician. A standard biography is Th. M. Fries, *Linné* (1903), trans. Jackson (1923), written from a national-romantic point of view. Linnaeus's prideful statement, incidentally, is given support by the eminent philosopher of science William Whewell, who argued in his *Philosophy of the Inductive Sciences* (1840) that modern systemic science could be said to have begun with Linnaeus. It should be noted, however, that Linnaeus was hardly without predecessors; for the tradition of classification in which he operated, see Ernst Mayr, *The Growth of Biological Thought* (Cambridge: Harvard University Press, 1982), chapter 4.

5. W. Blunt (with the assistance of W. T. Stearn), *The Compleat Naturalist: A Life of Linnaeus* (London: Collins, 1971), 122.

6. Gessner's name has been given various spellings, for example, Gesner (and the first name as Konrad). For an informed treatment, stressing his work as a bibliographer as well as a natural historian, see Hans H. Wellisch, *Conrad Gessner: A Bio-Bibliography* (Zug: IDC, 1984).

7. For further details, see Carl Linnaeus, *Travels*, ed. David Black, illustrated Stephen Lee (New York: Charles Scribner's Sons, 1979), the section labeled "Linnaean Classification" by William T. Stearn. This is a very pretty book. For an authoritative brief treatment of Linnaeus's achievements, see the entry "Linnaeus" by Sten Lindroth in *Dictionary of Scientific Biography*, ed. Charles Coulston Gillispie (New York: Charles Scribner's Sons, 1973), vol. 8.

8. Quoted in Blunt, *The Compleat Naturalist*, 34. The next quotation is from p. 224.

9. Ibid., 120. The next quotation is from p. 56.

10. As another scholar puts it, "With his hot sensuousness the young Linnaeus was as though obsessed with love, the mysterious drive that kept all living things in motion" (*Linnaeus*, ed. Frangsayr, 10). Love and sex for Linnaeus, I would argue, were generally commingled.

11. Compare the interesting article by Janet Browne, "Botany for Gentlemen: Erasmus Darwin and *The Loves of the Plants*," *Isis* (1989), 80.

12. As early as 1661, the Englishman Nathaniel Homes wrote that "the plants and trees and herbs have their passions or affections; their love appearing in their sympathy as . . . in the ivy and oak, etc.; their hatred in their antipathy, as in the vine and colewort, that will not prosper if near each other; their sorrow in pining and withering; their joy in blossom and flowering" (quoted in Keith Thomas, *Man and the Natural World* [New York: Pantheon, 1983], 179). The difference between Homes and Linnaeus is that the former was using affective terms while the latter also employed the sexual analogy, subjecting it to scientific purposes, and making it the basis of his scientific classification. Janet Browne, "Botany in the Boudoir: Plant Sexuality in the Late Eighteenth Century," *Journal of the History of Biology* 22 (1989), offers an interesting tracing out of the sexual theme in Linnaeus and both Darwins. Incidentally, as Frangsayr points out, "Both of the Darwins, grandfather and grandson, devoted themselves to a study of *Politia Naturae* and closely related writings by Linnaeus" (*Linnaeus*, 18).

13. Blunt, *Compleat Naturalist*, 194.
14. See Aram Vartanian, *Diderot and Descartes: A Study of Scientific Natural-ism in the Enlightenment* (Princeton, N.J.: Princeton University Press, 1953), 283.
15. The first quotation is from *Linnaeus*, ed. Frangsayr, 170, and the second from Goerke, *Linnaeus*, 61.
16. Arthur O. Lovejoy, *The Great Chain of Being* (Cambridge, Mass.: Harvard University Press, 1953), 234. Oddly, in this great classic, this is the only mention accorded by Lovejoy to Linnaeus.
17. Quoted in Blunt, *The Compleat Naturalist*, 122. The one that follows is from *Darwin*, selected and edited by Philip Appleman, 2nd ed. (New York: W. W. Norton, 1979), 316, and the one after that again from Blunt, *Compleat Naturalist*, 154.
18. Quoted in Blunt, *The Compleat Naturalist*, 154.
19. See Charles Le Brun, *Resemblances, Amazing Faces* (New York: Quist, 1980).
20. Compare Jacob Bronowski and Bruce Mazlish, *The Western Intellectual Tradition* (New York: Harper & Row, 1960), 12.
21. David Erdman, *Blake: Prophet Against Empire* (Garden City, N.Y.: Doubleday, 1969), 103–104.
22. A useful book on this subject is Roger Cooter, *The Cultural Meaning of Popular Science: Phrenology and the Organization of Consent in Nineteenth-Century Britain* (Cambridge: Cambridge University Press, 1984). It is interesting to note the connection of phrenology to Robert Chambers's *Vestiges of the Natural History of Creation* (1844) and thus to evolutionary theory; for Chambers's *Vestiges* was a popular evolutionary work before the *Origin of Species*. For details, see the closely reasoned article by J. A. Secord, "Behind the Veil: Robert Chambers and *Vestiges*," in *History, Humanity and Evolution*, ed. James R. Moore (Cambridge: Cambridge University Press, 1989).
23. James Paradis, *T. H. Huxley: Man's Place in Nature* (Lincoln: University of Nebraska Press, 1978), 124. The next quotation from Huxley is on p. 135.
24. The literature on Darwin is, not surprisingly, enormous. And, given his impor-tance in developing the evolutionary perspective that informs this book, some extended reference to that literature seems in order. Citations are necessarily highly selective, and many others than given here could be named. However, see the magnificent edition of *The Correspondence of Charles Darwin* (Cambridge: Cambridge University Press, 1985–) with seven volumes already in print (and containing such delicious entries as Darwin's comment in a letter to his friend W. D. Fox that he has "nearly finished Clarissa Harlowe, the most glorious novel ever written" [vol. 1, 96]); Silvan S. Schweber's astute "Essay Review: The Correspondence of the Young Darwin," *Journal of the History of Biology* (Fall 1988); and Howard E. Gruber, *Darwin on Man: A Psychological Study of Scien-tific Creativity, Together with Darwin's Early and Unpublished Notebooks*, transcribed and annotated by Paul H. Barrett (New York, 1974). For Darwin's life, see *The Autobiography of Charles Darwin*, ed. Nora Barlow (London: Collins, 1958); *Life and Letters of Charles Darwin*, 3 vols., ed. Francis Darwin (London: John Murray, 1887); John Bowlby, *Charles Darwin, A Biography* (New York: W. W. Norton, 1991); Gavin De Beer, *Charles Darwin: Evolution by Natural Selec-tion* (Edinburgh: Nelson, 1963); and the popular Alan Moorehead, *Darwin and the Beagle* (Harmondsworth: Penguin, 1971). For assessments of Darwin's scien-tific work and its position in biological thought, see *The Darwinian Heritage*, ed.

David Kohn (Princeton: Princeton University Press, 1985); Ernst Mayr's magisterial *The Growth of Biological Thought: Diversity, Evolution, and Inheritance* (Cambridge: Harvard University Press, 1982), with an exhaustive bibliography; and, to select a few more almost at random, David L. Hull, *Science as a Process: An Evolutionary Account of the Social and Conceptual Development of Science* (Chicago: University of Chicago Press, 1988), especially the chapter "Up from Darwin"; Peter J. Bowler, *Evolution: The History of an Idea* (Berkeley: University of California Press, 1984); and Michael Ruse, *The Darwinian Revolution* (Chicago: University of Chicago Press, 1979).

25. Charles Darwin, *The Voyage of the Beagle* (London: Dent, 1960), 303.

26. Ibid., 219.

27. See Frank Sulloway, "Darwin and His Finches: The Evolution of a Legend," *Journal of the History of Biology* 15 (1982), for a critical look at Darwin's work in this regard.

28. In fact, Darwin himself never used the term *evolution* in the original editions of his work—the term he used was *transformation* or *descent with modification.* The closest he came was in the last line of the *Origin,* where he writes of "forms . . . being evolved." The term *evolution* (from the Latin *evolvere,* to unroll) was coined by Albrecht von Haller (Linnaeus's old friend) in 1744 to describe the theory that embryos grew from preformed homunculi enclosed in egg or sperm—quite a different meaning from Darwin's "descent with modification." I will say more about the term *evolution* in chapter 11.

29. For the effect of Malthus on Darwin, and why Darwin was prepared to read him as he did—for example, as a result of earlier having studied Adam Smith—compare Silvan S. Schweber, "The Origin of the *Origin* Revisited," *Journal of the History of Biology* 10 (1977), and Stephen Jay Gould, "Darwin's Middle Road" (chapter 5), *The Panda's Thumb* (New York: W. W. Norton, 1980).

30. Darwin, *Origin of Species* (London: Oxford University Press, 1951), 65.

31. It is interesting to compare Darwin's approach with that of Adam Smith (who had helped prepare him for his reading of Malthus). Smith, of course, talks of an "invisible hand," and before that of Providence, as ordering the competitive struggle. Both Smith and Darwin, however, were continuing the elaboration of laws of nature, replacing arbitrary (and often homocentric) acts of God with a sense of impersonal regularity.

32. Darwin, *Origin of Species,* 63.

33. Ibid., 116.

34. Ibid., 64.

35. Ibid., 75.

36. Ibid., 89.

37. Ibid., 560.

38. Ibid., 128, 545.

39. Ibid., 548, 557.

40. Ibid., 556, 546, 558.

41. Ibid., 551, 560.

42. *The Autobiography of Charles Darwin and Selected Letters,* ed. Francis Darwin (New York: Dover, 1958). The first quotation is 249, and the next, 59.

43. See the fascinating treatment of this issue by Stephen Jay Gould, "Not Necessarily a Wing," *Natural History* (October 1985), 12–25.

44. In Germany, Ernst Haeckel was a powerful exponent of Darwinismus. See Paul Weindling, "Ernst Haeckel, Darwinismus and the Secularization of Nature," in

*History, Humanity and Evolution*, ed. James R. Moore (Cambridge: Cambridge University Press, 1989).

45. In fact, the event may have been less dramatic than as recounted subsequently.
46. Quoted in Paradis, *T. H. Huxley*, 11.
47. Ibid., 120.
48. Ibid., 136. Compare Konrad Lorenz's comment, "Man as a purely rational being, divested of his animal heritage of instincts, would certainly not be an angel— quite the opposite" (*On Aggression*, trans. Marjorie Kerr Wilson [New York: Harcourt, Brace & World, 1966], 247).
49. See Mario A. di Gregorio, *T. H. Huxley's Place in Natural Science* (New Haven: Yale University Press, 1984), for a discussion of the paradox that, though Huxley was serving as a champion of Darwin, he was not comfortable with the idea of evolution by natural selection; prior to about 1868 it was actually Ernst Haeckel's work on morphology that had persuaded him to believe in evolution.
50. Appleman, *Darwin*, 315.
51. Ibid., 319, 320.
52. Darwin, *Origin of Species*, 82.
53. Paradis, *T. H. Huxley*, 150.
54. Charles Darwin, *The Origin of Species and The Descent of Man* (New York: The Modern Library, no date), 391 and 390.
55. Ibid., 414.
56. Francis Dalton, *Hereditary Genius* (London: Collins, 1962; orig. pub. 1869, with 2nd ed. 1892), forepage. The earlier quotation is from p. 23.
57. Darwin, *Descent of Man*, 412.
58. Ibid., 431, 915.
59. Ibid., 446, 458.
60. Ibid., 462.
61. Ibid., 478.
62. Ibid., 494.
63. Compare Robert J. Richards, *Darwin and the Emergence of Evolutionary Theories of Mind and Behavior* (Chicago: University of Chicago Press, 1987). In this important work, Richards has sections on William James and James Mark Baldwin, as well as a chapter on "Transformation of the Darwinian Image of Man in the Twentieth Century," but, interestingly, nothing on Freud or Pavlov.
64. Darwin, *Descent of Man*, 391.
65. In fact, Lavater and Le Brun are further connected in that Lavater edited one of Le Brun's works, the "Conférences sur l'expression des différents Charactéres des Passions."
66. Charles Darwin, *The Expression of the Emotions in Man and Animals* (Chicago: The University of Chicago Press, 1965), 364–365.
67. Incidentally, perhaps the first daguerreotype taken in England, in 1835—the daguerreotype itself was invented in France in 1834—appears to be the picture of the infant who grew up to be Sir John Lubbock, one of Darwin's followers and an early ethnographer; this mechanical extension of human powers is, of course, an important subject in its own right. Here we merely note its use as a scientific aid and add that Darwin's cousin Francis Galton also used it in the form of photo composites.
68. Darwin, *Expression of the Emotions*, 17.
69. Ibid., 28, 29.
70. Ibid., 31.

71. Ibid., 309, 315, 320.
72. Ibid., 339–340.
73. Ibid., 350.
74. For further development of this line of thought, see Frank Sulloway, *Darwin: Biologist of the Mind* (New York: Basic Books, 1979), and chapter 1, "Darwin: Bedrock of Psychoanalysis" in my book *The Leader, the Led, and the Psyche* (Hanover, N.H.: Wesleyan University Press, 1990).

### Chapter Six: Freud and Pavlov

1. See further my treatment of this assertion in my book *The Leader, the Led, and the Psyche* (Hanover, N.H.: Wesleyan University Press, 1990), chapter 1, "Darwin, the Bedrock of Psychoanalysis."
2. Sigmund Freud, "An Autobiographical Study," in *Standard Edition*, vol. 20, 8.
3. For details of Freud's university education, and much more, see William Mc-Grath, *Freud's Discovery of Psychoanalysis: The Politics of Hysteria* (Ithaca: Cornell University Press, 1986). See further Lucille B. Ritvo, "Carl Claus as Freud's Professor of the New Darwinian Biology," *International Journal of Psycho-analysis*, 53 (1972).
4. Quoted in Frank Sulloway, *Freud: Biologist of the Mind* (New York: Basic Books, 1979), 14. In fact, however, by the time Freud was studying with Brücke, it was clear that in practice the model didn't work. As Paul F. Cranefield has shown, "Freud's work under Brücke was histological in nature," not physiological (Paul F. Cranefield, "Freud and the School of Helmholtz," *Gesnerus*, 23 [1966] Heft 1/2, 37).
5. Jones, *Life and Work of Freud*, vol. 1, 38.
6. Freud, "An Autobiographical Study," 10.
7. Freud, "Project for a Scientific Psychology," in *Standard Edition*, vol. 1, 295.
8. Sigmund Freud, *The Origins of Psychoanalysis: Letters, Drafts and Notes to Wilhelm Fliess*. ed. Maria Bonaparte, Anna Freud, Ernst Kris (Garden City, N.Y.: Doubleday, 1957), 149.
9. Freud, "An Autobiographical Study," 29.
10. In fact, James Strachey, editor of the *Standard Edition*, reflects that "Freud's attempted approach seventy years ago to a description of mental phenomena in physiological terms might well seem to bear a resemblance to certain modern approaches to the same problem. It has been suggested latterly that the human nervous system may be regarded in its workings as similar to or even identical with an electronic computer. . . . It has been plausibly pointed out that in the complexities of the 'neuronal' events described here by Freud, and the principles governing them, we may see more than a hint or two at the hypotheses of information theory and cybernetics in their application to the nervous system" (Editor's Introduction, "Project for a Scientific Psychology," in *Standard Edition*, vol. 1, 292).
11. For an informed treatment of Freud's life and work, see Peter Gay, *Freud* (New York: W. W. Norton, 1988). The classic work, though outdated and highly partial, is Ernest Jones, *The Life and Works of Sigmund Freud*, 3 vols.
12. I spell the last use of *man* uncapitalized to signal that, in fact, Freud's Oedipus complex really only applies to males; a so-called Electra complex is a pale version of the original. The psychology of woman in Freud is obviously one of the weaker parts of his work. It hardly needs comment that Freud was rarely able to rise above the male-oriented perspectives of his late Victorian world.

13. Compare Freud's letter to Einstein, "Why War?" *Standard Edition*, vol. 22, 211, for his comment, "But does not every science come in the end to a kind of mythology. . . ? Cannot the same be said to-day of your own Physics?"

14. Alex Comfort, "Darwin and Freud," in *Darwin and the Naked Lady* (New York: George Braziller, 1962), 35.

15. For a more subtle and also extended treatment of the stages, see Erik Erikson, *Childhood and Society* (New York: W. W. Norton, 1963).

16. For the difference between Freud's effort at a science and, for example, Nietzsche's wonderful intuitions, see my "Freud and Nietzsche," chapter 3 in *The Leader, the Led, and the Psyche*.

17. See Freud's treatment of the case of Schweber, *Standard Edition*, vol. 12.

18. A fuller treatment of "cure" in Freudian therapy, of course, would have to take up such subjects as transference and empathy, the latter attracting more and more attention on the part of present-day analysts. I am neglecting these elements in Freudian therapy simply to establish a clear line of argument.

19. Lili E. Peller, "Biological Foundations of Psychology: Freud versus Darwin," *Bulletin of the Philadelphia Association for Psychoanalysis* 15 (1965), 90. In much of what follows in this section, I am drawing on a revised version of what appears in chapter 1, "Darwin, the Bedrock of Psychoanalysis" in *The Leader, the Led, and the Psyche*.

20. Compare Wolf Lepenies, "Transformation and Storage of Scientific Traditions in Literature," in *Literature and History*, ed. Leonard Schulze and Walter Wetzels (Lanham, Md.: University Press of America, 1983). The quotation that follows is from p. 44.

21. Sigmund Freud, "Studies on Hysteria," in *Standard Edition*, vol. 2, 160–161.

22. *Letters of Sigmund Freud*, ed. Ernst L. Freud (New York: McGraw-Hill, 1964), 59–60, 65.

23. Carl Schorske, *Fin-de-Siècle Vienna* (New York: Vintage Books, 1981), 10–11.

24. George Eliot, *Middlemarch* (1872) (New York: The New American Library, 1964), 162–163.

25. Darwin, *Origin of Species*, 559. In fact, Spencer had already published his *The Principles of Psychology* in 1855. He had high hopes for it; as he confided to his father, "In my private opinion it will ultimately stand beside Newton's *Principia.*" The book's reception was tepid, however, and this may have contributed to Spencer's subsequent breakdown in health. According to one scholar, however, "It had a profound effect on the neurological thinking of John Hughlins Jackson and through him influenced the neurology, psychology, and psycholinguistics of the twentieth century" (C.U.M. Smith, "Evolution and the Problem of Mind: Part I. Herbert Spencer," *Journal of the History of Biology* 15, no. 1 [Spring 1982], 62).

26. Cyon is a rather intriguing, and mysterious, figure as George F. Kennan shows in his article "The Curious Monsieur Cyon," *American Scholar* 55, no. 4 (1986). A skilled surgeon and dramatic lecturer, holder of Russia's most distinguished chair of physiology, he suddenly disappeared, emerging in Paris as a journalist and secret agent until his death in 1912.

27. In chapter 3, "Automata," we mentioned Vaucanson's mechanical duck, contrived in the eighteenth century, which also had a see-through stomach. In his *Invisible Man*, H. G. Wells also created a character who has to cope with the problem of having a see-through stomach (see Peter Kemp, *H. G. Wells and the Culminating Ape* [New York: St. Martin's Press, 1982], 49).

28. "General Types of Animal and Human Nervous Activity" (1935), in I. P. Pavlov, *Selected Works* (Moscow: Foreign Language Publishing House, 1955), 317.
29. "Types of Higher Nervous Activity, Their Relationship to Neuroses and Psychoses and the Physiological Mechanism of Neurotic and Psychotic Symptoms" (1935), in ibid., 482.
30. Compare ibid., 341.
31. "Physiology and Psychology in the Study of the Higher Nervous Activity of Animals" (1916), in ibid., 391.
32. See Jeffrey A. Gray, *Ivan Pavlov* (Harmondsworth, England: Penguin Books, 1979), 104.
33. See William Sargant, *Battle for the Mind* (Baltimore: Penguin Books, 1961), 114, for the way men and women imitate the barking of dogs during religious revival meetings. Why they do so, or what kind of identification is involved in this action, is not made clear by Sargant.
34. Quoted in the article on Pavlov in *Makers of Modern Thought*, with an introd. by Bruce Mazlish (New York: American Heritage Publishing Co., 1972), 386. A comparison with Descartes's attitude, in an earlier time, discussed in chapter 4, is in order here.
35. As one scholar puts it, historians of psychology "have noted how early psychologists stressed the usefulness of their discipline and emphasized their ability to engineer people's behavior into useful channels. Behaviorism, as it was initiated by John B. Watson in 1913, and neo-behaviorism, as developed by B. F. Skinner, were exemplars of this ideal. Behaviorism was explicitly designed to predict and control human behaviour" (Deborah J. Coon, "Standardizing the Subject: Experimental Psychologists, Introspection, and the Quest for a Technoscientific Ideal" [ms., 2], to appear in *Technology and Culture* [Summer 1993]). Incidentally, this same author has published an article demonstrating that an American, Edwin B. Twitmyer, "independently discovered the conditioned reflex at approximately the same time" as Pavlov, but got little credit for it because of the differences between American and Russian social and intellectual contexts ("Eponomy, Obscurity, Twitmyer, and Pavlov," *Journal of the History of the Behavioral Sciences* 18 [July 1982], 255).
36. "Experimental Psychology and Psychopathology in Animals" (1903), in Pavlov, *Selected Works*, 155.
37. B. P. Babkin, *Pavlov, A Biography* (Chicago: University of Chicago Press, 1949), 65. The next quotation is from p. 66.
38. Ibid., 86.
39. Quoted in Gray, *Ivan Pavlov*, 19.
40. "Reply of a Physiologist to Psychologists" (1932), in Pavlov, *Selected Works*, 446–447.
41. Quoted in the introduction by Kh. S. Koshtoyants to Pavlov, *Selected Works*, 21–22.
42. *International Encyclopedia of Social Sciences*, 484.
43. Quoted in Babkin, *Pavlov, A Biography*, 86. The philosopher Gödel, however, has formally proved this to be impossible.
44. Gray, *Ivan Pavlov*, 4. The statement is actually that of the French ideologist Cabanis. It should be compared with Darwin's comment in his *Notebooks:* "Why is thought being a secretion of the brain, more wonderful than gravity a property of matter? It is our arrogance, our admiration of ourselves."
45. Quoted in Babkin, *Pavlov, A Biography*, 45. The next quotation is from "Natural Science and the Brain" (1909), in Pavlov, *Selected Works*, 206.

46. "A Letter to the Youth" (1934 or 1935), in ibid., 55.
47. Pavlov was obviously impatient—time driven—and truly obsessive in his work. His single-minded pursuit of facts, impersonally carried out, accords with his depersonalizing of Man—and himself—into a machine. For the way in which another behaviorist's basic assumptions about human behavior were rooted in his own life and character, see Alan C. Elms, "Skinner's Dark Year and *Walden Two*," *American Psychologist* 36, no. 5 (May 1981).
48. I say the later Freud, for in his *Project for a Scientific Psychology* (1895), his language was not all that different from Pavlov's.
49. "Essay on the Physiological Concept of the Symptomology of Hysteria" (1932), in *Selected Works*, 539.
50. Pavlov, "Reply of a Physiologist to Psychologists," 421, and Freud, *Standard Edition*, vol. 15, 28.
51. Pavlov, *Lectures on Conditioned Reflexes*, trans. W. H. Gautt (1928), 41, quoted in Babkin, *Pavlov, A Biography*, 86.
52. Freud, *Standard Edition*, vol. 16, 451.

## Chapter Seven: Babbage, Huxley, and Butler

1. Thomas Carlyle, *Sartor Resartus* (London: Chapman and Hall, 1910), 103.
2. Indeed, we have a story from Charles Darwin, who recalled a dinner at his brother's house at which even Babbage, who "liked to talk," was outdone by Carlyle. See *Charles Babbage and His Calculating Engines*, ed. Philip and Emily Morrison (New York: Dover, 1961), xiii.
3. Quoted in Maboth Moseley, *Irascible Genius: The Life of Charles Babbage* (Chicago: Henry Regnery Co., 1964), 65.
4. Clearly, Babbage thought of his "engine" as analogous to the "steam engine," say of Thomas Savery, dating back to 1698, or James Watt, dating to around the 1770s to 1780s.
5. In fact, the great Henry Maudsley was involved in the working up of the necessary tools, although Babbage himself did most of the actual designing, using one of Maudsley's trainees, Joseph Clement, as his assistant.
6. Quoted ibid., 262. For more attention to this pioneering woman in science, see Joan Baum, *The Calculating Passion of Ada Byron* (Hamden, Conn.: Archon Books/The Shoe String Press, 1986).
7. Morrison, *Charles Babbage*, 305.
8. Charles Babbage, *Passages from the Life of a Philosopher* (London: Dawsons of Pall Mall, 1968), 115.
9. Ibid., 17. The next two quotations are from pp. 17 and 365.
10. Ibid., 467.
11. Moseley, *Irascible Genius*, 261.
12. Compare Morrison, *Charles Babbage*, xx.
13. Ibid. This difference seems to correspond to the distinction today between what is called information processing and emergent AI. Lady Lovelace envisions the computer as remaining solely in the domain of information processing; Morrison is prepared to consider it within the context of emergent AI. Compare Sherry Turkle, "Artificial Intelligence and Psychoanalysis: A New Alliance," *Daedalus* (Winter 1988), 251.
14. Babbage, *Passages*, 114.
15. Morrison, *Charles Babbage*, 244.

16. Charles Babbage, *On Economy of Machinery and Manufactures* (Philadelphia: Carey & Lea, 1832), v. It should be noted, in passing, that Karl Marx read this work carefully; there is no evidence, however, that he paid any attention to Babbage's work on the Calculating Engine, any more than did most of his contemporaries. On the other hand, Charles Darwin's sister, Susan, wrote to him that "I have just got 'Babbage on Machinery' & shall certainly study it very diligently as a preparation" (15 August 1832, *Correspondence of Charles Darwin*, vol. 1 [Cambridge, 1985], 257). She does not say for what it is preparation.

17. Taxonomies, of course, can be of all kinds. For example, Linnaeus based his system on characters instead of functions. Although birds, bats, and insects all fly, he grouped them in different classes. A taxonomy emphasizing function might place them all in the same class.

18. Babbage, *Passages*, 104.

19. Morrison, *Charles Babbage*, 215–216, reprinting the account given by Babbage's friend Dr. Dionysius Lardner.

20. Ibid., 210.

21. Ibid., 145.

22. Adam Smith, *Lectures on Jurisprudence*, ed. R. L. Meek, D. D. Raphael and P. G. Stein (Indianapolis: Liberty Classics, 1982), 566. The quotation that follows is from p. 567.

23. Moseley, *Irascible Genius*, 132–133.

24. *Economy of Machinery*, 278. The quotation that follows is from Moseley, *Irascible Genius*, 20.

25. Charles Darwin, Thomas Henry Huxley, *Autobiographies*, ed. with introd. Gavin de Beer (London: Oxford University Press, 1974), 103. Huxley's Autobiography, incidentally, was written grudgingly and is very short. Mario di Gregorio, "The Dinosaur Connection: A Reinterpretation of T. H. Huxley's Evolutionary View," *Journal of the History of Biology* 15, no. 3 (Fall 1982), stresses the names of Von Baer and Ernst Haeckel and concludes that their "strictly mechanistic view of biology (based upon physics and chemistry) was entirely shared by Huxley" (416).

26. *The Essence of T. H. Huxley: Selections*, ed. Cyril Bibby (London: Macmillan, 1967), 80.

27. T. H. Huxley, "On the Physical Basis of Life" (1868), in *Selections from the Essays of T. H. Huxley*, ed. Alburey Castell (New York: Appleton-Century-Crofts, 1948), 19.

28. *Essence*, ed. Bibby, 66.

29. T. H. Huxley, "The Genealogy of Animals" (1869), in *Essence*, ed. Bibby, 63.

30. T. H. Huxley, "Prolegomena," *Evolution & Ethics: T. H. Huxley's "Evolution and Ethics," with New Essays on Its Victorian and Sociobiological Context*, James Paradis and George C. Williams (Princeton: Princeton University Press, 1989), 69. Huxley's comment appears reminiscent of that of Francis Bacon, quoted in chapter 1.

31. T. H. Huxley, "On the Hypothesis That Animals Are Automata, and Its History," in *Collected Essays*, 9 vols. (London: Macmillan, 1893–94), vol. 1, 218. The next quotation is from the essay on Descartes, 186.

32. "On the Hypothesis," 222. The next quotation is from p. 226.

33. Ibid., 228, 229, 235.

34. Ibid., 230, 234. The continuing quotation is on p. 235.

35. Ibid., 237. The next quotation is also from this page.

36. Ibid., 238, 239.
37. See also his essays "Agnosticism" (1889) and "Agnosticism and Christianity" (1889).
38. Huxley, "On the Hypothesis," 244.
39. Descartes does play, however, with rooting thought in the pineal gland.
40. In fact, Butler was also a painter of some real ability, having various of his works hung in the Royal Academy. For examples of his talent, see especially his self-portraits in Elinor Shaffer, *Erewhons of the Eye: Samuel Butler as Painter, Photographer and Art Critic* (London: Reaktion, 1988).
41. Samuel Butler, "Darwin Among the Machines," in a *First Year in Canterbury Settlement and Other Early Essays*, 20 vols. (London: Shrewsbury Edition of the Works of Samuel Butler, 1923), vol. 1, 186. The next two quotations are from pp. 201 and 187.
42. It should also be pointed out that the Darwins and the Butlers lived in the same town of Shrewsbury, and that Charles Darwin, in fact, had attended Dr. Butler's school.
43. Butler, "Darwin Among the Machines," 208 and 209. George W. Stocking, Jr., tells us that Colonel Lane Fox (better known as Pitt Rivers), "classifying the 'various products of human industry' into 'genera, species, and varieties' . . . discussed their development explicitly in terms of Spencerian evolutionary psychology and the processes of natural selection" (*Victorian Anthropology*, [New York: The Free Press, 1987], 180). Lane Fox was writing in 1874, suggesting either that he had read Butler or that the idea was in the air. The 1851 Crystal Palace Exhibition, with its arrangement of exhibits along a line of progress for both peoples and machines, lends support to the "in the air" hypothesis.
44. Butler, "Darwin Among the Machines," 210.
45. Ibid., 212.
46. Samuel Butler, "Lucubratio Ebria," in *A First Year*, 217 and 219.
47. Ibid., 215.
48. Samuel Butler, "The Mechanical Creation," in *A First Year*, 231–232.
49. Ibid., 232, 233.
50. Ibid., 236.
51. See Samuel Butler, *Erewhon or Over the Range*, ed. Hans-Peter Brewer and Daniel F. Howard (Newark: University of Delaware Press, 1981), for the authoritative scholarly edition; it also has an excellent introduction, offering a context and an analysis for the book. See also Butler's preface to the Second Edition for his own view of the correlations between his book and Lord Lytton's *The Coming Race* (41).
52. Compare Ralf Norrman, *Samuel Butler and the Meaning of Chiasmus* (Houndmills, Basingstoke, Hampshire: Macmillan, 1986).
53. Compare Henry Festing Jones, *Samuel Butler, Author of* Erewhon *(1835–1902): A Memoir*, 2 vols. (London: Macmillan, 1919), vol. 1, 20.
54. Charles Lamb had the following to say on this matter: "Alas! Can we ring the bells backward? Can we unlearn the arts that pretend to civilize and then burn the world? There is a march of science; but who shall beat the drums for its retreat?" (quoted in the frontispiece of Noel Perrin, *Giving Up the Gun: Japan's Reversion to the Sword, 1543–1879* [Boston: David R. Godine, 1979]). Perrin's book is a lovely little exploration of an actual "regression" in technology. Compare Arnold Toynbee's statement: "If a vote could undo all the technological advances of the last three hundred years, many of us would cast that vote, in

order to safeguard the survival of the human race while we remain in our present state of social and moral backwardness" (quoted in Perrin, 80–81).

55. Samuel Butler, *Erewhon* (Harmondsworth, Middlesex: Penguin Books, 1954), 161–171.
56. Jones, *Samuel Butler,* 1:156.
57. Samuel Butler, *The Way of All Flesh* (New York: The Modern Library, 1950), 531.
58. In fact, Butler was a declared Lamarckian and could well have entertained the view just stated. But Butler was in no way a serious scientist, systematically developing his ideas, and though he thought his book *Life and Habit* a major contribution to the theory of heredity, it was hardly so; as Peter Morton says, in judgment: "the whole corpus of Butler's 'evolutionary' writings are, as serious contributions to the sum total of knowledge, absolutely spurious" (*The Vital Sciences, Biology and the Literary Imagination* [London: George Allen & Unwin, 1984], 162).

### Chapter Eight: The Biogenetic Revolution

1. Irenaus Eibl-Eibesfeldt, *Love and Hate,* trans. from the German by Geoffrey Strachan (London: Methuen, 1971 [orig. pub. in Ger., 1970]), 32.
2. A statement by Alfred W. Crosby gives one pause. He argues that "if the Europeans had arrived in the New World and Australasia with twentieth-century technology in hand, but no animals, they would not have made as great a change as they did by arriving with horses, cattle, pigs, goats, sheep, asses, chickens, cats, and so forth. Because these animals are self-replicators, the efficiency and speed with which they can alter environments, even continental environments, are superior to those for any machine we have so far devised" (*Ecological Imperialism: The Biological Expansion of Europe, 900–1900* [Cambridge: Cambridge University Press, 1986], 173). Crosby's is an impressive book; and one must take his argument seriously. It certainly states part of the truth. However, in the perspective of a longer time span, the alteration of the environment by migration of humans and animals is small in comparison to the environmental effect, independent of humans, on all existing life of a Permian or Cretaceous extinction. As for machines, again over the perspective of a long time, they are increasingly replacing animals, *and* their effect on the environment is becoming more and more significant, perhaps even overwhelming. Final judgment in this debate may have to rest, in fact, in terms of one's view of the direction of development.
3. *GEO,* July 1984, 112.
4. Quoted in Peter Steinhart, "Synthetic Species," *Audubon,* September 1986, 10.
5. Ibid.
6. *Maine Times,* November 13, 1987, 6. Drury, it is interesting to note, taught at the College of the Atlantic, where human ecology is the only degree given.
7. Quoted in *The New York Times,* November 22, 1981, 8.
8. C. D. Darlington, *The Evolution of Man and Society* (New York: Simon & Schuster, 1969), 33.
9. Jon Luoma, "Prison or Ark?" *Audubon,* November 1982, 104.
10. In fact, zoos are more and more breeding and then releasing into the wild endangered species. The difficulties in doing so are, of course, great.
11. I cannot resist noting that while on a visit to Bangkok, Thailand, I picked up the local newspaper, with a lead story entitled "Genetic Horror Is Only One False

Step Away" asserting that genetic engineers were about to produce a disease that kills only blacks, destroys the eyes of enemy soldiers, and so forth (*Bangkok World,* August 11, 1984, 4). The American-based *National Enquirer* can thus be said to have its clone in Asia. This story also supports the point made earlier that the Western reaction to machines is becoming worldwide.

12. See the text for the exhibit "Beasts, Machines and Other Humans" in the Cecil H. Green Library, April–June 1987. I am indebted to Michael T. Ryan, Curator of Special Collections, for putting this text at my disposal.

13. In fact, Aristotle saw the mother herself as a departure from the norm of maleness, and thus a monstrosity, though a useful and necessary one. For a most helpful treatment of this point and its extension into seventeenth-century French thought, see Marie-Hélène Huet, "Monstrous Imagination: Progeny as Art in French Classicism," *Critical Inquiry* 17, no. 4 (Summer 1991).

14. The Young Man with Scales is described, with an illustration, in an advertisement reproduced in *The Times Literary Supplement,* April 18, 1980, 1.

15. Stephen Jay Gould, *The Panda's Thumb* (New York: W. W. Norton, 1980), 188, commenting on Richard Goldschmidt, *The Material Basis of Evolution* (New Haven: Yale University Press, 1940).

16. Eibl-Eibesfeldt, *Love and Hate,* 38.

17. Quoted in Stephen Jay Gould, "The Egg-a-Day Barrier," *Natural History,* July 1986, 16. Georges Canguilhem correctly points out that Darwin's interest in, and inspiration from, domestic breeding importantly distinguishes him from Alfred Russel Wallace, who also put forth the theory of evolution by natural selection in 1858. See Canguilhem, *Etudes d'histoire et de philosophies des sciences* (Paris: J. Vrin, 1983), 106.

18. James L. Gould, reviewing Ernst Mayr, *The Growth of Biological Thought: Diversity, Evolution, and Inheritance* (Cambridge: Harvard University Press/ Belknap, 1982), in *The New York Times Book Review,* May 23, 1982, 34. Mayr's book itself is an indispensable source.

19. See *The New York Times,* October 30, 1987. In fact, goats and sheep can interbreed in the ordinary way.

20. See again *The New York Times,* June 12, 1988 (while, admittedly, the *Times* does not have the authority of a biological serial, it does indicate the state of general public knowledge, even though sometimes erroneous, and thus serves my purpose here). Another, later story in the *Times* tells how hatchery trout released into a stream where wild trout have already established a stable social order become a highly disruptive force, charging around in schools and provoking fights. One result is that both types of trout dwindle in numbers (the hatchery trout are less adept at feeding on wild fare), and another result is that serious genetic problems ensue (July 23, 1991, p. C1). This story underlines the fact that genetic breeding still has to face the evolutionary selective process once the "product" is released from the laboratory.

21. See *The New York Times,* February 6, 1988, February 22, 1988, and April 17, 1987. It is worth noting that words such as *tinkering,* regularly applied to genetic "engineering," underscore the conflation of the animal and the mechanical.

22. For example, the dairy industry paid for research at MIT to discover the optimum rate at which cow embryos must be cooled, because it "is interested in replacing its 11 million Holstein cows with six million 'supercows' that may produce twice as much milk on the average," a process accelerated by embryo transfer (*The MIT Report,* vol. 11, no. 7, July 1983, 2).

23. See *The New York Times*, July 5, 1981.

24. See note 20.

25. Robert Owen, *A New View of Society and Other Writings* (London: J.M. Dent & Sons, 1949), 9.

26. "On the Queerness of Social Evolution," a summary of a talk by Edward O. Wilson to the American Academy of Arts and Sciences, October 1972, in *Bulletin* of the organization 26, no. 3 (December 1972), 5–6.

27. Melvin Konner, *The Tangled Wing: Biological Constraints on the Human Spirit* (New York: Holt, Rinehart, and Winston, 1982), 15. See Richard Dawkins, *The Selfish Gene* (New York: Oxford University Press, 1976). For a more sophisticated treatment of the selfish gene, and of biogenetic and AI matters in general, see Herbert A. Simon, *Reason in Human Affairs* (Stanford, Calif., Stanford University Press, 1983).

28. Edward O. Wilson, *Sociobiology: The New Synthesis* (Cambridge: Harvard University Press, 1975), 3, quoted in Mary Midgley, *Beast and Man: The Roots of Human Nature* (Ithaca, N.Y.: Cornell University Press, 1978), 90.

29. For an extension of Wilson's work to human sociobiology, see, for example, *Evolutionary Biology and Human Social Behavior: An Anthropological Perspective*, ed. Napoleon A. Chagnon and William Irons (North Scituate, Mass.: Duxbury Press, 1979); and to show how far this work can go, Laura L. Betzig, *Despotism and Differential Reproduction: A Darwinian View of History* (Hawthorne, N.Y.: Aldine, 1986), as well as the review of the latter by Lee Cronk in *Critical Review*, vol. 2, no. 1, 103–110. For devastating criticism of the overextension of sociobiology, so that the genetic serves as the basis for cultural practices (as opposed to behavioral potentialities), see various works by R. C. Lewontin.

30. Konner, *The Tangled Wing*, 11.

31. Quoted in Paul F. Cranefield, "The Organic Physics of 1847 and the Biophysics of Today," *Journal of the History of Medicine and Allied Sciences* 12, no. 4 (1957), 407, 408. The quotation that follows in the next paragraph is from p. 420. This is an important article.

32. Wilson, *Sociobiology*, 562, 575, quoted in Midgley, *Beast and Man*, 169–170.

33. I follow the synopsis given in Midgley, *Beast and Man*, 255. Further on Wells, see Peter Kemp, *H. G. Wells and the Culminating Ape* (New York: St. Martin's Press, 1982).

34. See Freeman J. Dyson, *Infinite in All Directions* (New York: Harper & Row, 1988), and a review of it by Roger Penrose, *New York Times Book Review*, July 24, 1988, 24.

35. William Day, *Genesis on Planet Earth: The Search for Life's Beginning* (East Lansing, Mich.: House of Talos, 1979), 390–392.

36. J. Lederberg, in *Towards Century 21*, ed. C. S. Walla (New York: Basic Books, 1970), 52; and Francis Crick, *Life Itself: Its Origin and Nature* (New York: Simon & Schuster, 1981), 118, all quoted in Mary Midgley, "Evolution as a Religion: A Comparison of Prophecies," *Zygon* 22, no. 2 (June 1987), 180, 183, 185.

37. Compare Susan L. Farber, *Identical Twins Reared Apart* (New York: Basic Books, 1981).

38. For the thyroid gland equivalent, see *Tech Talk*, December 14, 1983, 5.

39. C. S. Lewis, *Studies in Words* (Cambridge: Cambridge University Press, 1961), 46. Lewis's discussion of the meaning of *Nature* is one of the most suggestive available.

40. The same U.S. Patent and Trademark Office that approved the patenting of genetic improvements, and the consequent payment of royalties for their use, declared that its ruling does not apply to humans: "The grant of a limited but exclusive property right in a human being is prohibited by the Constitution" (*The New York Times*, February 22, 1988, 18). Of course, change in this ruling is possible; but I doubt it will occur.

41. It should be noted that the eminent scientist Freeman Dyson would appear to have a different opinion, as when he states that "when I compare the biological world with the world of mechanical industry, I am impressed by the enormous superiority of biological processes in speed, economy and flexibility" (*Infinite in All Directions*, 155). Perhaps it is this belief, however, that gives him his faith in the future coming of an "astrochicken" (see this chapter).

### Chapter Nine: The Computer-Brain Revolution

1. Ralph Waldo Emerson wrote that "the soul in man . . . is not a function, like the power of memory, of calculation, of comparison, but uses these as hands and feet" (*The Oversoul*, quoted in Arthur Lovejoy, *The Reason: The Understanding and Time* [Baltimore, Md.: Johns Hopkins University Press, 1961], 88–89). Emerson was presumably not thinking of the computer (though Babbage's calculator was already in existence), but his words could obviously apply to it. The computer, carrying with it the age-old fear of the machine's depersonalization, did inspire directly the more recent expression of this anxiety on a protest sign: "I am a human being; do not fold, spindle, or mutilate."

2. Sherry Turkle, *The Second Self: Computers and the Human Spirit* (New York: Simon & Schuster, 1984), 321. Compare especially p. 90. The subsequent citation from Turkle is from p. 155. This book, by a colleague at MIT, is a pioneering empirical study, enhanced by psychoanalytic and sociological insight. Implicitly, it touches on many of the same reactions that we have been studying in the present book, though from a less historical perspective. It is essential reading on the topic of computers.

3. Compare Keith Thomas, *Man and the Natural World* (New York: Pantheon, 1983), 29, 38.

4. Bernard Knox, "The Theatre of Ethics" [review-essay of Martha C. Nussbaum, *The Fragility of Goodness*], *The New York Review of Books*, December 4, 1986, 52. The quotations from Plato are also in Knox.

5. Again, I have used the paraphrase of Knox, who so well expresses what I have in mind. His entire review-essay touches, although with a different intent, on much of what we have been concerned with throughout this book.

6. Martha C. Nussbaum, *The Fragility of Goodness: Luck and Ethics in Greek Tragedy and Philosophy* (Cambridge: Cambridge University Press, 1986), 420.

7. Huxley, of course, was an evolutionist. As we have seen, however, he conceived of the animals, including Man, that were part of the evolutionary process as basically being machines. Or at least as operating on mechanical principles. In opting to become a machine in order to be moral, Huxley was actually asking only to be a more perfect machine.

8. A. M. Turing, "Computing Machinery and Intelligence," *Mind* 59, no. 236 (October 1950), 449.

9. Compare the discussion in Turkle, *The Second Self*, 302; Pamela McCorduck, *Machines Who Think* (New York: W. H. Freeman, 1979), 171; and especially

Douglas R. Hofstadter, *Gödel, Escher, Bach: An Eternal Golden Braid* (New York: Basic Books, 1980). The implications of Gödel's theorem for theology are mind boggling, for even God in these terms could not be all-knowing and perfect.

10. Ernst Haeckel, *The History of Creation* (1867), 1876, vol. 2, 367, quoted in I. F. Clarke, *The Pattern of Expectation, 1644–2001* (New York: Basic Books, 1979), 141.

11. Darwin, *Origin of Species*, chapter 3, no. 2, 63.

12. Hans Koning, "Onward and Upward with the Arts," *The New Yorker*, March 2, 1981, 80. This is an interesting article on the eleventh edition of the *Encyclopaedia Britannica*, noting the change in science since 1911 and the advent of the computer.

13. Robert Jastrow, *The Enchanted Loom: Mind in the Universe* (New York: Simon & Schuster, 1981). I confess that my faith in Jastrow's predictions was earlier shaken by his misguided statements about the space effort. See *The Railroad and the Space Program*, ed. Bruce Mazlish (Cambridge: MIT Press, 1965), 38.

14. Edward A. Feigenbaum and Pamela McCorduck, *The Fifth Generation: Artificial Intelligence and Japan's Computer Challenge to the World* (Reading, Mass.: Addison-Wesley, 1983), quoted in Joseph Weizenbaum's review-essay in *The New York Review of Books*, October 27, 1983, 62. This review should be read in its entirety.

15. The term *artificial intelligence* was coined by John McCarthy of Dartmouth in 1952 to denote computers capable of solving real-world problems. The whole of the Winter 1988 issue of *Daedalus* is devoted to artificial intelligence.

16. Quoted in William Stockton, "Creating Computers That Think," *The New York Times Magazine*, December 7, 1980, 41. The quotation that follows is from Jeremy Bernstein, "When the Computer Procreates," *The New York Times Magazine*, February 15, 1976, 38. Minsky does add the qualification that the actual silicone chips on which the circuitry is printed must still be supplied from the outside, and that at the present moment a truly self-replicating automaton would have to be the size of a factory. In principle, however, miniaturization is possible. And anyone who remembers that Norbert Wiener's original conception of a chess-playing computer was the size of Rockefeller Plaza and is now in a nice compact size will hesitate to dismiss the idea out of hand (or should it be mind?).

17. Turing, "Computing Machinery and Intelligence," 456.

18. This is a convenient chart given by Rony Sebok, "How Computers Affect the Way We Live," *Radcliffe Quarterly*, December 1983, 24, though already outdated. Other ways of classifying the generations are, of course, possible, and, indeed, by the time this book appears a new generation will undoubtedly have been born.

19. Eugene Zamyatin, *We*, trans. Gregory Zilboorg (New York: E. P. Dutton, 1924), 89.

20. William Delisle Hay, *Three Hundred Years Hence* (1881, p. 354), quoted in Clarke, *The Pattern of Expectation*, 157.

21. A more recent Daedalus is to be found in the "mechanist," as he is called in Samuel Johnson's *Rasselas* (1759), who designs wings in order to fly out of the happy valley in which the Prince is imprisoned—and immediately drops into the lake. Johnson's mechanist rhapsodizes how "with what pleasure a philosopher, furnished with wings, and hovering in the sky, would see the earth, and all its inhabitants, rolling beneath him, and presenting to him successively, by its diurnal motion, all the countries within the same parallel" (Samuel Johnson,

*Rasselas, Poems, and Selected Prose,* ed. Bertrand H. Bronson [New York: Holt, Rinehart and Winston, 1952], 517–518). This was written a few decades before the actual advent of balloon flight. Johnson's novel as a whole is worth reading in regard to our general topic.

22. Sébastien Mercier, *The Waiting City: Paris, 1782–88,* trans. and ed. Helen Simpson (1933), 314, quoted in Clarke, *The Pattern of Expectation,* 30.

23. Walter A. McDougall, *The Heavens and the Earth* (New York: Basic Books, 1985), 17.

24. I have used here the paraphrase of Wiener's ideas in *God and Golem, Inc.* (Cambridge: MIT Press, 1964) as made by Martin Gardiner in his *Order and Surprise* (Buffalo, N.Y.: Prometheus Books, 1983), 256.

25. I might add that long before *Invasion of the Body Snatchers,* Homer, in the *Iliad,* has the Olympian gods constantly and casually occupying human bodies.

26. Biosphere II is a closed, self-sustaining ecosystem, a "built environment," so to speak, imitating the earth in microcosm.

27. Gerald O'Neill, *Nature,* August 23, 1974, quoted in Clarke, *The Pattern of Expectation,* 312. See further O'Neill's *The High Frontier: Human Colonies in Space* (New York: Morrow, 1977).

28. For what it's worth, two of my favorites are Ursula K. LeGuin and Orson Scott Card. I will avoid entering into a discussion of science fiction, in order to avoid writing another book.

29. Philip K. Dick, *Do Androids Dream of Electric Sheep?* (New York: Ballantine Books, 1991), originally appeared in 1968. The quotation that follows is from p. 125. In the book, almost all real animals have disappeared from the earth, being replaced by electrically operated versions; hence the title.

30. In a recent American television serial called "Mann and Machine" (in which Mann is a detective and the machine is an android, named Eve, gifted with seven-year-old emotions, but learning, who acts as his partner), there is also lots of sex play and innuendo between human and android. The serial can be seen as an android "soap opera" and will probably have vanished from the air waves by the time this book is published. A sign of the times.

31. Quoted in an interview in *'GBH,* July 1988, 11.

32. Searle's article, "Minds, Brains, and Programs," espousing his views, originally appeared in *The Behavioral and Brain Sciences,* vol. 3 (Cambridge: Cambridge University Press, 1980), and is reprinted in *The Mind's I,* composed and arranged by Douglas R. Hofstadter and Daniel C. Dennett (New York: Basic Books, 1981), 357–373. See also Searle's review-essay of *The Mind's I* in *New York Review of Books,* April 29, 1982, from which the quotation is taken, p. 6, and his book *Minds, Brains, and Science* (Cambridge: Harvard University Press, 1984). For Turing, of course, see "Computing Machinery and Intelligence."

33. Sherry Turkle, "Artificial Intelligence and Psychoanalysis: A New Alliance," *Daedalus* 117, no. 1 (Winter 1988), 248. This is an intelligent article on both subjects.

34. Gerald M. Edelman, "Through a Computer Darkly: Group Selection and Higher Brain Function," *Bulletin of the American Academy of Arts and Sciences,* 36, no. 1 (October 1982), 21 and 48. This is an earlier and simpler statement of the theories and work that are contained in his book *Neural Darwinism: The Theory of Neuronal Group Selection* (New York: Basic Books, 1987).

35. A good account of Darwin III, with illustrations, is to be found in David Hellerstein, "Plotting a Theory of the Brain," *The New York Times Magazine,* May 22,

1988. The use of the term *automaton,* however, is taken from Edelman in the *Bulletin,* "Through a Computer Darkly." To employ a different use of "selection," however, it should be pointed out that machines do not have to "eat" other animals (or at least not directly; they do consume energy in other forms), nor compete with them for food.

36. These statements are taken from James Gleick, "Exploring the Labyrinth of the Mind," *The New York Times Magazine,* August 21, 1983, 26.

37. One early attack on the limitlessness of computer development that has received a good deal of attention and refutation is Hubert L. Dreyfus, *What Computers Can't Do: A Critique of Artificial Reason* (New York: Harper & Row, 1972). Dreyfus weakened his critique by announcing in 1972 that further progress in AI was "unlikely" (197); nevertheless some of his substantive arguments still have general force (though I find myself at odds with the tone of his book). Joseph Weizenbaum is himself a computer scientist—Dreyfus is a philosopher—and his book *Computer Power and Human Reason* (San Francisco: W. H. Freeman and Co., 1976), is an important contribution to the debate.

38. Heinz R. Pagels, *The Dreams of Reason: The Computer and the Rise of the Sciences of Complexity* (New York: Simon & Schuster, 1988), discusses the way the computer is the new version of scientific instruments—the telescope and the microscope preceding it—that mark the great transformations in Man's grasp of nature.

39. This analogy is made in an article by Brad Leithauser, "The Space of One Breath," *The New Yorker,* March 9, 1987, 45. A good deal of what follows draws on his excellent account.

40. The figures in 1980, for example, were over 3,000 being used in the United States, with 1,170 being produced in that year alone. (See Thomas B. Sheridan, "Computer Control and Human Alienation," *Technology Review,* October 1980, 63; this article, in general, is an informed and thoughtful piece, though much has happened since it was written.) In that same year, however, Japan was producing just under 20,000. The implications, incidentally, of robot labor in place of the previously cheap labor of underdeveloped countries are important to consider. That route to economic development may, in the future, simply be closed off. (I might add that at the moment of this book's publication, the rate of robot growth has slowed; I believe this to be a temporary phenomenon.)

41. *MIT Reports on Research* 8, no. 2 (September–October 1980), note by Davis Pan.

42. Phil Berger, *The State-of-the-Art Robot Catalogue* (New York: Dodd, Mead, 1984). The second quotation is from p. 100. This is an engaging book, giving off-the-shelf prices for available robots as well as an overall treatment of the subject.

43. Ibid., 102.

### Chapter Ten: The Beginning of a Conclusion

1. Quoted in Martha C. Nussbaum, *The Fragility of Goodness: Luck and Ethics in Greek Tragedy and Philosophy* (Cambridge: Cambridge University Press, 1986), 73. The quotation that follows is from p. 52.

2. Recent paleoanthropology has apparently cast some doubt on this chronology, for example, a large brain may have preceded upright posture. The evidence is still inconclusive; and in any case does not affect my essential point.

3. *Homo erectus* apparently lived, with little structural change, from about one and a half to half a million years ago and was the first undoubted fabricator of

implements (it is not known who made the crude "Olduvai" tools of two million years ago). See Richard Leakey, *The Making of Mankind* (London: Michael Joseph, 1981).

4. Georges Canguilhem, "Charles Darwin," in his *Etudes d'histoire et de philosophies des sciences* (Paris: J. Vrin, 1983), 125.

5. David S. Landes, *Revolution in Time* (Cambridge: Harvard University Press, 1983), 15.

6. Gregory Benford, *Great Sky River* (New York: Bantam Books, 1987), 284.

7. Compare Norbert Elias, *The History of Manners*, vol. 1: *The Civilizing Process*, trans. Edmund Jephcott (New York: Pantheon, 1978), 120.

8. One of Claude Lévi-Strauss's informants told him that "to be a man it was necessary to be painted; to remain in the natural state was to be no different from the beasts" (*Tristes Tropiques*, trans. John and Doreen Weightman, New York: Atheneum, 1981, 188). It may be unkind to point out that, in contrast to most animals, many humans are "out of shape," or at least think of themselves in that way, and quite ugly. Persistently getting drunk and taking drugs—abuses of the body—may also be unique to humans.

9. Melvin Konner, *The Tangled Wing. Biological Constraints of the Human Spirit* (New York: Holt, Rinehart and Winston, 1982), 320.

10. C. D. Darlington, *The Evolution of Man and Society* (New York: Simon & Schuster, 1969), 50, 52–53, 57–58, and 59.

11. In fact, elephants and apes may also sometimes recognize grandchildren as such; again, we are faced with a matter of degree.

12. Again, we must hedge a bit and stress the matter of degree: pigs, for example, are alleged to be conscious of their impending deaths, and parrots to be "aware" of the death of their mates and offspring.

13. There are stories of elephant mothers trying to cover up their dead offspring— perhaps a form of burial?

14. Clearly, the question of "consciousness" is crucial here. *The* essential book in this regard is Julian Jaynes, *The Origin of Consciousness in the Breakdown of the Bicameral Mind* (Boston: Houghton Mifflin, 1976). This is truly a path-breaking work, deserving close and critical reading of its avowedly innovative and controversial theses. One of these is that consciousness in humans is itself a late evolutionary development, occurring sometime in the last three thousand years.

15. Quoted in Nussbaum, *The Fragility of Goodness*, 2.

16. Konrad Lorenz, *On Aggression*, trans. Marjorie Kerr Wilson (New York: Harcourt, Brace & World, 1966), 218. On the general subject of animal feelings, language, consciousness, and so forth, compare Donald R. Griffin, *The Question of Animal Awareness: Evolutionary Continuity of Mental Experience*, rev. and enl. ed. (New York: Rockefeller University Press, 1981).

17. In terms of our earlier discussion of monstrosities, a person without pity can be regarded as a monster—thus, there can be a moral in contrast to a physiological dimension to monstrosity.

18. Mary Midgley, *Beast and Man: The Roots of Human Nature* (Ithaca, N.Y.: Cornell University Press, 1978), 107. Compare Jaynes, *The Origin of Consciousness*, for the way volition and consciousness are necessarily tied together.

19. In this matter, I am in agreement with Marvin Minsky, who writes that "our culture wrongly teaches us that thoughts and feelings lie in almost separate worlds." In fact, "beyond a certain point, to distinguish between the emotional

and intellectual structures of an adult is merely to describe the same structures from different points of view" (*The Society of Mind* [New York: Simon & Schuster, 1986]).

20. Compare J. Bronowski, *The Identity of Man* (Garden City, N.Y.: The Natural History Press, 1965), 48–49.

21. See Griffin, *The Question of Animal Awareness*, 9, 18, 19, 26–27, 43, and 76–77. See, too, Eugene Linden, *Apes, Men, and Languages* (Harmondsworth, England: Penguin Books, 1981). I have also found useful Carol Grant Gould, "Out of the Mouths of Beasts," *Science* 83 (April 1983).

22. Konner, *The Tangled Wing*, 171. The next quotation is from Lorenz, *On Aggression*, 68.

23. Joseph Weizenbaum, *Computer Power and Reason: From Judgment to Calculation* (San Francisco: W. H. Freeman, 1976), 209. In fact, change in language as a unique human attribute is again a matter of degree; birds, for example, learn to change their calls.

24. For an expansion of this idea, compare my book *The Leader, the Led, and the Psyche* (Hanover, N.H.: Wesleyan University Press, 1990), especially chapter 1, "Darwin, the Bedrock of Psychoanalysis."

25. Charles Darwin, *The Origin of Species and The Descent of Man* (New York: Modern Library, n.d.), 471.

26. In this connection, I have already noted the recent construction of Biosphere II (in contrast to Biosphere I, which is the "natural" environment, earth). Biosphere II, as I said earlier, is an artificially constructed "nature," supposedly ecologically balanced, which is intended as a prototype for a module to be transported into space, where it will serve as the habitat for human space colonies. Noteworthy is that this "built environment" seeks to be as naturelike as possible rather than as artificial.

27. Again, compare Griffin, *The Question of Animal Awareness*, 109.


### Chapter Eleven: The Ending of a Conclusion

1. J. H. Plumb, in Neil McKendrick, John Brewer, and J. H. Plumb, *The Birth of a Consumer Society* (London: Europa Publications Ltd., 1982), 316.

2. Elaine Pagels, *Adam, Eve, and the Serpent* (New York: Random House, 1988), 84.

3. Harold F. Searles, "Unconscious Processes in Relation to the Environmental Crisis," quoted in David Lavery, "Departure of the Body Snatchers, or the Confessions of a Carbon Chauvinist," *The Hudson Review,* Autumn 1986, 383. Lavery's article is an intriguing takeoff on the theme of the movie *Invasion of the Body Snatchers.*

4. *The Standard Edition of the Complete Psychological Works of Sigmund Freud,* ed. James Strachey (London: Hogarth Press, 1968), vol. 21, 92. Freud's whole passage is worth reading.

5. Norbert Wiener, *God & Golem, Inc.* (Cambridge: MIT Press, 1964), 76.

6. The early twentieth-century Futurists lyricized about the possible mixture of Man, energy, and machine. Thus, in one of Boccioni's sculptures, as Stephen Kern recounts, "The head is a montage of skull, helmet, and machine parts" (*The Culture of Time and Space, 1880–1918* [Cambridge: Harvard University Press, 1983], 122). Taylorism, or scientific management, can also be seen as a further attempt to turn humans, as workers, into machine parts.

7. See Sherry Turkle, *The Second Self: Computers and the Human Spirit* (New York: Simon & Schuster, 1984), 338. Such hybrids of machine and organism are

generally called cyborgs. Cyborgs, androids, and robots are sometimes used as synonyms; technically, the android is a robot that looks like a human, while a robot can have any form. Some notice must be given here to Donna Haraway's "A Manifesto for Cyborgs: Science, Technology, and Socialist Feminism in the 1980s," *Socialist Review,* no. 80, March–April 1985, and her book, *Simians, Cyborgs, and Women: The Reinvention of Women* (New York: Routledge, 1991).

8. Quoted in Lavery, "Departure of the Body Snatchers," 391–392.

9. Ibid., 386. This form of possession raises the fundamental philosophical question of personal identity through time. Those of a philosophical bent should read Robert Nozick, *Philosophical Explanation* (Cambridge: Harvard University Press, 1981), where there is in fact a long footnote discussing the two film versions of *Invasion of the Body Snatchers* (58–59), and Bernard Williams, "The Self and the Future," in *Problems of the Self* (Cambridge: Cambridge University Press, 1973).

10. Herman Melville, *Moby-Dick,* ed. Harrison Hayford and Hershel Parker (New York: W. W. Norton & Co., 1967), 390.

11. Diderot, "D'Alembert's Dream," in *Rameau's Nephew and Other Works,* trans. Jacques Barzun and Ralph H. Bowen (Garden City, N.Y.: Doubleday Anchor, 1956), 120.

12. Ibid., 128.

13. Darwin, *The Descent of Man,* 920.

14. Quoted in James Eli Adams, "Women Red in Tooth and Claw: Nature and the Feminine in Tennyson and Darwin," *Victorian Studies,* Autumn 1989, 20.

15. For an interesting attempt at an empirical study of the effect of computers on humans as workers, see Shoshana Zuboff, *In the Age of the Smart Machine: The Future of Work and Power* (New York: Basic Books, 1988).

16. One other possibility, of course, is a new, genetically engineered human. I am not including that possibility here for reasons given earlier and because I am concentrating on the Butlerian machine-type extrapolations.

17. Wiener, *God & Golem, Inc.,* 12–13 and 29. John Von Neumann is credited with working out the principles of this reproductive possibility. In spite of the technological hyperbole in the Prologue—"a future . . . best described by the words 'postbiological' . . . It is a world in which the human race has been swept away by the tide of cultural change, usurped by its own artificial progeny" (1)—Hans Moravec, *Mind Children: The Future of Robot and Human Intelligence* (Cambridge: Harvard University Press, 1988), is an informed and sober exposition of our present knowledge in regard to self-reproducing robots.

18. Joseph Weizenbaum, *Computer Power and Reason: From Judgment to Calculation* (San Francisco: W. H. Freeman, 1976), 210.

19. Stephen Jay Gould, *Ever Since Darwin* (New York: Norton, 1977), 257.

20. Stephen Jay Gould, *Wonderful Life: The Burgess Shale and the Nature of History* (New York: W. W. Norton & Co., 1989), 323.

21. *The New York Review of Books,* June 14, 1990, 4.

22. Robert J. Richards, *The Meaning of Evolution: The Morphological Construction and Ideological Reconstruction of Darwin's Theory* (Chicago: University of Chicago Press, 1992), 167. Chapter 6, "The Meaning of Evolution and the Ideological Uses of History," is especially worth reading in regard to the general issue. The next quotation is also from this book, p. 167.

23. See, for example, the controversial book by Stephen Jay Gould, *Ontogeny and Phylogeny* (Cambridge: Harvard University Press, 1977).

24. David L. Hull, *Science as a Process: An Evolutionary Account of the Social and*

*Conceptual Development of Science* (Chicago: University of Chicago Press: 1988), 41.

25. See my treatment of Hegel in *The Riddle of History* (New York: Harper & Row, 1966), especially 147.

26. Hull, *Science as a Process*, 76.

27. Ibid.

28. Thomas S. Kuhn, *The Structure of Scientific Revolutions* (Chicago: University of Chicago Press, 1962), 171.

29. George Basalla, *The Evolution of Technology* (Cambridge: Cambridge University Press, 1988), and Joel Mokyr, *The Lever of Riches: Technological Creativity and Economic Progress* (New York: Oxford University Press, 1990). As for economics, Milton Friedman weighs in when he writes, "Let the apparent immediate determinant of business behavior be anything at all—habitual reaction, random choice, or whatnot. Whenever this determinant happens to lead to behavior consistent with rational and informed maximization of returns, the business will prosper and acquire resources with which to expand; whenever it does not, the business will tend to lose resources. . . . The practice of 'natural selection' thus helps to validate the hypothesis—or, rather, given natural selection, acceptance of the hypothesis can be based largely on the judgment that it summarizes appropriately the conditions for survival" ("The Methodology of Positive Economics," in *Essays in Positive Economics* [Chicago: University of Chicago Press, 1953]).

30. Let me hasten to add that my own pride does not extend to imagining myself alongside Copernicus (or Galileo), Darwin, and Freud. They, with their path-breaking scientific work, ended the first three discontinuities and created new theories to explain the new continuities; I have merely sought to write some of the history and to describe the possible ending of the fourth discontinuity.

31. For some idea of work in this interdisciplinary area, see "The Computation and Neural Systems Series," ed. Christof Koch, and the first volume in this series, Carver Mead's book, *Analog VLSI and Neural Systems* (Reading, Mass.: Addison-Wesley, 1989). As stated in the foreword: "Over the past 600 million years, biology has solved the problem of processing massive amounts of noisy and highly redundant information in a constantly changing environment by evolving networks of billions of highly interconnected nerve cells. It is the task of scientists—be they mathematicians, physicists, biologists, psychologists, or computer scientists—to understand the principles underlying information processing in these complex structures. At the same time, researchers in machine vision, pattern recognition, speech understanding, robotics, and other areas of artificial intelligence can profit from understanding features of existing nervous systems. Thus, a new field is emerging" (viii). Mead's book, whose technical aspects I do not claim to understand, is worth attention by the general reader for its sober, well-written, and informative short introduction. (I owe knowledge of this book to my student Robert Codell, who *is* able to understand the technical part.)

# Index